contents

Acknowledgements

The chapter 'The Voids of Berlin' has appeared earlier in the journal *Critical Inquiry*, vol. 24, no. 1, in the autumn of 1997. Chicago University Press.

The chapter 'Capitalism and the City' has appeared earlier in *Cities for the New Millennium*, edited by Marcial Echenique. Routledge.

The chapter 'Milan: Urban Footnotes' has appeared earlier in Italian in the catalogue of the exhibition 'Milano senza confini' (curator Roberta Valtorta).

Introduction
Jürgen Rosemann

This is a book about cities – cities as the dominant form of human settlement for the future. It is about the transformation that cities are presently undergoing, and about the making of cities – about the ability to influence or even define the urban future by planning and design. Never before has human society gone through a comparable process of urbanization, never before have cities expanded as today. Within a few decennia the process of urbanization has led to agglomerations of unprecedented dimensions. In 1950 New York was, with 12 million inhabitants, the largest city in the world. Today metropolises like Mexico City, São Paulo, Tokyo and Mumbai have far surpassed New York with inhabitants numbering sometimes way beyond 20 million.

Most of the new super-agglomerations are situated in the so-called developing countries. The process of urbanization in these countries is accompanied by fundamental economical, cultural and social changes; impoverished farmers and land workers try to find a new livelihood in the fast developing urban economy, and a growing number of refugees seek escape from escalating conflicts worldwide. As a result the new mega-cities are faced with an unprecedented stream of mostly poor and unschooled rural migrants that threatens to undermine the conditions of economical development as well as social life.

In the industrialized countries, cities are, at first sight, confronted with the opposite problem. They are not growing, but losing population to the suburban areas that are spreading out into a diffuse sprawl. In particular, higher income groups are leaving the core cities and are settling in the better secured and often gated communities of the suburbs. At the same time though, the urban sprawl extends into metropolitan areas and new models of urbanity. Edge cities and network cities are expanding the boundaries of the traditional cities and are creating new urban entities and new dimensions of urban life.

Thus the process of urbanization has not only led to new dimensions of cities, their form and structure are subject to great changes too. Technological innovations such as the automation and digitalization of industrial production as well as the wide scale introduction of ICT are changing the locational conditions for enterprises and employment. New traffic- and transport systems enlarge the reach and area of impact of cities and lead to new forms of centrality. Globalization and internationalization give rise to an increase in competition between urban agglomerations. Parallel to this cities are confronted with growing social contrasts. Yet in industrialized countries too urban developments are characterized by fragmentation and segregation.

Within this thematic Future City focuses specifically on the issue of the conceptualization of inherently dynamic urbanization processes. In his introductory text Stephen Read elaborates on this theme, criticizing the formal utopianism of many of our planning and design ideas and suggesting a possible outline of an urban utopianism of process, which explicitly acknowledges change as a fundamental state and makes, in Sennett's words, "…provision for the fact of history, for the unintended, for the contradictory, for the unknown". Understanding the ways alignments of power and control are articulated within these processes and their products is seen as being vital for understanding the ways human creativity can be given back its priority, as the foundation of empowerment, and as the source of a continual progressive change and development.

The form and structure of the book responds to this emphasis on the conceptualization and experience of contemporary urban conditions. The body of the publication is formed by three sections: a collection of 10 city case studies, ranging from the highly planned (the Dutch Randstad or Deltametropolis) to the highly spontaneous (Belgrade); a series of theoretical pieces dealing with some fundamental conceptualizations of contemporary urban society and urbanization, and an image essay made by NEXT Architects in which the appearance has been recorded of the meeting of the global and the local in 18 metropolitan centers around the world.

These three parts are intended to lie loosely against each other, illuminating each other in ways sometimes intended, sometimes accidental. The juxtaposition of these different pieces will we hope challenge the reader to consider and reconsider the way in which they look and think about the urban environment as it surrounds us and constitutes the framework for our daily lives.

The Form of the Future
Stephen Read

It has become almost obligatory to begin introductions to books such as this one with statistics about the rates of urbanization we are experiencing in the world today. Everyone by now knows the bottom line: we have apparently – silently in the sense that we did not mark the exact point, but with a lot of noise about the impending moment of it – passed the 50 percent mark. From this moment forward our world is unequivocally an urbanized world. And given the rates at which this process is proceeding – there are various projections about where we will be at 2010, 2025 and 2050 – it in any event seems clear that by the turn of the next century there will be no argument about the fact that we live in a world which is fundamentally different to the world we have known over the history of mankind up till now. And all this has happened in the mere twinkling of an eye in the overall time span of human history.

Making projections about urban futures is a notoriously fraught terrain, littered with the wrecks of previous attempts shown to be trite and superficial and ignorant of the evidence which is later known to have been staring the predictors in the face. Nevertheless we seem compelled to mark moments in this calamitous urban adventure with projections about where it is all leading. Not least, of course, because it is not all a roller-coaster ride with our hands off the controls. We have the power to affect the way that the story of the city goes forward, and we have to go on theorizing so that we may, to some degree at least, exercise our responsibility to steer that progress in directions which we hope will be not only equitable in terms of the way opportunities for livelihood and self-realization are distributed and mediated within this vast and encompassing urban framework, but also enabling, liberating and supportive of the human spirit. These moments of accounting come with such frequency these days that we feel we can afford some level of excessive speculation, of intellectual indulgence which is almost bound to run aground on quite obvious, yet unseen (by us), rocky shores. Because not to indulge in fairly radical speculation – if not on the exact form of the future, then at least on the underlying principle of this form and how we may be able to affect it – at this moment also seems inappropriate, given the scope and the dynamism of the changes that are upon us; given the enormity of the changes that the next twinkling of an eye seems bound to bring.

Change occurs at many different levels, of course, some of it very substantial and obvious, some of it difficult to account for, much of it in locally specific forms which may obscure more general underlying trends. Urbanization in developing lands at this moment consists of a massive flow of people out of rural areas and towards centers, while in the industrialized lands the recent past has seen an emptying of urban centers as people with means drifted to the suburbs. These suburbs are however themselves urbanizing, and everywhere the change is to more urban forms of life, embedded in formal and informal urban economies. The changes in the qualities of modern life have much to do with technologies that have become ubiquitous in many or most parts of the world; personal and collective mobility, communications through the telephone, the Internet and the broadcast media. Quantum leaps in instantaneity – in the space-time compression that processes of globalization so depend on – have come with the telephone, with high-speed travel, and then the Internet and other more specialized technological networks. And these promise to be eclipsed in the next century as networks become ever more thickly laid over each other and ever more integrated, ultimately perhaps becoming those global 'technological skins'[1], which offer, besides ubiquitous connectivity, the possibilities of instantaneous monitoring and feedback of economic, environmental and urban processes. For the first time we see the possibility – indeed the necessity – of the development of technologies less directed to overcoming and exploiting our world and its natural riches, more towards understanding and managing its processes.

But while technological probabilities and the demand for connection explode, pressures on the earth's resources seem bound to mount, as will pressures tending to social polarization and inequity. In the last 20 years, annual world production has grown from 4,000 to 23,000 billion dollars, while in the same period, the number of the world's poor has increased by 20 percent. As growing world production is coupled with falling employment, the share of the world's income available to the poorest 20 percent of the world's population has fallen, from 2.3 percent in 1960 to 1.1 percent in 1997.[2] The classical opposition between capital and labor of Marxian economics is replaced by an opposition between those who participate in the circuits of the primary economy (and in the growing prosperity), and those who are shut out of those circuits and have to survive on their wits and creativity in the informal sector and in temporary work. Growing social polarization emerges at all scale levels; within cities, where issues of access dominate and local networks divide territories increasingly into protected areas of privilege, and the no-go areas of the excluded; regionally, where, for example, the poor may become trapped in inner-city areas while the better-off and more mobile occupy suburban areas; between regions, which compete to position themselves within the circuits of the global economy; and at the global scale, where large sections of the world become excluded from global economic networks, while others dominate and control these circuits to their own advantage.

Multiple layerings of change, while presenting urgent problems that need to be dealt with at their own levels, are not all equally significant in terms of an understanding of the whole. Certain issues emerge out of others, and the problem of theorizing the city also becomes one of knowing, or of proposing, the nexus of change, proposing also what is product and what by-product of the processes that drive the urban machine. But implicit in how we understand the mechanics of this thing, is a choice and a judgment. Reservations about 'totalizing discourses' notwithstanding, we are still compelled, if we are to achieve some kind of crisis management towards a purpose, to understand our living environment in terms to which we can ascribe a directionality.

[1] As proposed by Derrick de Kerckhove, for example in his paper 'Architecture and Plasma' in *Archis 5*, 2002

[2] *Human Development Report 1997*, New York: Human Development Report Office, 1997

The Form of the Future **Stephen Read**

We need to understand it in terms which we may understand as progress towards certain value-laden goals. Definitions and directions at this level are no politically neutral zone; rather, they are a matter of priorities and points of view with strong political and ethical dimensions. We will inevitably need to unwrap many of our half-conscious, half-examined presumptions about the city, and the values these notions incorporate and often conceal. There exist mental habits, presumptions of the obvious, which have themselves contributed to many of the predicaments we find ourselves in.

We need in particular to get beyond those habits which have made the city a thing to be engineered with the aim of containing and controlling social processes. Planning methods, with their strongly utopian antecedents, have often presumed a fixed spatial order underpinning an idealized social stability. They have conceived an ideal correspondence between spatial form and a regular, mechanical social process, and have imposed that form, fixing futures in an often banal or repressive caricature of the exact utopia concerned. What we need – more today than ever before, it seems – is a framework for understanding the city in terms that transcend the limitations imposed by static and utopian conceptualizations about the city and its products; the rule-of-thumb components and ensembles that have become so familiar we regard them as natural. What we need is a framework built explicitly around a principle of urban change and a framework for knowing how we can influence that change; a framework which itself explicitly incorporates an acceptance of continual process, development and change in historical time, and which can be cast in terms of continually ongoing processes of urbanization, and of social formation and transformation.

The urbanization of our world implies so much more than more buildings, more surfaces covered with asphalt, fewer green fields and woods to walk in, significant though these surface manifestations of the encroaching urban state might be. It has to do with the deep structures of our lives as individuals and as members of this ambiguous slippery thing we call 'society'. Because while we are by all accounts becoming more individualistic, less bound by bonds of family, neighborhood, community, nation and so on, we are simultaneously ever more immersed in a world which is constituted by variously media-ted relationships with other human beings, and the institutions we and they construct. Moments of real isolation from densely inter-meshed webs of relatedness are becoming increasingly rare; our lives are more and more conditioned by the hyperconnective world in which we are immersed and an increasing density of interrelationships with people, places and institutions – and this even while our consciousness registers an increasing detachment from real social involvement and belonging. The behavior of certain species of ants becomes social by some process we are quite unable to account for, when their world is constituted by the presence of other ants. As we enter deeper and deeper into these fields of intense social interconnectivity and intersubjectivity we have no means of knowing what the outcomes of this process will be.

Possible surprises in store for us don't stop at the necessary indeterminacy and openness of relational effects – which are as capable of course of reordering society into increasingly homogeneous pockets as they are of maintaining powerful interconnective and trans-scalar effects. These fluid effects are capable themselves of supporting the formation of stabilizing institutional structures and may also possibly contain checks and balances; attractors in their virtual spaces which continue to hold the whole in some recognizable enough, society-like, configuration. Possible other effects though, when we consider the increasing mediation of our experience by technological networks, include those of a de-skilling of the body's own perceptual capabilities. When perception is a 'creative addition' built around experience's self-referencing to its own ongoing event in a state of continual bodily movement, "[t]he more impoverished the conditions for feedback-enabled cross-referencing, the flightier will be the creative addition of the more to reality."[3]

Society and City seem bound to become ever more inseparably bound up with each other, destined to reveal perhaps eventually in each other their essential natures. As Simmel has pointed out:

> Life as such is formless, yet incessantly generates forms for itself... although these forms arise out of the life process, because of their unique constellation, they do not share the restless rhythm of life... They acquire fixed identities, a logic and lawfulness of their own; this new rigidity inevitably places them at a distance from the spiritual dynamic which created them and which makes them independent.[4]

Things, entities to which we ascribe unity and 'thingness', never comprise nothing but themselves. Their unity and autonomy hide an emergence out of processes, often of great complexity and even apparent disorder, at the level below that at which the unity is revealed. This idea is formalized by Whitehead in the notion of 'permanences' – "practically indestructible objects"[5] constituted out of flows, processes and relations operating within bounded fields. The mathematical study of complex systems has revealed a similar logic[6] and pulled the rug out from under Newton's vision of a deterministic clockwork universe. The clockwork cities of Le Corbusier and of the Garden City movement, in their pure forms at least, have all but gone the same way. We now know that things, entities, and phenomena emerge in much the same way as standing waves in a fast-flowing river; their seeming stability hiding the fact that they are generated out of dynamic relations. Processes and things are tied up together in a complex nested relationship of interdependency; things to which we ascribe stability are only provisionally 'permanent' and are liable to come under stress and to change as the conditions and forces and flows that generated and support them change. And we live in the midst of change, much of it surprising and unaccountable at first sight, all of it probably eventually to reveal its logics of emergence long after the critical moments of transformation. Our anxieties in the face of the changes taking place around us reveal how difficult this process is to absorb. Our sense of belonging has much to do with living in a world which we feel we can understand –

3] B. Massumi, *Parables for the Virtual*, Durham: Duke University Press, 2002, p. 156

4] G. Simmel, 'The conflict in modern culture', in K.P. Etzkorn (ed. and trans.) *Georg Simmel: The conflict in modern culture and other essays*, New York: Teachers College Press, 1968, pp. 11–12

5] A.N. Whitehead, *Science and the Modern World*, Lowell Lectures, Cambridge University Press, 1926

6] J. Cohen & I. Stewart, *The Collapse of Chaos: Discovering Simplicity in a Complex World*, London: Viking/Penguin, 1994

The Form of the Future **Stephen Read**

and in which we feel understood by others.[7] In a world where what appears solid and certain to the youth of one generation has a tendency to dissolve into thin air before that generation reaches middle age, such a sense of being familiar with the world is going to be a rare state indeed, and we will surely have to learn to deal in our urban future with the condition of provisionality as being routine. Explicitly recognizing this need for a mental and cultural acceptance of provisionality as a normal state of existence may be one of the most difficult but necessary tasks for building a future which does not feed on a fear which leads to insularity and to social and territorial segmentation and polarization.

In fact, many of the strategies we have devised and use in making the city, have as their underlying motive the avoidance or control of this intrinsic logic of formation and transformation. As Jane Jacobs has so powerfully argued, the neighborhood and the urban center of the planning manuals, are often areas which seek distance from the edgy and uncontrollable – from the contaminating power of the city itself. In the massive building boom of the last century, these forms achieved a status of normality and are often better known to newer generations of urban dwellers than are Jacobs' streets and sidewalks of former times. They have achieved their highest forms in the modern interiorized shopping environment – to be found now equally in center and periphery as a sort of generic plug-in element – and in the separated suburban or even gated 'community'.

But these forms, in their determination to define a safe and predictable inside, just as emphatically define an outside; a space beyond the consideration of highly localized spatial and social designs, and a space which has become the other defining environment of the contemporary city as we have made it. The "incongruous rims of ratty tattoo parlors and second-hand stores"[8] of the edge of center, and the strange, deserted, unnamable spaces of the periphery, are just as much a product of a now generic way of making the city as are its more conscious products. And paradoxically – or maybe not, given the forthright anti-urbanism of many of the twentieth century's planning utopias – these days, it is often these spaces which shout to us about the potentials of the urban, of an environment which is open to shifting valences, to expedient and practical appropriation, and to an unprogrammed and unpredictable vitality. It is these spaces that are occupying the attention of some of the most original minds in urban research and design[9] and it is these spaces that often seem to hold out the promise of a future open to surprising new potentials, and to the way human need can be served through empowering human creativity and resourcefulness. These spaces, beyond the constraining limits of institutionalized consumption and cast-in-concrete social patterns, may offer some individuals and groups the opportunities they seek. Again it was Jacobs who pointed out to us that "there is a quality even meaner than outright ugliness and disorder... the dishonest mask of pretended order, achieved by ignoring or suppressing the real order that is struggling to exist and to be served."[10] As protected, programmed, imaged and designed urban spaces are opposed to those left-over spaces, which by the fact of their being unprogrammed represent potentials for creative appropriation, so the regimentation

[7] See M. Ignatieff, 'There's no place like home: The politics of belonging', in S. Dunant and R. Porter, *The Age of Anxiety*, London: Virago, 1996

[8] J. Jacobs, *The Death and Life of Great American Cities*, Harmondsworth: Penguin, 1965, p. 35

[9] For example, S. Boeri, 'Notes for a research program', *Mutations*, Barcelona: arc en rêve centre d'architecture & ACTAR, 2000

[10] J. Jacobs, op. cit., p. 25

of programmed lives within a rapidly globalizing order of corporate economics and consumption is opposed by the restless spirit of masses of individuals, within marginal territories at all scale levels (from that of the suburb or slum to that of the third world), struggling either to survive by necessity outside this (for them) excluding order, or simply to be creative and to realize themselves.

It is tempting to take from all this – besides the fact that cities can be in and of themselves divisive, and that it can be us and our ways of building that can make them divisive – a rather naive conclusion that the processes of the city themselves, if allowed their own freedom of expression and working, offer the best bet we have for human opportunity and self-realization. This is a thesis that has been taken up in diverse forms on both sides of the political spectrum in the past by those who have reacted against the utopian fixity of modernist planning. The 'invisible hand' is a notion with which we are all too familiar, and we need to be wary of straightforwardly recycling conceptual habits about transformation dynamics, and projecting these wholesale onto the city. Wherever we start in thinking about urban process we will almost surely, if we are honest and diligent, be confronted with heterogeneity, not just in the products of the processes but also in the nature of the processes themselves. Within the nested interdependency of processes and things referred to earlier, particular configurations of processes and things will actively reproduce these configurations to serve their own interests. The urban world is as much an ecology of competing power interests capable of manipulating the field in a top-down fashion, as it is an ecology of synergetic agents who evolve structures from the bottom up.

The division of channels of social and economic process and flow into so-called 'trees' and 'semi-lattices' (if one is listening to Chris Alexander)[11], or 'hierarchies' and 'meshworks' (if one is listening to Manuel de Landa)[12], or 'trees' and 'rhizomes' and 'striated' and 'smooth' space (if one is listening to Deleuze and Guattari)[13] – especially if we recognize that network systems can operate in different modes at different scale levels, as well as at different levels of integration and interaction across scale levels – could offer a means of understanding how we may influence and direct processes of urbanization and social formation towards ends which are in the end liberating and enabling. It is well known that networks have fundamentally different ways of distributing control, depending on their tree-likeness or semi-lattice-likeness. But here again a word of warning is called for; meshworks/semi-lattices exist in the real world always in combination with, and in hybrid forms with, hierarchies/trees, and their properties, even in their pure form, are almost impossible to determine by theory alone. The fact is that we need both forms if we are to achieve the ends of both liberation and intelligibility. As Deleuze and Guattari assert; "rhizomes also have their own, even more despotic, hierarchy... there are despotic formations of immanence and channelization specific to rhizomes, just as there are anarchic deformations in the transcendent system of trees".[14] De Landa warns that "meshworks grow by drift and they may drift to places we do not want to go. The goal-directedness of hierarchies is the kind of property that we may desire to keep at least for certain institutions."[15]

11] See C. Alexander, 'A city is not a tree', in G. Bell and J. Tyrwhitt, Human Identity in the Urban Environment, Harmondsworth: Pelican, 1972

12] See M. De Landa, Meshworks, Hierarchies and Interfaces. Online. Available <http://www.t0.or.at/delanda/meshwork.htm>

13] See G. Deleuze and F. Guattari, A Thousand Plateaus: Capitalism and Schizophrenia, Minneapolis: University of Minnesota Press, 1987

14] Ibid., p. 20

15] De Landa, op. cit.

The Form of the Future Stephen Read

We are making a transition from a world where the urban represents a condition of social life, to one where it represents *the* condition of social life. The urban was once an interval of concentration in a life space-time which included the countryside and the home. Both these non-urban conditions have been progressively infiltrated, to the point where, for some of us at least, almost all the activities and functions we used to think of as being urban can be, and are being, performed everywhere. We shop and work at home, at our computer screens or on the telephone. We drive to out-of-town business parks and malls and haul files and laptops, or shopping bags, back to our cars, parked on spots where cows recently grazed. But at the same time as the urban is becoming the condition of modern life, the properties of urban places are assuming all manner of hybrid and newly-emergent forms. The obvious variety and differences both between and within cities in the manner of emergence of the local condition, needs for a moment to be considered against the incongruous nature of the local under the process of globalization. The apparent disappearance of a strong local place condition in many situations can be contrasted with the fact of a simultaneous emergence of places whose power is precisely a consequence of their alignments within global networks.[16] As far as designers and planners are concerned today, the lesson may be one of understanding the problem in terms of a less superficial, less pictorial, perhaps less object-oriented and certainly more process-oriented, understanding of the condition of the urban and of urban place. While the effect of the global on the local may suggest another way of understanding the emergence of local conditions, the local and the global are not the only scales in the modern city, and are certainly not the only scales which bear on particular urban conditions.

There is hardly a place – certainly no urban place – in our world which is not touched by the global, but the influence of this and other scales depends very much on the particular conduits of their transmission. While these conduits, in our contemporary world, need not all be physical networks, one of our particular tasks is to understand the mechanics of the city in terms of urban scale relationships and the networks which mediate them. As Bruno Latour reminds us, the lengthening of our technological networks has had enormous scaling effects, enabling interrelationships between the local and the global and all scales in between. We should not however make the mistake of thinking of the local and the global in terms of the old opposite categories of universal and contingent. We can follow the pathways of all networks, whatever their scale, in the local; all networks are fabricated, used, guarded, adjusted, controlled and maintained in the local, and to the service of particular interests which find their place in the local, and while there are today "... continuous paths that lead from the local to the global, from the circumstantial to the universal, from the contingent to the necessary ...", these paths remain, and remain continuous "... only so long as the branch lines are paid for."[17] When considered in this way, it's not difficult to see that many interesting questions of the contemporary city, as far as they concern us, revolve not so much around issues of local adjacency supplemented by the transmission of a generalized global onto every local surface, but rather around the diagonal paths interrelationships take through nested scale levels. The pathways producing the local condition, are woven through an urban-social space which

16] S. Sassen, *The Global City: New York, London, Tokyo*, Princeton: Princeton University Press, 2001

17] B. Latour, *We have never been Modern*, Cambridge, Mass.: Harvard University Press, 1993, p. 117

spans, and is modified by, networks operating within and between adjacent and not so adjacent urban scales. It is no longer sufficient to think of locality as being a simple given, defined by its coordinates in Cartesian space – nor is it sufficient to think of the scale issue as one of the simple penetration of a generic global into all lives and all places. Rather, the local needs to be seen as a production of the real social and economic interconnections that people and their transactions trace through the physical and virtual network spaces of the city at a variety of speeds and scales, up to and including that of the global.

Such a perspective, if taken seriously, is bound, we feel, to take us beyond the conventional planners' and designers' wisdoms of 'community', 'neighborhood', 'urban village' and so forth, which see the local as a refuge, as the psychological home of the disaffected modern urbanite, to be made as a sort of protective buffer or fortress against the contaminating and disturbing influence of the city. An approach which seeks to support processes which empower people - and especially those people whose power is limited within existing social and economic orders - is almost bound, we feel, to find value in those spatial processes which tend to 'globalize' (or at least 'de-localize'); which tend to offer opportunity and power to people with respect to a wider world around them. People need to participate in the dynamics of change, and they need to participate through places (both virtual and 'physical', though we feel the importance of face-to-face social relations should not be underestimated) situated within and energized by a non-local space which is open, connected to streams of urban, regional and global power while not being controlled by them. If this begins to sound like the space of the city promoted by Jacobs, then what we seek are ways to uphold the virtues of Jacobs' open, connective, socially thick and layered, traditional city within a rather different sort of urban state. We can do this only by understanding the ways in which the processes of people's lives and livelihoods today connect the local to the global and to all the scales in between.

All this involves processes and mechanics which are difficult to predict, and difficult to theorize using current ideas about the city. They may be by their nature processes which depend for their outcome on finely-adjusted thresholds so that we are left with the familiar dilemma of having to try things out before knowing if or how they work. Simulation of urban processes within virtual environments as well as the monitoring of processes in the real world are two obvious ways forward. What we also need to do, though, is consider and reconsider our ways of looking at and thinking about urbanization and urban and social formation processes and the networks they exploit, as well as our understanding of their abstract categories, so that we can begin to develop a deeper insight into the way all of this works – and of how power relations are embedded in ideas of urban stasis and change, and how they are distributed within the urban social and economic field.

This is a subject for a research program to which we can at this point give only indications. The city is an environment, an ecology rather than a neutral setting for social practices; it is itself a part of the 'habitus', the "durably installed generative principle

The Form of the Future **Stephen Read**

of regulated improvisations" producing practices which reproduce the generative principle.[18] We need to know more about the ways in which different urban spaces influence the "conductorless orchestration which gives regularity, unity, and systematicity" to practices.[19] And we need to understand how this can be influenced to happen in a way which imparts form and pattern, with opportunity, without coercion, and holding futures open for continuous change and development. As people who attempt to build living environments which empower people, we need to build an understanding of the ways people's surroundings are integral with their lives and how these surroundings may liberate and enable people to search for and find their own realization in a continuing cycle of creative adaptation. Research to this end has hardly begun, but the blind spots and neglected domains in our discipline seem, to us at least, to be clustered around this general zone. We believe that the stories of our cities from this point forward will be marked more and more by the way they deal with and make provision for the factor of change. Research needs to focus not just on the procedures of city building but also on the conceptual apparatus that we bring to bear on the problem, and we will need to measure this apparatus not only against values of justice and equity, but also against sets of values that incorporate an idea of an urban future which makes "provision for the fact of history".[20] We do not claim to have answers at this stage, and propose here only to pose questions around the general theme of transformation as a permanent urban state.

The cities collected here look at processes of change from the perspectives both of the author and of the particular conditions of that city. We make no claims to comprehensiveness; indeed we hope to follow these stories at regular intervals with new stories about new cities. What we hope they do is illustrate some of the spectrum of urban development and change at this point in history, as well as surveying some of the conceptualizations by which these processes of change are understood.

The contributions
The extraordinary historical circumstances of the Dutch, and their centuries-long collective struggle to wrest productive and habitable land from the water, have produced in their turn not just a huge planning bureaucracy, but also a collective mind-set conditioned to the idea of planning. It is a landscape that is quite literally made from the foundation up, but made also to a definite aim. This landscape is no blank sheet of paper, no smooth space waiting to be written; it has been measured and marked from the beginning, rendered unavailable for the casual appropriation that has delivered sprawl in other parts of the world. It is subject from the beginning to a highly regulated institutional framework which defines fitness of purpose.

The land, as a mental as much as a physical construct, is subject to change within this context. The power of an idea as a guiding principle for change is the subject of the paper by Dirk Frieling. Here the process of urbanization is conceived quite explicitly in terms of the mental constructs of policy-makers and planners, and it is to the end of the coordination of diverse planning sectors towards an explicit aim of reshaping of the urban landscape that this idea refers. Where in other parts of the continent

[18] P. Bourdieu, *Outline of a Theory of Practice*, Cambridge: Cambridge University Press, 1977, p. 78

[19] Ibid., p. 80

[20] R. Sennett, *The Uses of Disorder*, New York: Norton, 1992, p. 99

cities are transforming seemingly by default, first into carpets of amorphous sprawl, which glue together around infrastructural works into whole urbanized regions, in the Netherlands the transformation process has to be conceived first as being necessary in order to maintain competitiveness at a European level, and then the idea guided through a complex process of lobbying, exploration and consensus-forming before being incorporated into planning documents at government, provincial and municipal level. Even in the Netherlands, however, there has long been a sense that the game has changed. The master plan is a museum relic, and strategies and private-sector partnerships are the order of the day. Still the regular assessments of the planning 'notas' or green papers, are less catalogues of achievement than of missed aims and inadequate means (often at the level of conceptualization and of the understanding of the relation between changing life patterns and expectations, and the plan). Chief among the difficulties seems to be the translation of people's expectations of urban quality and amenity into a reality in terms of a densely supportive living environment. The transportation plan is one of the chief instruments used for affecting change, and the conceptualization of this plan is perhaps indicative of the difficulty. Its effectiveness at the higher scale levels is reasonably clear, but at the finer scales - in the way different scales of network interpenetrate and interact, and the way these affect the characters and social structures of living environments - understanding remains still stuck in conceptions which neglect the dense layerings of social and economic relationship between the scales of the regional and the local.

Modernist planning treated the city as something to be rationalized, as an instrument of social betterment, efficiency and hygiene. A plan is always to some extent a diagram, holding people and things in some kind of relation to each other for a particular social purpose. The modalities of the plan reveal assumptions about the way things are supposed to relate and interrelate, and the modernist plan pinned these normative relationships and divisions in place, positively excluding other possibilities. The dynamic, swarming mechanisms of the looser, more traditional city were seen as chaotic, unpredictable and dangerous. The story of the beginning of planning in Johannesburg in the paper by Lindsay Bremner has all the resonance of foundation myth. Here, in the sorting pens of the hospital camp lie the beginnings of the city as instrument of control and cleansing. The society it supported, obsessed with purity, partitioned the landscape in the ultimate exercise in social cleansing. The connective network was set up as a system of valves and switches, controlling relationships between zones, making it efficiently governable and becoming part of the administrative and policing machine. It was not just race that was partitioned, but also the violence of prejudice, fear and grievance. This was and remains a landscape of planned holding tanks for all manner of tensions and loathing. In a society obsessed with control, the lifting of the guard at the political level has had explosive and unpredictable consequences. The minds of the population, or that part of the population that planning served, has become conditioned to fear, to conflate real and imagined danger, and to setting up fortress walls around insular fantasies of order and propriety. The extraordinary banality of the fortress interiors contrasts now with the relative lawlessness of the more open spaces of urban centers. The sclerotic effect of this vicious heritage remains a weight around the neck of possible new futures, still fixing social orders in the shapes of an unhappy past.

The forces of economic globalization are having a powerful effect on the shapes of cities, transforming many in a decade or less from national centers in economies structured around the nation state, into places competing for position in the regions and networks of a global economy. It is perhaps in this global game of jockeying for positions of power that one perceives most clearly the primacy of process over the static material of the city. In the story of the marketing of Sydney, Penelope Dean tells of the coordination of policy and planning effort towards the ends of achieving an image designed to promote the city on a global stage. The image, built around the theme of leisure, has to be distinctive and recognizable against those of other cities competing against Sydney in the global region. With the stakes so high, it is not only local places but also all the power of information and media channels which become appropriated to global strategies. In Sydney it is the central zone of the city itself, with all its natural advantages – but also as a vibrant cosmopolitan living environment – that is being marketed. Public policy supports investment and the concentration of business, commerce, high-rise and high-priced housing, and entertainment to the center in support of this strategy. The image of the city becomes a marketing feature for housing as well – real-estate is shifted on the basis of skyline or harbor views rather than on the basis of their footprint locations and public environments. In the rush for immediate gain at the global level, relationships at the lower scales are overlooked; public space loses continuity, becoming fragmented into highly particularized, imaged and no doubt variably exclusive and excluding spaces.

Cities, even the most brash and new, do not become global out of nothing. Rather, their transformation is built on improvisations around and adaptations of past habits and practices. Cities are built by people, and those that are positioned closest to the circuits of money and power, attract the attentions of dynamic and inventive people. Stories of urban generation and reinvention are threaded through with individuals intent on positioning and repositioning themselves and their cities within axes of money and power. The notion of the adaptation of highly local conditions and practices to the end of the repositioning of a city relative to global networks is perhaps even stronger in the case of Kuala Lumpur. Ramesh Biswas describes how a place of bustling entrepreneurship at a crossroads of eastern trade routes repositioned itself opportunistically within the circuits of global capital, while maximizing profit in a frenzy of grandiose overreach. Here is a place that has grown out of local cultural patterns; the network of social relationships and favors has itself been the structure supporting the success stories.

The lives of the common people appear to be caught in the same whirlwind of optimistic freewheeling dynamism, as the city pins its global image to a few spectacular, iconic and popular projects. Commercial interests feed a dynamic which is more or less given free rein, spilling out of the center and into the region, into an extensive, uneven post-metropolis, which thickens around points of high regional accessibility.

In both Kuala Lumpur and Sydney we hear about a strategy of connection, knitting the city together at the metropolitan scale through infrastructural works, while at the same time there is the increasing loss of connectivity at the lower scales, as commercial development concentrates on its own relatively narrow field of interest. The fragmentation of public space and interconnectivity at this scale translates into Dean's "spaces of publics", which while being distinctive and selective, also represent a loss of continuity at lower speeds and scales, and a breaking of the tissue of interrelationship at this scale that the more traditional city supported; a tissue of interrelationship which expanded social space from the very local level towards the scales of the city above.

If Kuala Lumpur represents the case of the new city repositioning itself opportunistically in relation to global flows of capital – and presenting itself through a brash new image to international investors, "simple minded folk" who need to be persuaded to fill the empty skyscrapers – then the case of Berlin represents a marketing exercise at a far more historically and culturally layered level. In particular, Andreas Huyssen investigates a city whose meanings and presences in modern consciousness echo thunderingly in the voids that the city presented to us in its recent contemporary form. According to Huyssen, one of these voids is the authentic "real Berlin of today", squeezed out by a vacuous debate on the future form of the city, between two camps who promote "banal images of a national past against equally banal images of a global future". For Huyssen the massive building projects at the Potsdamer Platz and Leipziger Platz are an exercise in forgetting, and especially in erasing, the pregnant, even eloquent, silences which the voids represent.

At the same time, the life of the city is in the process of becoming encaged as corporate structures "confine their visitors, rather than recreate the open, mobile, and multiply-coded urban culture that once characterized this pivotal traffic hub." The fact is that the global marketeering interests behind these structures see no advantage in creating the city and district scale synergies and interactivities which were the basis of this urban culture, and the public open conduits which transmitted these active relationships become anachronistic at the feet of global corporate behemoths with their eyes on a transnational or transcontinental, certainly not local or city-scale, horizon.

Ultimately the city cannot be the detached, objective, stable instrument, the "prism through which we can focus issues of contemporary urbanism, national identity and statehood, historical memory and forgetting". The prism and the issues of being and identity are so wound up with each other, and with the shifts and drifts of the circumstances of life within a particular urban place. The city, perhaps the 'real Berlin', and the living cultures it incorporates in the end reassert themselves, develop dynamics of their own, and move forward along unexpected pathways and against unimagined contours. On the other hand, these developments are often quite unremarkable when experienced in real time, as they happen, as products of ever-mobile global and local conditions playing out in real urban place.

Jim Masselos traces the identities emergent out of the extraordinary social cauldron of Mumbai over the 10 years since the terrifying upheavals at the beginning of the 1990s. Once again the issue of local lives and practices dominates a story of massive growth and an alignment within the flows of a global economy. The concurrent realignment of Mumbai with identities embedded in the region coincides with a shift away from another global orientation – that of the colonial empire with its center in Europe. This simultaneous reorientation of the city relative to a global economic network and relative to the region is reflected also in a redirection of consciousness towards a sense of local pride and self-sufficiency. There is evidence from other places as well, with a reassertion of regional identities the world over, that these identities and a powerful but non-centrifugal global pattern of power may work in a curious, mutually reinforcing relationship with one another. Certainly in the case of former colonial territories, the sense of cultural allegiance to the former colonial power has been difficult – still is difficult in truth – to throw off. But the issue is by no means straightforward, with contemporary patterns of global power being potentially just as oppressive as previous ones, while being more difficult to deal with because of their lack of an easily identifiable center. Mumbai, like many of the hugely expanding world cities, tries pragmatically to optimize its position within the global network, while relying on the city and its surroundings for its particular sense of its own self.

The outward spiral of urban scales towards the metropolitan, regional and the global is clearly not the only tendency in today's cities. In some of the most surprising places we begin to see a reassertion of scales closer to those of the body and its unmotorized movements. The reassertion of place and of scales moving from the local to those just above is a tendency identified by Kazys Varnalis in Los Angeles of all places, the original city of the car. LA, with its two or three cars per household, is becoming a victim of its own success; here the growing costs and other difficulties in maintaining, expanding and adapting the freeway network has already led to gridlock at many strategic points of the system. People are responding by seeking out places where more locally centered living patterns are possible. It is perhaps not surprising that this tendency to more locally scaled living patterns is finding its most fertile conditions within spatial patterns which grew when these sorts of scales predominated. Many of the old towns on the streetcar lines are reasserting themselves as centralities, becoming the new hotspots in the overall urban field, as new living patterns reappropriate the historical street grids which served those scales before. The demographics of these places are also under transformation, as society in general splits along lines of ever-finer distinction. A society of atomized minorities identifies itself less and less along the traditional shear planes of class and ethnicity, and relies less and less on class or ethnicity for choices when it comes to dwelling location or consumption patterns. The social homogeneity of many neighborhoods is being eroded as demographic clusters share locations, opening the possibility of more socially diverse living areas, more closely linked to workplaces.

This lower scale of urban movement is the dominant subject also of my own contribution, on the central space of Amsterdam. Here, in a spatial field composed of multiple overlapped individual and group lived spaces, local place, rather than being seen as a blank canvas supporting social writing, is proposed instead as being itself a product of patterns of (mainly low-speed) movement. Urban existence becomes dynamically embedded in the material networks of the fabric, which itself constitutes the immediate framework of identification and orientation, the 'condition of perception' as Merleau-Ponty might have it. When considered as 'extended local' connectivities – as a meshwork of routes that produces local conditions through their relations towards the larger scales – the physical fabric can be shown to support social-spatial forms in place, including for example interfaces of copresence between local inhabitants and strangers, and street-edge economic viability. These 'provisional permanences' in place are literally supported by the flux of real movement which passes through these places – like the standing waves in the river – and are liable to shift or change as the conditions of flow and the stuff flowing through change. Certain environments are identified which appear to structure without coercion, imparting identity and particularity while remaining open to fresh appropriations which overlap with the old. Here the quality of the place is imparted by movements relating urban part to a larger scale whole through the spatial grid of the city. Places, relating simultaneously to local and wider central urban scales, produce conditions which appear to be particularly conducive to a diverse and vibrant activity in place. The rather more rigid structures we are creating out of the larger-scale movement patterns in our cities today have yet to produce an equivalent power of place, while as planners and designers we neglect the scales *between* – the middle scales, between the most local and the new metropolitan scales – which have supported these constructions of place in the past.

A city which deals very explicitly with the energy of new orders, and with some new kinds of emergent forms in the city, is Hong Kong. Gary Chang takes us on a tour of a place which constantly dazzles and surprises; a city of energy, light and movement rather than of steel and concrete, suspended directly between the local and the global. Hong Kong has become, out of the creative energy of its inhabitants and the power of global finance, a place which absorbs all; which offers seemingly no resistance to the new. Anything seems possible here as the effects of global flows are captured in an extraordinarily absorbent local place. Moments of quiet and stillness are poised precariously between the humming webs; the most violent juxtapositions are taken up by the everyday – the constructions that people make of them testifying to the continuing adaptability of the human animal and to his ingenuity in improvising out of necessity and out of contingent circumstance the most surprising and unlikely of constructions.

The local dominates in Douala, Camaroon, where Abdou-Maliq Simone describes a place where each individual has to cut their own way through knotted local webs to the networks which support their livelihood. There are no larger-scale political or civil institutions capable of representing the everyday interests of residents. Also lacking are the social-spatial forms which mediate the local and the larger city, undermining collective understandings of the city as an identifiable social and political entity. The city forms a highly complex and disarticulated social patchwork of local identities, founded in residential patterns organized around small clusters of ethnic and familial solidarity. At the same time, urbanized behavior patterns mean that the burden of survival is incumbent on individuals and households. The relative lack of networks moving from the local to the larger scales mean that relations on scales above the local become a matter of dealing with delicate border situations within mazes of territories. The lack of a city-level identity means issues of the larger scales become clouded in the consciousness of the population. Urban life becomes enmeshed in a web of urban mythology, where fact and fantasy intermesh and may be manipulated to ends that remain opaque or even sinister. The complexity and opacity of the way to the non-local becomes an opportunity for those with skill and ambition to gain at multiple unseen points, while offering to the weak "turbulent spaces of some autonomy [through] navigating an array of spectral worlds and multiple temporalities that are as real as anything else in the city." There are "no clear maps; no grand visions for a viable future" as people inhabit a space poised between but detached from both their traditional affiliations with their deep structures and rhythms, and the modernity that the city has promised but not yet delivered.

Another city in crisis, but one which is delivering in unexpected ways, is Belgrade. Whereas the lack of a broader institutional and identifying framework has turned the social and political space of Douala into an underworld of intrigue and manipulation, in Belgrade it is with the breakdown of normal institutional frameworks that the dynamics of urban change are breaking explosively out of a condition of stasis. The vibrant informal economy that is emerging seems to have found a way of breaking out of the local that Douala has not, and it seems that the city itself is playing a part in this process. In spite of the emphasis on the micro in the story told by Ana Dzokic, Milica Topalovic, Marc Neelen and Ivan Kucina, it seems to be the city's crossings and most powerful axes, and the everyday life-patterns they organize and make legible, which coordinate this process, becoming an armature on which micro-effects condense and solidify. Belgrade, while demonstrating the fluidity of city structures and their possibilities for reordering the social and economic fabric, at the same time also demonstrates by default – by the fact that it doesn't happen in other times and other places – that there are as many forces, solidified institutions and practices, and interests, working for stasis as there are working for change.

Number of inhabitants [p]	6,058,943
Area [km²]	4,408
Density [p/km²]	1,375
Population urbanized (national) [2003]	66%

kanje

Maeskantkering

Harrel Kanaal

Nieuwe Waterweg

Schieveningen

Wassenaarse slag

1809

Rijn - Schie kanaal

126

ndscherm sluis Rozenburg

1245

Hartelkering

De Schie

Nieuwe Maas

De Rotte

De Noordplas polder

Spui

1340

Zuidplaspolder

Gouwe

⊗ - 6.8 n.a.p

Oude Maas

Stormvloedkering Capelle a/d IJssel

Hollandse IJssel

1272

uizen

De Krimpenerwaard

Lek

De Vlist

e Kil

<1220

e Diep

From Randstad to Deltametropolis
Dirk Frieling

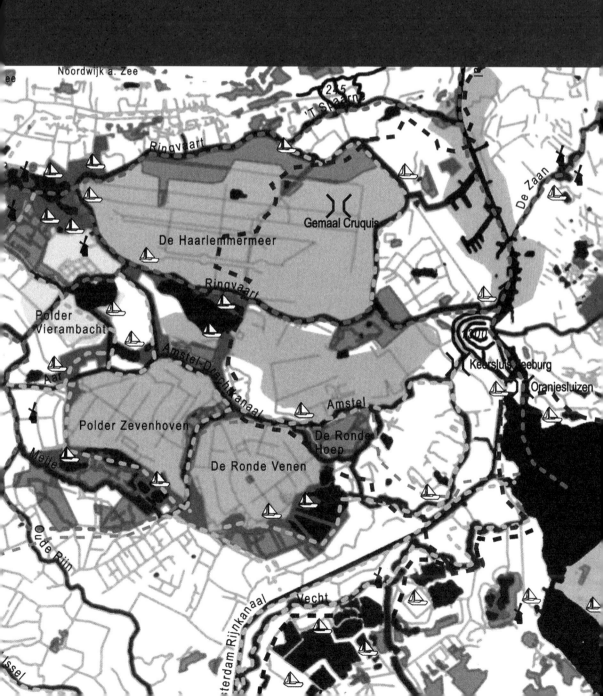

This text is about the eventual transformation of that loose collection of towns and cities known as the Randstad into an interconnected urban constellation to be called 'Deltametropolis' – 'Delta' deriving from the natural system it is part and parcel of, and 'metropolis' referring to the cultural system of world cities in which it might partake, the global network in which these metropolises are the focal points of human interaction. It is not certain that this will happen. It may happen. This text is about what it may take to let this happen. Questions that arise, then, are how a metropolis is conceived, how society can become pregnant with this idea and how this idea may grow and materialize in the outside world.

The birth of Deltametropolis has to start with conception, like any other birth. To transform the Randstad into Deltametropolis you first have to change the concept in which planning policy in the Netherlands is rooted. This concept is that the Dutch live in the most densely populated country of the world and that the western part is the densest of all – so densely populated, indeed, that it cannot accommodate its own growth and has to export this to the south, east and north. Recently the minister of Housing, Planning and Environment made an official statement in this tenor in the papers. This statement is in line with central government planning policy of the last 40 years.

If, however, one looks at these western lowlands as a potential metropolis, what one sees then is an extremely low-density type of metropolis, where most of the area is reserved for cows – holy cows, because they embody the Dutch paradise of milk, butter and cheese.

The main topic to be discussed here is understanding the role of design in this change of concept, its role in the change of mindset with which people look at the world around them, and its role in whether people experience the reality of the Netherlands as a high-density country or as a low-density city.

Concepts are the seeds of action, but as we know from nature, seeds need fertile soil to come to anything. As any farmer knows, if you want to harvest you should cultivate the soil before you start sowing. So this is the third part of the transformation this text will dwell on: the strategy of winning others to your ideas.

The story that is told here is not the perception of an outsider but the story of a participant. Do not expect the observations of a scientist who wants to discover the truth, but rather the analysis of an engineer who wants to invent something that works.

The research that is done on the subject is an active, forward-looking research and takes place in three stages:
1984-1989: design of political perspectives,
1993-1997: design instruments and tools for interactive decision-making in design,
1998-2002: introducing processes that lead quicker to better decisions.

Political perspectives

In the 1970s, the Netherlands was influenced rather heavily by the coincidence of the Club of Rome study *The Limits to Growth* and the first energy crisis triggered by OPEC. At the end of that decade there seemed to be no limit to the growth of unemployment. Cabinets tried to fight unemployment with more public spending, in social security as well as in housing. Public finance got out of hand. This led to a political coalition that took 'no nonsense' as its motto.

What this meant was that public spending changed into public saving. At once planning, which means spending for the future, became politically incorrect. Planning departments were dissolved, consultancies closed down and the whole planning machinery came more or less to a standstill. Politicians declared that 'society cannot be made' to cover up this destruction of planning organizations.

In the same period, the Scientific Council for Government Policy tried to reorient cabinet, parliament and interested political parties to the future by means of three substantive studies. These policy-oriented surveys of future development, however, fell on barren ground. Some professional people became so angry about what they considered political escapism that they initiated a five-year project called 'The Netherlands Now As Design'. Following the lead given by the studies of the Scientific Council for Government Policy, they decided to design four political perspectives for the Netherlands in 2050, halfway through the present century. With this they aimed to kill three birds with one stone: redesign the Netherlands for the time when growth wouldn't be an issue anymore, revitalize politics and put the focus back on planning.

The 'Netherlands Now As Design' Foundation enlisted the support of government departments, the participation of universities and private research organizations, collected 4 million guilders and engaged the *fine fleur* of the design profession. It then organized a three-year design program in which more than 200 professionals participated, meeting every three months to discuss designs and progress. An exhibition of these four political perspectives was held in Amsterdam and Rotterdam. The State Printing Office published an exhibition catalogue in two volumes: one with all the designs, the other with background research.[1]

[1] Hans van der Cammen (ed.), *Nieuw Nederland*, Den Haag: Staatsuitgeverij 's Gravenhage, 1987

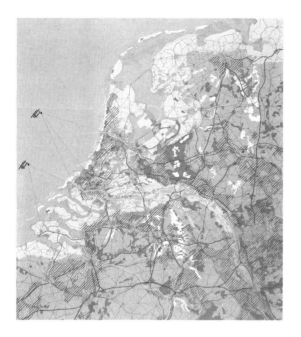

Four basic designs of the Netherlands in 2050 were developed. In each one, a different region was selected to demonstrate how the design would work out in that area. These regional designs were then elaborated via between five and 10 architectural designs for specific objects within that region.

figure 1 Careful

figure 2 Dynamic

The first design, entitled **Careful**, was the perspective from a Christian Democratic point of view. This was the only perspective that showed the Netherlands as a part of Europe, leaving out sharp state boundaries. This European orientation gave the eastern and southern parts of the country a more central position, whereas the western part became more peripheral. The network of roads and railroads was transformed from the present star like shape, radiating from the west, into a grid connecting all parts of the country to each other and to the European mainland. Agriculture and nature were integrated, farmers maintaining both. The Eindhoven area was chosen as the subject of regional design.

The second design, **Dynamic**, was the perspective of those people that the Dutch call liberal but that elsewhere are called conservative. It was a market-oriented perspective which strengthened the western constellation of cities by way of three interventions in the transport system: a new international airport in the sea, high-speed railway connections with the rest of Europe and a new circle rail line to interconnect the main cities in the west. The country as a whole was in a way considered as a city, with the Central Business District (CBD) in the west and the living areas on higher and drier grounds in the south and east. The lower parts of the country were transformed into large-scale wetlands for reasons to do with water management. Farming was to become large-scale factory farming. Amsterdam was chosen for the regional design.

figure 3 Critical

figure 4 Relaxed

Critical, the third design, was the perspective of the left of centre point of view. Society was changed radically in three ways: energy systems were based on sunlight, wind and biological bulk, working hours were reduced to three days per week and all regions were connected to the European high-speed transport network. A combination of less work and better connections would extend the job market for inhabitants of the Netherlands to Hamburg, Berlin, Frankfurt, Paris and London.

The western part of the country was transformed into an area of ecological balance, with the former Green Heart changed into a huge wetland and cities and wetland integrated into one ecological system. Elsewhere as well, large areas were transformed into wetlands and nature reserves. Agriculture for the international market was concentrated in the clay areas in the north, the middle and the southwest. East Groningen was chosen for the regional design.

These three perspectives were based on political scenarios, put forward by the Scientific Council and then translated and elaborated into socio-economic programs and territorial settlement patterns by Rob Gastelaars and Leo de Klerk of the University of Amsterdam.[2]

The fourth design, called **Relaxed**, was the perspective of the initiators of the project themselves. The essence of the perspective was that technological and political transformations would lead, not to ongoing urban dispersal but, on the contrary, to a new period of urban concentration. This was also the conclusion of Manuel Castells in his book *The Informational City* of 1989 and of Saskia Sassen in 1991 in her book *The Global City*.[3] The central technological breakthrough was to be the availability of cheap energy by nuclear fusion and by harvesting sunlight, and for which 2,000 sq km were allocated. Energy being no problem, the speed of transport could be multiplied. In this

[2] Ibid., pp. 41–63

[3] Saskia Sassen, *The Global City: New York, London, Tokyo,* Princeton, NJ. : Princeton University Press, 1991

perspective of a full energy economy and transcontinental magnetic train systems, the
Rotterdam area was the region to concentrate on: it would no longer serve only as a main
port for Germany but also for Poland, Russia and the middle-European economies. The
political breakthrough (envisaged a few years before the fall of the Berlin Wall) was that
technology would be the driving force to break through old world political boundaries.

figure 5 Changes between
present and projected land use
(1987–2015)

figure 6 Investments per
hectare for the whole period
1987–2015

The two years after the exhibitions in 1987 were used, among other things, to develop
an investment strategy. The central government's fourth report on planning policy, published in 1988, was taken as a starting-point.[4] The existing physical shape of the country
was then compared to the future shape proposed by the cabinet. The difference was
then used to calculate the costs of transformation. The first figure maps the difference
between present and future shape. The second maps the investments per square km
needed for this transformation.

Following the logic of their political priorities, one could then show that Christian
Democrats would invest in rural areas and provincial towns everywhere, Liberals would
invest in infrastructure and Labor in the larger cities. The planning policy document
showed an almost perfect correlation with these different political priorities. Another
result of this analysis was that at a regional level, investments per person were more or
less the same all over the country. As one can see on the map, investments show the
same pattern as population patterns.

Interactive decision processes

What can one learn from these exercises with regard to metropolitan development, the
role of design and the way to form strategic alliances with other actors in society?
What had to be the next step in research?

4] Min. van VROM, Vierde
Nota over de Ruimtelijke
Ordening: op weg naar 2015,
's Gravenhage: SDU uitgeverij,
1988

The arguments for metropolitan development are quite pronounced in the Dynamic, Critical and Relaxed perspectives, although for different reasons: economic in the Dynamic worldview, ecological in the Critical, and the outcome of technological development in the Relaxed perspective. The Labor priorities were misinterpreted by the participants, however. Labor allied with the Christian Democrats in an anti-metropolitan policy. This became clear in the difference between the fourth planning report of 1988 and a fourth planning report 'extra' of 1990.[5] The original report, issued by a Liberal minister of planning, had as its main issue the urban development in the west. Three years and a cabinet crisis later, the Labor minister issued a fourth report extra in which the three main urban concentrations in the west were replaced by 13 cities all over the country.

All four perspectives were internationally-oriented. In political reality however, not the international future but the provincial present won the day. From this experience we may conclude that there may be reasons of international competition and economic, ecological and technological arguments that point to metropolitan development, but the popular mood of the time, expressed by the political majority, is still very much in favor of urban sprawl.

Design has been the main instrument in this project: to survey the future, to clarify political priorities and to regain attention for planning. In 'The Netherlands Now As Design' project, design has been shown to be an excellent medium to do all of these three things.

First of all, many issues raised in these four designs look very familiar now. But they were quite new 15 years ago. Who had ever seen maps with new lines of defense for the coast and vast stretches of inundated lowlands behind these coasts of islands, floating barriers, dunes and dykes? Who dared to think then that agriculture would lose ground, not because of urbanization, but for reasons generated by the world market for agricultural products? Who dared to allocate 2,000 km^2 for harvesting of sunlight? This does not imply that the designers discovered or invented these changes all by themselves. What is important is that these designs made all of these scientific forecasts and expectations visible, publicly debatable, subject to planning and subject to decisions on investment priorities.

The strategy the initiators of this project chose in creating alliances was clear and simple. Their collaborators would be other designers and those research institutions whose work on energy, water, coastal defense, transport systems, etc. influences the shape of the country. This part of the strategy succeeded.

The other collaborators had to come from the body politic and from the world of economics. Engaging politicians or political parties in the project proved difficult, due to their unwillingness to commit to the scenarios. Unequivocal declarations of intent would have conflicted with a new media sensitivity.

5] Min. van VROM, *Vierde Nota over de Ruimtelijke Ordening extra: op weg naar 2015*, 's Gravenhage: SDU uitgeverij, 1990

Engaging economic parties did not succeed either. The building industry was the major sponsor of the project but did nothing with the results. The institutional investors paid for the investment strategy on condition that the Minister of Planning would then create a public-private committee on national investment policy as a part of national planning policy. The committee was duly formed but after a few years was dissolved. Summing up these experiences one can say that the project had a great influence on the fourth report on planning policy issued by a coalition of Christian Democrats and Liberals and was then turned down by a coalition of Christian Democrats and Labor, who did not want to change the successful policy of urban dispersal they had embraced in the 1950s.

Evidently, something had to be done in the process of making and taking decisions on planning policy and investment priorities. The focus of research thus had to be directed to this process of interacting public and private decisions that are the main causes of transformations in the material world. This led to a second research project, beginning in 1966, which focused on interactive decision processes.

The metropolitan debate

Again, the initiators started with design exercises by teams of urban planners and designers from Amsterdam and Rotterdam, provincial and national planning departments and the Universities of Delft and Wageningen. Their subject was no longer the Netherlands as a whole but only the most urbanized western part of it. The exercises were carried out in a series of workshops, the main aim of which was to focus on the potential for transforming the existing situation into an urban system that might behave like a metropolis. This metropolitan behavior has been defined as responsiveness in relation to planning matters.

figure 7 The Metropolitan Debate logo

Parallel to these design exercises a more fundamental approach was initiated by asking academics to comment on design approaches for areas of this size. Many considered the existing physical structure of the metropolitan area as the outcome of a historical process, analyzing strong and weak points in this structure with regard to future development and proposing interventions to adapt it to future use.

At the same time work was done on analyzing the object being designed as the outcome of interactive forces – that is interventions in the existing balance between situation and program – as well as the keepers of continuity, people we elect to invent rules and regulations and to maintain law and order under circumstances of continuous change. As these interacting forces are all embodied by human beings, organizing the decision-making process means structuring their interaction. This is done by acknowledging that change is the result of an interaction between a continuous stream of private projects and politically-generated public perspectives. The investors compete for investment money for their projects at the same time as the political parties compete for the public vote on their perspectives. Organizing both competitions in the same process, one could conceivably create conditions for quicker and better decisions.

From Randstad to Deltametropolis **Dirk Frieling**

If you take public perspectives seriously, then you need an instrument to penetrate the metaphorical disguises of political ideology and unmask the designs to have a look at the physical reality beneath them. One participant invented an instrument to do just that, based on a legend of only four main units: urban areas, rural areas, water networks and road networks. The method distinguishes in a systematic way between sizes of areas of consideration and hence scale of observation. Using such a vocabulary would help to overcome the enduring misunderstanding in public debate about matters like concentration or dispersal.

An analysis of 25 designs for the Randstad area, from different authorities and interest groups, convinced the elected representatives of Amsterdam, Rotterdam, The Hague and Utrecht that all these perspectives were uniformly directed at ongoing urban dispersal. They then decided to join forces and to design a perspective of their own. It was decided to use the passenger transport system as the main instrument of strategic planning.

The essence of urbanity was seen as human interaction. So improving the conditions for human interaction, accommodating a growth in volume and frequency of people meeting each other, was the basic component of the metropolitan concept. These contacts differ functionally, territorially and temporally, giving rise to a system of transferia, multimodal nodes in the different networks of transport systems.

Quicker and better decisions

What lessons did we learn in this last period and what consequences does it have for present research?

In 1997 the stage was set for putting metropolitan development back on the political agenda. Design approaches were collected that were capable of tackling the dilemmas of design at the metropolitan scale. A method of analysis was invented to compare public perspectives. A method of deciding on private projects interacting with public perspectives was developed and tested several times with different groups of participants.

What is lacking, however, are compelling designs for interventions the size of strategic projects. Student projects can fill this gap excellently because the best of them combine the freshness of youth with the ingenuity of the engineer, originality with fertility. Architecture and planning schools can play a vital role in the public debate.

To be able to influence future development it is essential to be able to show participants in the decision-making process images of what that future might look like and what choices may be made. It is not enough then to have different perspectives to choose from. Strategic thinking means deciding on what interventions in the existing order will lead to the desired transformations.

Deltametropolis

In February 1998 the elected representatives of the four main cities issued the declaration 'Deltametropolis' as a political statement and as an invitation to others who were in favor of metropolitan development.[6] They had already decided to give priority to the systems of water and of passenger transport to clarify their intentions and make their proposals more specific.

Priority for the water system is a matter of survival. The water system is also seen as the main component of the metropolitan park system. The combination of ongoing urbanization along the Rhine with climatic change over the next 100 years may create the need for an extra storage capacity of around 600 million cubic metres of water. This is around 0.5 percent of the 100 billion cubic metres of water that flows into the country per year, either by river or rain.

One solution is to exploit the soil itself for storage, using the peat as a sponge. This is what nature has done for centuries. It means turning agricultural land into a nature reserve of wetland, exactly as was proposed in the Critical perspective 15 years ago. Another solution is to create a supplementary network of storage capacity in addition to the existing intermediate level between the fixed water level of the polders and the dynamic water levels of rivers and the sea.

[6] D.B. Stadig, G.A. Noordanus, J.C. Kombrink, A.M. Rijckenberg, *Verklaring Deltametropool*, Rotterdam: dS+V, 1998

From Randstad to Deltametropolis **Dirk Frieling**

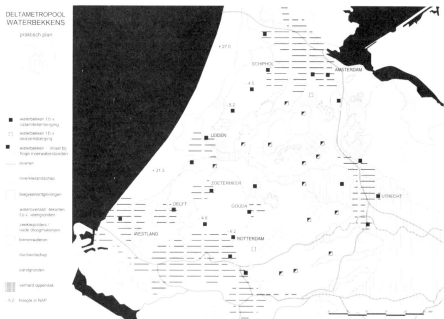

DELTAMETROPOOL
WATERBEKKENS

praktisch plan

■ waterbekken t.b.v.
  calamiteitenberging
□ waterbekken t.b.v.
  seizoensberging
■ waterbekken - inlaat bij
  hoge rivierwaterstanden
  rivieren
  rivierkleilandschap
  laagveenontginningen
  wateroverlast/ -tekorten
  t.p.v. veengronden
  zeekleipolders /
  oude droogmakerijen
  binnenwateren
  duinlandschap
  zandgronden
═══ verhard oppervlak
- 5.2 hoogte in NAP

gure 9 Holland without dikes

gure 10 Holland without
ikes: water basins

A third solution has been proposed, consisting of a system of reservoirs with capacities of 1 million cubic metres each, areas of 1 square km and up to 10 metres difference in water level. This solution is more efficient with regard to land use. It is proposed that the relationship between lowlands and metropolis could define the international image of the Deltametropolis.

The second priority is for passenger transport. As I mentioned before, human interaction may be seen as the essence of urbanity, and improving the transport system is a way to improve the conditions for this interaction. The Deltametropolis declaration states that to this end the motorway system and the railway system should be interconnected by multi-modal transfer nodes. A design based on connecting and disconnecting nodes in the transport networks creates a hierarchy of multimodal nodes, regulating intensive and extensive use of space. The images show the same system in two ways: as a territorial network with a pattern of nodes of different character, and as a system of nodes, clar-

gure 11 Transport system in
he Deltametropolis with multi
nodal nodes and their poten-
al development

gure 12 Delta net: trans-
ortation system with stations

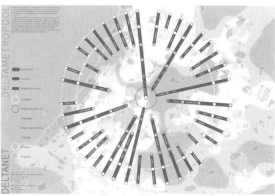

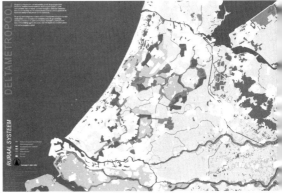

ifying this different character by showing the different sorts of transport systems that interconnect in these nodes.

figure 13 Urban System Deltametropolis

figure 14 Rural system Deltametropolis

At the moment, around 80 billion passenger km are traveled per year in this area: 60 billion by car, 12 billion by public transport, mainly rail, and 8 billion on foot and by bicycle. In 10 years' time this will be 100 billion passenger km: the aim is to hold car travel at 60 billion km, raise public transport by rail and taxi to 30 billion and travel on foot and by bicycle to 10 billion km.

The design of the rural and urban landscape is based on this transport system. Additional urban program is concentrated as much as consumer preferences allow in and around the nodes. Those parts of the metropolitan area that will stay agricultural and so will be used very extensively, should be disconnected from the system.

As the maps show, even in the so-called 'densely populated' western part of the country, urban land use is less than a third of the total area. Agriculture alone occupies twice the area taken up by urban uses.

To conclude this story in scientific tradition let us review what kinds of questions remain unresolved. To list them all would take much longer than it took to explain what has been discovered and invented. So this summary is restricted to two big questions that have to be attended to. Both have to do with coming to grips with time as an instrument of design in the composition of space. We are experimenting with graphical representations of space-time. Two images from a design of the Deltametropolis may serve as examples.

One question has to do with the future. If it is true that we have entered the information age and have the technology to send and to receive information all over the world, an interesting question then is: who are the sources of information? Where does new information – whether discovered by science, invented by art, produced by economic actors, decided by judges, chosen by politicians or selected by the media – come into existence? If ideas like 'information age' and 'global cities' mean anything at all, then the metropolis should be a concentration of sources of new information. But this general statement

From Randstad to Deltametropolis **Dirk Frieling**

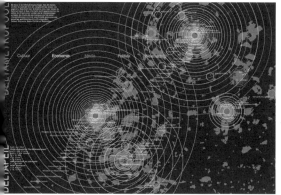

does not give a clue as to the eventual interaction between this pattern of sources of information and the territorial composition of the metropolis. So this is an open question.

The other question has to do with the past. These lowlands have been cultivated for a few thousand years – long enough to leave an imprint on the face of the earth. Digging in the soil we find ships and traces of Roman settlements from 2,000 years ago, beads and fireplaces of 5,000 years ago. Looking at the landscape we may see parcellations from the Middle Ages, dykes, polders and canals from the sixteenth century onward, lakes left after extracting peat and the whole machinery necessary to regulate water levels to a precision of a few centimeters.

This delta landscape, cultivated for centuries, has been more or less erased by urbanization in the last 50 years, fragmented by sloppy planning and careless design. So a big question is how we can create a new cohesion in this cultivated landscape and pay due respect to the legacy of the past. An up-to-date water system is of ultimate importance to the sustainability of the Deltametropolis. So we have to find a way to compose a new system that retains the valuable components of the old one. This necessary transformation can best be triggered by deciding to conceive the landscape of the delta as a metropolitan park system. How to design this, is an as yet unresolved question.

Number of inhabitants [p]	2,833,225
Area [km²]	1,626
Density [p/km²]	1,742
Population urbanized (national) [2003]	57%

Remaking Johannesburg

The city of Johannesburg, South Africa, is a multilayered landscape of intersecting, overlapping and conflicting geographies, places and identities. Until recently, these were shaped almost exclusively by geological and political conditions – influences that have been replaced today by the dynamic of unbridled economic forces.

This essay, a reading of several episodes from Johannesburg's history and observation of contemporary practices, reveals the logic of its past performance and theorizes the strategies of the present.

The geology of place

Like Isaura, Italo Calvino's city of a thousand wells,[1] Johannesburg's visible landscape is conditioned by an invisible one. Under the low, parallel, east-west running ridges which make up its visible topography, lie layer upon layer of sedimentary rock. These include pebbly layers or conglomerates containing gold in abnormally high concentrations.[2]

In 1886, while building a house for a friend, Mr George Harrison, a builder by trade, made the first discovery of gold, in an outcrop of conglomerate lying close to the surface. Within a matter of days, nine farms were declared public diggings, prospectors flocked to the site and the mining of the world's richest gold reserves began.

Early miners found gold containing ore close to the surface in long outcrops, known as reefs, running east–west along the valley floor. Mined in shallow trenches, these outcrops were soon exhausted. It became necessary to get down to deeper strata of conglomerate

figure 1 Looking west from downtown Johannesburg, 1999

figure 2 A present day mining landscape

figure 3 Subterranean map of Witwatersrand mine

figure 4 Mine worker's compound, circa 1908

[1] I.Calvino, *Invisible Cities*, London: Pan, 1974, p.19

[2] F. Mendelsohn and C.T. Potgieter (eds), *Sites of Geological and Mining Interest on the Central Witwatersrand*, Johannesburg: Geological Society of South Africa, 1986

Remaking Johannesburg **Lindsay Bremner**

figure 5 Johannesburg Street, 1938

figure 6 Soweto, black working class township, 1994

figure 7 Waterfront theme park in a white residential suburb, 1994

figure 8 Upper-middle-class white residence, 1987

which fell away sharply to the southwest. Shafts were sunk to the south of the first reefs and deep level mining began. In the process, unexpected difficulties presented themselves – deep-level mining needed vast amounts of capital. It required machinery, water, and infrastructure. It was also labor-intensive, requiring large reserves of unskilled labor. Ore brought to the surface required elaborate machinery and chemical processing to extract the gold.[3]

These difficulties and the measures taken to overcome them constructed the early contours of the city of gold. Shafts were sunk and new mines opened. The subterranean landscape was surveyed and mapped. Mining headgear, ore dumps, battery stamps, reduction works, slime dams and railway lines traced this underground geography onto the surface of the earth. Ridges and valleys were translated into a churning metallurgical landscape. Syndicates, consolidations and new financial institutions sprang up to bankroll mining operations. The grid of the city was laid out on a triangular piece of land between farm portions. Mining compounds, municipal locations and slums spread around its edges. The city soon became one of the world's richest and most rapidly growing centers, attracting a global network of interest and capital.

From its inception, Johannesburg was constructed in the image of Western modernity. Its building boom before the turn of the century drew on the style of *fin de siècle* Europe, while the boom following the Boer War (1989–1902) produced monumental Edwardian buildings, consolidating the relationship between the gold-mining industry and the British homeland.[4] The Depression of the 1930s, which saw the abandoning of

[3] Department of Mines, Union of South Africa, *The mineral resources of the Union of South Africa*, 4th edn, Pretoria: Government Printers, 1959

[4] C. Chipkin, *Johannesburg Style*, Cape Town: David Philip, 1993

NATIVE TOWNSHIPS OF MOFOLO, DUBE AND IN TOP RIGHT-HAND CORNER, ORLANDO WEST EXT.

the gold standard in 1932, resulted in foreign capital flooding into the country and transformed Johannesburg into a little New York (or if not New York, then at least Chicago or Saint Louis).[5] By 1936, at the time of the British Empire Exhibition in Johannesburg, the city was described as the "largest and most densely populated European city in Africa" with "fascinating shops and smartly dressed shoppers".[6] It claimed for itself the status of "the Empire's great gold centre".[7] Straddling the 130-km-long gold reef that was the source of its wealth, lay the prosperous business district and industrial suburbs. To the south was housed the black working class, temporary residents in the urban system under apartheid's grand scheme of things, while to the north stretched leafy, Whites-only, residential suburbs.

The geography of race
Early Johannesburg lay on a saddle of land between two ridges. It stretched for 13 km in an east-west direction, crisscrossed by small watercourses, the biggest of which formed a swampy hollow to the west of the town. Here the poorest inhabitants had been forced to settle, in what were known as the Kaffir and Coolie locations. These city slums were not only crowded and unsanitary, but also sites of racial cohabitation. W.C. Scully, a visitor to the city, was struck by what he called "slum warrens", in which lived "Europeans of various nationalities, Indians, Chinese, Arabs, Japanese, Kaffirs, and miscellaneous colored people of every hue".[8] The world the mine owners made was not, initially, a racially constructed one.

figure 9 Disinfecting an inhabitant's house during the plague, 1904

figure 10 The burning of the "Coolie Location"

figure 11 The Shower room in the compound at Crown Mines, circa 1930

figure 12 New housing in Soweto, circa 1950

[5] C.W. De Kiewiet, *A History of South Africa, Social and Economic*, Oxford: Oxford University Press, 1966, quoted in Chipkin, op. cit.

[6] *Times Weekly Edition*, January 1936, quoted in Chipkin, op. cit., p. 105

[7] C. Rogerson, 'Image enhancement and local economic development in Johannesburg', *Urban Forum* 7(2), 1996, pp. 139–158

figure 13 Postcard from "Living in Yeoville, Daily Life in a Johannesburg Suburb 1984–1988"

On 18 March 1904, pneumonic plague broke out in the Coolie location. With military precision, steps were taken to eradicate it. The area was cordoned off and patients removed to a temporary hospital set up 12 km to the east of the city. Every house from which a patient was taken was evacuated, disinfected and closed; all rats in the area were exterminated and a "special team of scavengers" was sent in to remove and burn rubbish.[9] The entire population was relocated to an area 20 km to the south of the city, where tents and latrines were erected and 3,100 people rehoused. The old location was burned to the ground: a corrugated iron fence was erected around it, all animals were killed, all belongings were removed and disinfected and the place was fired, from the outside in.

While I am sure that many cities are haunted by the memory of such events, in Johannesburg, the destruction of the Coolie location introduced into the geography of place a complex discourse of race, space and hygiene. When disease broke out, the extent of racial mixing was revealed: of the 113 cases of the plague, 25 were White, 55 Indian, 4 Colored and 29 Black. The steps taken to eradicate this curse articulated a racially-based administrative and political practice over a therapeutic practice. Race was coupled to hygiene as the master narrative of social control. Disease opened up the dark, impenetrable space of the slum and scattered its inhabitants across a color-coded landscape.

The emergency hospital erected to deal with plague patients modeled future practice. An enclosed 200 x 300m space, it was divided into two – one half for plague patients,

8] W.C. Scully, *The Ridge of White Waters*, London, 1912, quoted in C. Van Onselen, *Studies in the Social and Economic History of the Witwatersrand 1886–1914*, Vol. 1: New Babylon, Johannesburg: Raven Press, 1982, p. 39

9] W. Carr, *Plague on the Witwatersrand*, Johannesburg: Argus, 1905, p. 75

one half for plague suspects. Each of these divisions was subdivided into sections for Whites, Asians and Blacks, which were further subdivided into sections for each sex. Separate bathrooms were provided for each race and each sex. In the words of the Rand Plague Committee, "The difficulties attendant upon the equipment of an infectious hospital in the Transvaal are as great, if not greater than found elsewhere. Provision had to be made for the Whites, Asiatics and natives of each sex, so that there were 6 different camps, each separated either by barbed wire or corrugated iron. This fact made every detail of management more difficult and *inter alia* more expensive".[10]

The administrative absurdities and inefficiencies of this space nevertheless permitted a detailed and precise tabulation of and control over the burgeoning population. The slum yard, a great heterogeneous space, governed by threatening "creolised practices and imaginations"[11] was obliterated. In its place, an administratively useful landscape of fixed spaces and identities was created.

The subsequent development of the city charts the penetration of, and resistance to, this logic in all aspects of social space and life. Education, leisure, alcohol consumption, work, home - these and many more were partitioned on the basis of race. Civil liberties, such as mixed marriages, friendships across color lines, socializing in areas not for one's designated racial group, were criminalized. By 1933, the whole of the city of Johannesburg had been proclaimed white and by 1938, most of its former black population had been moved south.[12] Pockets remained, soon to be dismantled by the Nationalist Party Government in their efforts to permanently eradicate 'racial contamination' from society. Black people were reduced to being temporary, laboring sojourners in a white world. Their presence was a constant reminder that a creolized, heterogeneous world was only an administrative slip away.

The landscape of desire

I now turn my attention to a former rural area just to the north of Johannesburg, whose biography has become increasingly relevant in the changing political economy of the new South Africa.[13] For it is here, in former suburban nodes, that Johannesburg is being re-centered and its socio-political economy re-articulated. As the former center has been abandoned through disinvestment, the former periphery has attracted that investment, its peripherality seeming to offer a buffer against the messiness of the creeping urban decay associated with de-racialization. This has meant that the city has been turned inside out, its center and margin everywhere reversed.

Sandton (City of Sand) was inhabited by hunter-gatherers as far back as 30,000 years ago. Its modern existence began at the start of the twentieth century as a site of country estates and recreational activity for wealthy Johannesburgers. Leisurely pursuits like Sunday picnics, afternoon teas, duck shooting, fishing, hunting or gentlemen's farming transformed it into the playground of the moneyed classes. In keeping with this, a 'Lido' was planned for the area in 1936. While its restaurant, lake, beach, paddling pool and sporting facilities never left the drawing board, another scheme did: Sandton became the site of South Africa's first Grand Prix when its circuit was opened at Kelvin in

[10] Ibid., p. 78

[11] S. Nuttall and C. Michael (eds), *Senses of Culture*, Oxford: Oxford University Press, 2000, p. 22

[12] W.J.P. Carr, *Soweto –Its Creation, Life and Decline*, Johannesburg: South African Institute of Race Relations, 1990

[13] J. Carruthers, *Sandton–The Making of a Town*, Rivonia: Celt Books, 1993, p. 8.

figure 14 Sandton City, 2001

figure 15 Sandton building boom, circa 1995

figure 16 Sandton Square, center piece of the Sandton City Shopping Mall complex, 2001

figure 17 Corporatised community, Fourways Gardens, 2000

1937.[14] The particular mapping of wealth, pleasure, consumption and the images of country life and the romance of Italy which have subsequently been woven through the Sandton landscape were beginning to emerge.

Sandton was proclaimed a city in 1969. It promoted itself as offering a "relaxed open air lifestyle" to middle class citizens.[15] Associated with wealth and leisure, this lifestyle attracted property developers in unprecedented numbers to Sandton's large open spaces. In 1975, plans for developments to the value of R16.5 million were approved by the planning department; in 1993, not 20 years later, this had increased to R650 million in one year. Town houses and office parks displaced smallholdings and large residential lots. By 1997, the Johannesburg city center had lost 17 of the 65 top South African company headquarters to these northern developments or to other cities in the country. Most were clustered around the Sandton City Shopping Mall, built on a consolidation of suburban lots in 1973, and which inaugurated a new kind of shopping and a new kind of city center in South Africa – the car-dominated, enclosed suburban mall.

In this transient, rapidly transforming, commodified space, fantasy, meaning, memory and desire converge around two prevailing themes: nostalgia for a lost suburbia and desire for authentic citiness.

Suburbia, that idealized interface between city and country, eradicated through aggressive development, resurfaces in Sandton in the walled residential precincts to which its citizens retreat from the fast moving, car-dominated, hijacking craziness of the world

14] Ibid., p. 32

15] Ibid., p. 66

figure 18 Dainfern Estate
gatehouse, 2001

figure 19 The Michelangelo
Hotel, Sandton Square, 2001

figure 20 "Tuscany was never
so perfect" billboard

figure 21 Fourways Gardens
Estate, 2000

they have created. Within the security of these walls, images of a domesticated nature (neatly clipped lawns, picture book waterways, golfing greens) and a corporatized community (communing around tennis, biking, walking and golf) offer continuity between what Sandton was and what it is becoming.

In the prose used to market these new developments, the images of who people think they are and where they would like to be are portrayed and endorsed: "Dainfern: country-style living in a secure natural environment"; "Tanglewood Theme Village tucked away in a secret forest setting"; "High Meadow Grove: gather beneath the trees and the great blue sky – take a walk, ride a bike, play squash, swim or simply enjoy a lazy day with friends in the village estate"; "Needwood: paradise regained, tranquil country living, completely self contained".

At the same time, the public realms of this new city are almost without exception invested with meaning by being configured as little bits of Italy. Whether one is sipping cocktails in the lounge of the Michelangelo Hotel, favorite haunt of South Africa's new black bourgeoisie, eating pizza in the piazza of Sandton Square, gambling on the slot machines in the permanent twilight zone of the Monte Casino or arriving home to one's Tuscan town house, images of Italy proliferate, allowing one to pretend to be somewhere else. Consumption mingles with fantasy, with the magic, the allure and the romance of Italy. It allows the reality of this place to be temporarily forgotten. It externalizes the Europe in each one of us.

Remaking Johannesburg **Lindsay Bremner**

Figure 22 The Monte Casino complex, 2001

Sitting in Sandton Square's Fact and Fiction bookshop one afternoon, I witnessed a couple poring over a travel guide to Italy, discussing their forthcoming holiday. More interested in food and what their Rand would buy than in architecture, art or history, the young woman expressed reservations about going to Italy in summer because the cities 'smelled' at this time of the year. "I tell you," she said to her partner, "I smelled some pretty rich smells when I was there last summer". The Italy of Johannesburg's northern suburbs does not affront in this way. Reduced to a visual metaphor, it allows people to live in their fantasy, to be in Italy, without the intrusion of smells, Italian traffic, real Italians or a falling Rand. The romance of Italy is constructed and experienced as an idealized cultural icon in the comfort and the luxury of home. It is infinitely preferable to the real thing.

Why Italy, one might ask? In a city with very little past and an uncertain future, investing in images of Italy achieves a number of things. Firstly, it confers a sense of history on this place. Never mind that it is not our history, it is probably a history we wish we'd had and one which distances us from the real history going on around us. The imported landscapes of Italy allow us to locate ourselves in an illusion of the historical while freeing us from the burden of having to be agents in it. We can simply act out an eternal present. Secondly, Italy is invoked as a representation of all that is civilized, urbane and cultured in the western world. By living our lives in Italianate spaces, they take on the qualities those spaces represent to us. We become civilized, urbane and cultured. Our nagging cultural insecurities, our anxieties about being, or being thought to be, uncivilized, parochial, barbaric or wild are silenced. Thirdly, in a city which, despite increased densities and corporate investment, still maintains its suburban character, in a suburb

desperately trying to become a real city, Italy represents all that is authentically urban. By borrowing its image, our city becomes a real city, it gains an urban heart, it is authenticated.

figure 23 Private residence, Fourways Gardens Estate, 2000

figure 24 Adjacent estate gate-houses, Sandton area, 2001

figure 25 Street Closure, 2000

figure 26 Advertisement for Razor Wire

The architecture of fear

During the apartheid years, crime in South Africa was defined as crime against apartheid and criminality was confined largely to black townships. The state security system was designed almost exclusively to protect white South Africans. Horrific forms of violence were justified and not considered criminal by those waging the war on both sides of the apartheid divide. As this system has been dismantled and a new society reshaped, this violence has not disappeared. It has found new outlets in a widespread increase in all forms of criminal activity. Petty crime, organized crime, drug dealing, burglary, housebreaking, armed robbery, assault, hijacking, rape and murder lace the Johannesburg landscape. Exacerbated by unprecedented levels of unemployment, that landscape has become an intense network of violations.

In 1986, while to the south Soweto burned, the first-ever walled estate in South Africa was opened in the northern reaches of Sandton. Named Fourways Gardens, it comprised a walled precinct of 420 lots set in generous public gardens and incorporating a small game farm, home to African birds and buck. Its roads, lighting, water and sewer net-work, garden maintenance, refuse removal and other services were managed by a homeowners association, through which collective control over each other, the use of public space and, most importantly, who could lawfully enter and exit the precinct, was

Remaking Johannesburg **Lindsay Bremner**

exercised. In this innocuous civic-mindedness, segregation was about to be re-articulated.

Buying into this precinct was not just buying a piece of land or a house. It was buying into a closed, homogenous lifestyle, a fortified space. In it, one could ensure that those with whom one came into daily contact would be more or less the same as oneself and that anyone unknown or different could be shut out. Accessing such a precinct required familiarity and identification; strangeness was criminalized and the terrifying possibility of casual encounter eradicated.

This set the pattern for things to come. The closed, homogenous, fortified space of Fourways Gardens has become the way of life for most middle-class Johannesburgers. All over the city, walls, booms and security personnel transform parks, offices, shops, suburbs and entertainments areas into closed enclaves with controlled access. Citizens close off streets, wall off suburbs, excising whole neighborhoods from the public realm. For those living inside these barriers, an either triumphant or regretful sense of security and communality is regained. Gates are left open, children play in the streets again, and crime levels fall.

Those not so fortunate fortify their homes and businesses with walls, razor wire, electrified fencing, security gates, intercoms, concealed cameras and the human shield offered by private security companies. Low walls are raised and topped with spikes or glass chips. Razor wire (a particularly cruel form of barbed wire developed in South Africa for counterinsurgency purposes) unfurls around perimeter fencing. Live electrical wires designed to administer a shock when touched are mounted on garden walls; security gates transform homes into prisons. Fortified against crime, their fear of the other contained, residents reconfigure their lost Eden through the logic of exclusion.

These new frontiers, woven through and carving the city into a myriad of enclaves, have constructed a new spatiality of fixed identities and logics of discrimination. Attitudes are hardening as experience of crime causes a retreat into the known and new rigidities in the definition of self and the Other. While race is no longer privileged as the 'master signifier' in these definitions,[16] increasingly homogeneous enclaves operationalize and render productive the fear of the Other which haunts the South African psyche. Just as fear of disease opened up the creolized space of the slum and operationalized a racially-based administrative apparatus, so fear of crime negates the potential spatiality of the newly-democratized city, creating new separations and exclusions through the technologies of defense. Haunted by a fear of the heterogeneous, a new social landscape of fixed spaces and identities is being formed.

[16] Nuttal and Michael, op. cit., p. 12

In between

While mining operations in the city have long ceased and the geography of race has been superseded, both are deeply embedded in Johannesburg's psyche. Mining headgear and mine dumps loom over the city's skyline, and cut a swathe through its heart. Silent, unused and sinister, their poisoned earth contains and absorbs the most rabid of the city's crimes, the most cynical of its secrets.[17] While apartheid's spaces and identities have crumbled and race no longer provides the primary reading of the city, racial prejudices are embedded in the 'market forces' which are re-centering it. New practices have fixed memory and desire in old certainties.

In between these fixed encampments of desire and paranoia – the shopping centers, security suburbs, walled estates, office parks and the sealed capsules in which people move between them – lie ambiguous and ill-defined public spaces whose very fluidity and aterritoriality is providing opportunity for other practices to emerge. These spaces – streets, roads, parks, highways – released from the strictures of apartheid are becoming spaces where new livelihoods are being made and new experiences of the city lived. Individuals or groups are trying out, inventing new social or economic roles for themselves, and trying to make the city work for them. Some of these are brutal and terrifying - car hijackings and cash-in-transit heists turn roads and traffic intersections into places of violent contestation. Others make visible the highly complex networks of small-scale, informal, fluid social and economic associations and dependencies upon which an increasing number of people's lives depend. The very exclusivity of suburban enclaves, with their homogenous, sanitized reconstructions of idealized 'citiness', oper-

figure 27 Pavement restaurant, Woodmead, 2001

figure 28 Makeshift trading stalls outside the Johannesburg central station, 2001

figure 29 Pavement restaurant, Woodmead, 2001

17] A mapping of the city's crime in 1996 revealed that the mining belt remains the location for the highest incidence of rape, sexual assault and serial killing in the city (GJMC 1996)

ationalizes a metropolis without, where people's survival depends on both their ability to move, select a location, network, group or regroup and on the anonymity and chance encounter which metropolitan life offers.

For instance, on the highway adjacent to Woodmead, a rapidly expanding retail center in the north of the city, a woman has set up an outdoor restaurant next to the spot where taxis stop to transport workers in the formal retail sector to and from nearby Alexandra township. She lives in an inner-city suburb but commutes every day to this site, which she has identified as productive. Two or three other women work for her, preparing food at home or alternating with her on the pavement. Slightly to the west, snaking along both sides of a major arterial road, traders market their wares to passing traffic: large-scale curios, mirrors, furniture, garden umbrellas and instant lawn transform the road into a drive-by showroom for casino visitors or executives returning home from work. Makeshift enterprises trace the paths of ambulant people looking for opportunities or traveling to and from work at almost every intersection in the northern suburban landscape. Small tables are set up under trees or awnings; from them, vendors (nearly all of them women) sell cigarettes, sweets, bananas or tomatoes to passers by, engaging at the same time in child care, gossip or a game of cards. Streets and roadsides serve as gathering places for domestic workers, where, instead of being trapped in isolated lives on their employers' properties, they are able to engage in informal lotteries, supplement their meager incomes with informal trade or simply share stories about their employers' craziness. Church groups visibly occupy inner-city parks on Sundays; wedding photography is a thriving business the day before.

Lindsay Bremner Remaking Johannesburg   45

None of these activities rely on fixed infrastructure, fixed locales or fixed investment for their survival. They simply claim space for a while and, if necessary, move on. A fine balance between stasis (staying in one place for long enough to be recognized) and mobility (the ability to pack up and move on), between necessity and contingency, between structure and event, constructs peoples' relationship to the urban landscape.

Practices unfamiliar in the urban world have been introduced into this space. For instance, the intricate web of the maize trade on the streets of downtown Johannesburg overlays the quintessential colonial, modern urban grid with traditionally rural patterns of food consumption: women make fires in braziers, lay out raw maize on pavements, cook for passers-by, their colorful garments a contrast to the gray suits and ties of executives and government bureaucrats. Livestock is sold and chickens are slaughtered on the streets or in the apartment blocks of inner city suburbs. In a recent novel, Mpe[18] describes the hold of witchcraft over the lives of recent arrivals in these suburbs, tying their lives in the city inescapably to the values and traditions of rural life. People in Johannesburg and other cities in Africa often live their lives in multiple loca-

figure 31 Domestic workers engaged in an informal lottery, Killarney, Johannesburg, 2001

figure 32 Shembe church service, Pieter Roos Park, Hillbrow, Johannesburg, 2001

figure 33 Mielie traders on a street in downtown Johannesburg, 1999

18] P. Mpe, *Welcome to our Hillbrow*, Pietermaritzburg: Natal University Press, 2001

Remaking Johannesburg **Lindsay Bremner**

Figure 34 Long distance taxi rank, downtown Johannesburg, 1999

tions. Their movements increasingly cross borders, continents or even the globe.[19] Children move between parents, grandparents or friends. Sophisticated urban dwellers return to their tribal homes to undergo initiation rites, living as hunter-gatherers for weeks in the African bush before returning to 'civilization'. The idea of belonging in one location is foreign in a continent where the sense of being-in-the world is tied to the maintenance of links between multiple sites. The city in Africa, while arguably initially foreign,[20] has thus not disengaged people from their roots. It is simply another figure in the rich landscape of overlaid economic, social and cultural practices that constitute home.

These activities and others like them are transforming the city, remaking it and reinterpreting its found landscapes in new ways. Although officially excluded from the city by Western urban management practices, town planning codes and the legal and administrative systems of apartheid or market forces, these ordinary, everyday practices are nevertheless omnipresent, transforming the landscape of the city into an increasingly complex multiplicity of overlapping and intersecting social, cultural and economic transactions. It is in the tracing and mapping of these, in the narration of their intersections, the telling of their stories, that new, provisional images of the future and new conceptions of a different politics are emerging.

19] A. Simone, 'Globalisation and the identity of African urban practices', in H. Judin and I. Vladislavic (eds), Blank__ Architecture, apartheid and after, Rotterdam: NAi Publishers 1998, pp. 173–187

20] A. Adebajo, 'Cities in Africa - A search for identity and sustainability', paper delivered at African Solutions towards Sustainable Urban Development, conference, Pretoria, 27–28 March 2000, unpublished

Number of inhabitants [p]	4,154,722
Area [km²]	12,145
Density [p/km²]	342
Population urbanized (national) [2003]	92%

The Construction of Sydney's Global Image

Penelope Dean

Dateline opportunism

In December 2001, Sydney's fringe burned. The scene was apocalyptic: thick brown smoke obscured the sun, water-bombing helicopters battled twenty-meter high flames, residents threw possessions into cars and drove away. By the end of it all, half a million hectares of 'nature' had been destroyed, thousands of people had been evacuated and houses and parks were left smouldering in a scene that was like something out of a Mad Max film. At the same time, New Year's Eve was approaching and the fireworks spectacle over Sydney's Opera House and Harbor Bridge was planned as usual. But the local response was flat. Were these celebrations appropriate under such circumstances? While many Sydneysiders hesitated, the Lord Mayor took a decisive stance:

> ... it's important that it proceed ... we are the only major world city to have fireworks this year after September 11. New York is only dropping the giant ball in Times Square. London and Paris have cancelled their shows. It's important that we can show the world and ourselves that it's business as usual.[1]

And so, televised live, the fireworks went ahead, and the fact of Sydney choosing to market itself to a global audience exposed the pre-dominance of global presentation over local opinion. But what exactly was being marketed? Was it Success? Normality? Competence? The fires had already captured international attention through their severity and horror. As a counterpoint to this, the urban icons of Sydney's opera house, bridge and fireworks would be lifted out of their local context and transmitted as an optimistic live snapshot to the world: a signature image delivering global reconfirmation.

Competition deadline

Sydney's predicament is not unique. As cities become more competitive in global networks, their priorities shift. Modernization processes, the global economy and new flexibility of capital investment have led to a struggle between cities for investment and position in the emerging order of global cities. While the top tier of cities is defined: London, Tokyo and New York, the second tier is less clearly articulated and because of this, cities compete to establish and stabilize their position in city networks. It is exactly here that Sydney finds itself: positioned within the Asia-Pacific region and competing with other cities for economic dominance.[2] To advance this position, Sydney has spawned an enterprise culture that develops and promotes business strategies to attract even more capital. Sydney's Central Business District demonstrates the striking effect of such an agenda on urban form. Singled out as a global finance attracting, strategic device, it has undergone radical change, and the effect of this has cut across the whole spectrum of city production from urbanism to architecture. As the city has transformed physically, so too have its consumption practices. The marketing of such practices and the demand for architectural typologies to fulfill new lifestyle requirements have now taken on epic proportions.

Sydney is a city that became global.[3] This was not always the case. Any local discussion about Australian urbanism used to revolve around the continental divide between the urban and the natural landscape, the 'city' versus the 'non-city' and as far as com-

[1] H. Gilmore, Bushfires may spark cancellation of fireworks, *The Sydney Morning Herald*, 30 December 2001

[2] Sydney is in the same time zone as East and Southeast Asia. Australia plugs into the economic growth of SE Asia and fosters many interdependent relations. Offshore manufacturing and Australian exports go to SE Asia and a large amount of tourism along with foreign investment comes from SE Asia. In addition, many multicultural linkages occur between Asian populations residing within Australia and SE Asia

[3] Sydney is Australia's only global city. Saskia Sassen has written that despite a country having multipolar urban form, not every city rises to global status. In the case of Australia, characterized by such polarity, rather than the emergence of several highly internationalized financial and business centers, there is a concentration of international and financial functions in Sydney. S. Sassen, *Cities in a World Economy*, Thousand Oaks, CA.: Pine Forge Press 1994, pp. 85–97

petition between cities went, Sydney and Melbourne rivaled one another for national and cultural supremacy. In the last decade, both debates became irrelevant as Sydney displaced Melbourne, the city that had long held the position of national banking and wealth centre. And as Sydney continued to grow and attract a disproportionate number of enterprises and tourists, the city shifted into the Asia-Pacific orbit to compete with regional cities for economic investment.[4]

The criteria demanded of global cities tend to be generic, a standardized checklist of selling points: a skilled and educated labor force, education facilities, physical infrastructure, an international airport and communications technologies suited to international corporations. To be eligible, global city candidates should have these prerequisites from the outset. Yet to be competitive a city requires more than just the 'basics'. The basic selling points tend to be quantitative, functions of statistical equations where supportive infrastructures are measured against office floor area and numbers of corporate employees. These quantities are standardized, based on size, location, turnover and efficiency, and derive from abstract notions of supply and demand. To achieve a defining edge that will ultimately set one city apart from another seems to require the articulation of qualitative difference. It is around the qualitative that cities formulate their image and in relation to that image, globally market themselves as unique.

In order to achieve global distinction, cities subject themselves to self analysis. They need to not only be aware of their local 'identity' and recognizable qualities but also have the capacity to translate these assets into an 'image'. The translation encourages the use of artistic license; imagination and exaggeration re-shape the assets into mediated realities. Assets can be spatial, programmatic, cultural or social. Any city would then seem to have a choice: either it possesses enough qualities to make it easy to sell or it must undergo a change of image if it is to be competitive.[5] In combination with the right selling points, image and a marketing campaign, sellable trademarks are a further necessity. As Kim Dovey writes: "Local places become appropriated to global strategies. Urban marketing requires civic imagery that can identify places and cities as different products. In particular this stimulates the market for iconic imagery embedded in 'signature' projects that signify a 'sense of place' for global consumption. ... The Manhattan skyline, Westminster, the Eiffel Tower and the Sydney Opera House set the standards of urban iconography. Like corporations without logos, cities without icons are not in the market." [6]

Free time city, ASAP

Blessed with 'site luck', Sydney has obvious spatial attributes: a clean harbor, beaches, gardens, parks and nature. Yet only to define these as assets as such, is not enough. What do they translate into and what meaning should be attributed to them? In Sydney, green spaces translate as 'public space' or 'recreation'. These spaces become marketable for their 'leisurely', 'easy going' and 'relaxed' atmospheres. With waterfront gardens, parks, yacht clubs, hotels, beaches, Olympic sports facilities and a zoo, Sydney's harbor zone is and has always been, interpreted as the ideal leisure landscape.[7] Whilst such local assets may be diverse and consist in fragmented parts, when added together they

[4] Ever since the 1980s, advanced capitalist countries have undergone a globalization of markets in terms of services, finance and commerce. In the context of such forces, Australia reorganized itself: it massively increased foreign investment, shifted from agriculture, mining and manufacturing toward real estate and services, and reorientated itself away from the Atlantic towards the area surrounding the Pacific Ocean: the 'Pacific rim'. Following from this, Sydney emerged as the major beneficiary of regional investment in finance and real estate in Australia

[5] S.S. Fainstein and D.R. Judd (eds), 'Global Forces, Local Strategies and Urban Tourism', in The Tourist City, Yale: Yale University Press, 1999, p. 11

[6] K. Dovey, Framing Places, Mediating Power in Built Form, London: Routledge 1999, p. 159

[7] S. Jenkins, 'Sydney Harbour: A Leisure Landscape', in .. Finch, C. McConville (eds), Gritty Cities, Images of the Urban, Annandale: Pluto Press Australia Limited, 1999, pp. 201–216

figure 1 Sydney harbour

coagulate into a *theme* of leisure. When promoted as a dominant characteristic and foregrounded through marketing campaigns, the leisure dimension differentiates Sydney from other cities in the Asia Pacific region.

Peter Murphy and Sophie Watson have contended that Sydney markets itself from two platforms: tourism and business.[8] While Sydney's tourism assets are obvious: an airport hub, icons such as the Harbor Bridge and Opera House and major events (e.g. the Gay and Lesbian Mardi Gras), Murphy and Watson contend that there is also another element marketed. The urban metropolis recognized as a 'familiar' image, is critical. Sydney's downtown is 'modern'; it offers shopping, nightlife, skyscrapers, entertainment and neon. The cosmopolitan image of Sydney as being modern specifically attracts Asian tourists.[9] As a familiar image, modern city life supplements exceptional images (e.g. Sydney Opera House). The ideal urban image is therefore not a case of either this or that, but of the familiar and ordinary promoted alongside the exceptional and extraordinary.

In terms of business, Murphy and Watson also suggest that in addition to programmatic selling points (enough office space, apartments, restaurants and hotels) Sydney markets a *lifestyle* that is hedonistic and inexpensive.[10] This lifestyle, a meaning defined through Sydney's outdoor assets and atmospheres, becomes a theme that enables Sydney to position and market itself against its competitors in a 'compare and contrast' format.

[8] P. Murphy, S. Watson, *Surface City, Sydney at the Millennium*, Annandale: Pluto Press Australia Limited, 1997, p. 48

[9] Ibid., p. 44. Murphy and Watson also state that research has indicated that this is exactly the kind of urbanity Asian tourists want to consume whilst on holiday

[10] While the cost of living in Sydney is higher than anywhere else in Australia, it is considerably lower than that of the cities of the Asia Pacific region such as Hong Kong, Singapore or Tokyo

The Construction of Sydney's Global Image **Penelope Dean**

In a Discussion Paper released by the City of Sydney, Sydney classified as a 'living' city, takes on Hong Kong and Singapore:

> Although density and property values are high in the centre of these cities, there is little street life and access to open spaces and pedestrian amenity is a low priority in the planning process...
> Since 1991, the City of Sydney's Living City Strategy has encouraged high population growth in the CBD and greater pedestrian amenity and vibrancy on the streets.[11]

Sydney markets itself as a site-specific leisure-city that fuses lifestyle and international business. The notion of lifestyle as a desirable, achievable concept, has infiltrated almost every aspect of urban life. What began as a relatively modest practice became an image for the global marketplace. Lifestyle has now returned with boomerang effect in a magnified version, feeding back into consumption practices and the built environment. The demand for 'styled life' has forced Sydney to shift its urban design agenda and diversify its housing typologies.

Deadline urbanism

The urban model of Sydney has always been a great suburban expansion containing a centralized, high-rise CBD and a spread of low-density suburbs consisting of detached houses, gardens and double fronted garages, in an almost park-like setting. Over four million inhabitants now occupy the 12,145 square km of Sydney's statistical land area. But the city's topography has transformed. Shooting up from the spread are high-rise hot spots, defacto CBDs dubbed 'mini Hong Kongs'[12] for those who choose to turn away from suburban culture and move 'downtown'. The effect on Sydney has been to have it become a multi-polar city where clusters of high-rise activity interrupt the endless expansion of suburbs.

Sydney's urban planning agenda oscillates between fulfilling market expectations and managing market-led processes. To attract investment the state government has opted for urban outcomes geared to market forces, and this has resulted in a form of *deadline urbanism* where remedial interventions are carried out in fragments, as exemplified by the preparations for the 2000 Olympic Games where Sydney revamped only the parts of itself considered relevant to international tourist trajectories. The approach marks quite a shift in Sydney's urban policy. From the 1950s until the 1980s Sydney's metropolitan 'planning' was based on strategies of suburban growth, establishing transport corridors, green issues, incremental land development combined with medium density subdivision controls, urban consolidation and sustainability. The style of planning was 'urban management' with realistic objectives.[13] Since the 1990s, business needs, boosting of existing attributes and 'place' marketing have been driving urban planning. And to achieve a more compact city and reconcile investment opportunities, 'quality of life' criteria have come into play.[14]

[11] Council of the City of Sydney, 'Positioning Sydney as the Clever City', in *City of Sydney Discussion Paper, Living City Beyond 2000*, Municipal Brochure, 2000, p. 8

[12] A. Gripper, 'The duplexes that ate Willoughby's castles', in *The Sydney Morning Herald*, 3 May 2000

[13] M. Lennon, 'The Revival of Metropolitan Planning', in S. Hamnett, R. Freestone (eds), *The Australian Metropolis, A Planning History*, Sydney: Allen & Unwin, 2000, p. 149

[14] S. Hamnett, 'The Late 1990s: Competitive versus Sustainable Cities', ibid., p. 169

figure 2 Foodcourt entrance

The most radical transformation has been in Sydney's CBD, located in the east of the city, and occupying less than 1% of the total metropolitan figure. Here compaction is most evident and one finds a plethora of international business and financial functions. The CBD functions as a programmatic magnet, clustering, accumulating and increasing the density of built substance. Rather than seeking territory, new programs (offices, apartments and retailing) seek proximity and association. The 'new' includes not only similar programs, but constructs the whole urban scene: shops, nightlife, housing and offices. Distinguished by high-rises, offices, shopping malls, food centers and lobbies, the CBD has been transformed from a Monday to Friday, 9 to 5 work zone into a 24/7 work, eat and live zone. With its residential population growing at a rate of 14.5% per year, downtown Sydney has become the fastest growing urban area in Australia.[15] While Sydney has been exposed to the same forces of economic restructuring as other global cities, the urban and social result follows the model of *intensified centrality*. What this means is that despite Sydney's metropolitan area encompassing a vast terrain, services and business functions have tended to cluster heavily within its city centre. The traditional centre has become even *more* of a centre.

By contrast, North American cities have seen businesses and services piling up on the periphery, usually in specially zoned technology parks and technopoles. Concomitant with this, these cities have often experienced an emptying-out of their inner-city areas, resulting in growth on the fringes and population loss and an increasingly marginalized population in the city centre. Labeled the 'doughnut effect', this is a syndrome that Sydney has managed to avoid by attracting services and developments to the city centre itself. Sydney has turned the model inside out. If the doughnut effect is about inner-city decline, the intensified centre is about inner-city boom. In Sydney's case, several

[15] In the twenty years from 1976 to 1997, the workforce of central Sydney increased from 180,000 to 213,000. Between 1991 and 1997 the CBD resident population tripled to reach 20,000. As quoted in Council of the City of Sydney, 'Transport, City on the Move', in *City of Sydney Discussion Paper, Living City Beyond 2000*, Municipal Brochure, 2000, p. 8

The Construction of Sydney's Global Image **Penelope Dean**

REX
- LIVE IN STYLE -

Centrally located at the edge of COCKLE BAY, this CHIC
development is the ultimate in contemporary design.

Just a stroll to restaurants, cafes, QVB and
CENTREPOINT. Studio, 1 bedroom, 2 bedroom
apartments and penthouses featuring water views over
DARLING HARBOUR and the CITY SKYLINE

INSPECT 12-2 7 DAYS
Visit actual Display Unit 379 Kent St

- THE ULTIMATE -
• 26 levels of glorious living space
• 124 apartments all with balconies
• perfect location
• finest imported SMEG kitchen appliances
• floor to ceiling glass windows
• 2.7 ceilings
• air-conditioned
• GYM and POOL

THE IDEAL HOME OR INVESTMENT
MOVE IN OR LEASE OUT BY MID 2003
Mark Mitchell 9908 7887 0414 448 549
Gavan Kohen 9908 7887 0414 911 070

elite
PROPERTY BROKERS

urban assets have been repeated and upstyled to help this process along. This has meant not a change of image for Sydney but rather a bolstering of existing identity. Capitalizing on the success of its CBD, the City of Sydney has injected itself with even more city-centre exotica: public parks, swimming pools, urban gardens and cultural facilities. These programs have acted as urban stimulants that not only intensify the CBD as a cultural destination for the entire metropolitan area, but further confirm and legitimate the image of Sydney with even more 'leisure-lifestyle' specificity.

Check in, check out

The profusion of international corporate services and company headquarters in Sydney has created a market demand for more office space, and the new corporate focus has brought with it categories of resident professionals who are highly paid and have high price lifestyles. Their specific consumption practices have led real estate developers to change their marketing focus from low and medium-income housing to the rapidly expanding top-end market of luxury apartments. The result is a high-rise apartment explosion. The CBD, now a destination for fast turnover investment, has become an exuberant international property market.

Halfway between hotels and apartment blocks, several towers fall into the category of 'service apartments'. The towers have been adapted beyond the standard type to include swimming pools, private gyms, tennis courts and gratuitous landscapes. Controlled like business class airport lounges, they are highly monitored vertical enclaves, secure and exclusive. Elevators and key cards program the residents' trajectories. Sets of one-way routes from underground car park to lobby to apartment floor to privatized gym control the access of a diverse clientele: security staff, janitors, cleaners, tourists, residents

figure 4 Sydney's high-rise

and visitors. The multi-level car parks themselves become bizarre sites for security obsessed behavior. Although already designated and secure, paranoid residents construct cages around their allocated car spaces. This defense of private space suggests individualization at its most extreme and exemplifies an obsessive cocooning of the private into a multiplicity of privates.

The apartment buildings market themselves through illusory themed lifestyle packages: 'hotel' lifestyle, 'resort' lifestyle and 'penthouse' lifestyle. The promotional slogans equate with spatial and service benefits that range from collective facilities such as swimming pools and gyms, to the apartment interior itself. Glamorous lifestyles are legitimized through architectural elements and urban outlook: ubiquitous panoramic windows, enormous balconies and spectacular views, all uniformly guarantee the same lifestyle qualities at any position in the building. The effect of these new lifestyle aspirations has percolated throughout Sydney in an extraordinary way. What used to be the 'Great Australian Dream' of owning one's own detached dwelling with a garden somewhere out in the suburbs has turned around, as the shift towards denser living increasingly takes hold. The housing market now offers a diverse range, including town-houses, lofts, studios, and apartments. The increased diversity has maximized choice over Sydney's metropolitan area and enabled 'qualities of life' to be designed, marketed and chosen.

Clever marketing has made use of *quid pro quo* logics to make apartments seem more appealing. A development might offer less open space but include a gym, pool, and sauna; proximity to retail activity and parks may compensate for higher density living; a huge balcony is acceptable in place of a garden. The shift from home ownership to renting has been made more palatable by real estate agencies offering 'bonuses' such as a rent-free trial period to entice potential new customers. Another important element is *exclusivity*. What used to be socially affirmed through location and address has now zeroed down onto the building itself and what that object *looks at*. Marketing has foregrounded the object and its outlook while backgrounding the context. A view of Sydney's harbor, opera house or CBD skyline equates with luxury. Marketing catchphrases such as 'harbor glimpses', 'water vistas' or 'views never before seen from a Sydney apartment' often hype the view more highly than it deserves in order to feed the marketability of the image. Marketable image translates into a locally lived reality with economic and social status.

Underground Preservationism
Signature buildings designed by famous architects – for example Renzo Piano's Aurora Place and Harry Seidler's Horizon Apartments – add a branding dimension to the apartment market. The brands act as alibis for developers to promote their towers as 'exceptional', 'unique' and 'the best'. World Tower designed by the Melbourne architects Nation Fender Katsalidis, has 75 stories, 750 apartments, 3 swimming pools, a commercial gym, a private theatre and expanses of shops. Its developer, Meriton Apartments, promotes the tallest tower in the Southern Hemisphere as an exercise in design philanthropy:

> To design Sydney's highest and most prestigious residential apartment building was a task readily embraced by a team renowned for their architectural vision and innovative excellence, deeming architecture as an art form and then combining this with their mission to give something back to the community.[16]

Similar propaganda strategies apply to corporate office space to give added value to rental rates. Symbolic capital and locational advantage gives one office building a market advantage over another. As Kim Dovey writes: "The successful corporate tower offers a distinctive image to which lessees are invited to link their corporate image."[17] According to Dovey, office towers can claim distinction in a variety of ways: to be an artistic "masterpiece" (designed with an architect's signature), unique in form (a landmark in its context), or be "future looking".[18]

"The view available from the corporate tower is a primary selling point and the valued views are of two types. First are the long views of nature and landscape, the parks, gardens, lakes, river, bay, beaches and mountains. Second are the panoramic views of the city and its dominant institutions. The view, as advertised, is never onto a streetscape with people and city life. It is the city in the abstract, from above and at a distance – the surface, not the life."[19]

[16] Online. Available, http://www.meriton.com.au

[17] Op. cit. Dovey p. 108

[18] Ibid., pp. 108–112

[19] Ibid., p. 115

It is increasingly important that the skyscraper itself be iconic. As office lobbies and foyers increasingly connect to mall networks, what used to be a street address has become almost a back door exit. Access to buildings can be from anywhere as entrances have been absorbed above and below ground into spatial amalgams of department stores, food courts, retail passages and underground railway stations.

In Sydney, shopping is also lifestyle: the shopping malls, both interiorized and exteriorized, are enormous attractors. Malls split from street level into horizontal tube-like structures that absorb and collect all in their path together. Not just organizational devices to transport one from shop A to shop B, the malls are a synthesis of everything: food courts, specialty stores, car parks, cinemas, short cuts, banks, dry cleaners, hairdressers, beauticians, pet shops and office foyers. Sydney's malls are major public destinations in themselves. As consumption practices have changed to cater for individualization, self-expression and display, a shift in retail design and practice has also taken place. According to the design manager of one shopping mall, consumers want more shops, more parking, and more covered malls. Consumers are well informed and they understand trends. They seek a social context of image and lifestyle as a priority.[20] Because of this, Sydney has seen an increase in retail floor area dedicated to food.[21] Food retail now exists as a spatial continuum that incorporates malls, courts, sky-gardens, rooftop restaurants, podiums, streets, basements, pavement and atriums. The image of this food space is not trashy and cheap but sophisticated and cosmopolitan. What is sold is not food *per se* but the *food experience*.

In Sydney, lifestyle and consumption practices promise to produce architectural innovation. The subterranean extension to Sydney's Conservatorium of Music below the Botanic Gardens and the submergence of Sydney Aquatic Centre below Cook and Philip Park (a Church forecourt) are cases in point. Sydney's trademark parks, squares, and gardens, privileged with a 'preserve at all costs' status have in the face of impending developments, sent new buildings underground.

20] F. Alvarez, "Common Area" in *Debating the City: an anthology*, Glebe: Historic Houses Trust of New South Wales and University of Western Sydney, 2001, p. 220

21] B. Pritchard and D. Medhurst, "Eating Space", in *Debating the City: an anthology*, op. cit. p. 209

The Construction of Sydney's Global Image **Penelope Dean**

The future is too late

What can be learned from Sydney is how a city programs its identity towards the demands of a global market in order to remain competitive: identity – morphed into trademark – translates into image. Urbanism serves to legitimate this end and is carried out by way of a series of deadlines. This deadline urbanism exhibits two notions of deadline time: *Future and Perpetual. Future* deadlines reoccur with annual regularity like Sydney's New Year's Eve fireworks display or as one-off events such as Sydney's 2000 Olympic Games. Here time, date and place converge into dateline opportunism generating selective remedial urban projects. *Perpetual* deadlines make the future seem always too late. As Sydney globally competes with other Asian cities, markets its own image of a Free-Time City, and caters to a new check in, check out culture, urbanism is driven by a constant state of panic. The effect of these urban deadlines is a covert preservationism, conserving suburban values and transferring them from the horizontal sprawl into vertical stacks.

Deadline urbanism responds to issues in proportion to their perceived immediacy. Opportunistic decisions rather than long term plans react rather than pro-act. Unlike modernist rational planning that relied on the fixed, big picture Masterplan - an inflexible static model – deadline urbanism relies on fast response and feedbacks as perceived reality changes with development – it is a flexible, time-based and dynamic model. For deadline urbanism, the future is a void. Its technique is not a chronology of steps facilitating a predetermined outcome but a model driven and sustained by change itself as it constantly reinvents itself. It forces the city to innovate, developing new instruments and exploiting local assets to stay ahead of the competition. At the very moment when the gap between urban planning theory and practice is greatest, deadline urbanism presents a different, more dynamic model and new grounds from which to redefine an urban practice.

Number of inhabitants [p]	1,501,800
Area [km^2]	243
Density [p/km^2]	6,180
Population urbanized (national) [2003]	64%

Kuala Lumpur: an Allegorical Postmetropolis

Ramesh Kumar Biswas

The Petronas Twin Towers, opened in 1998 after a record building period of three years, are known to every taxi driver on the globe as the world's highest skyscrapers. This apparently megalomaniacal project, viewed with some skepticism before completion, has actually fulfilled its purpose admirably and precisely, which was to put Kuala Lumpur on the world map, to make it instantly recognizable. On 11 September 2001, minutes after the World Trade Center was attacked, tens of thousands of office workers were evacuated from the Petronas Towers due to a terrorist threat. Although nothing untoward happened, this fact was often repeated to me by several residents of the city with a certain amount of unconcealed pride – it was proof that Kuala Lumpur had arrived in the Big League; it was finally up there with the most important cities.

But this was only a punctuation mark in the story of a city that constantly reinvents itself, that deliberately strives to achieve a status beyond its natural size of only 3 million inhabitants in the entire urbanized Klang Valley, capital of a relatively small country of 22 million. That story moves on, the Asian economic crisis being overcome through sheer force of will, with new projects overtaking yesterday's news, much as Baron Munchhausen pulled himself out of the swamp by his own pigtails.

Kuala Lumpur, referred to by its inhabitants only by its initials, is a laboratory of urban form, of heterogeneous and shifting ethnic and political identities, a changing terrain of schizophrenia and megalomania. It is now part of the 'Multimedia Super Corridor' (a silicon valley with an Asian twist), engendering new forms of anonymous urban form and high-tech infrastructure, new consumption and employment patterns. It provides a new matrix of structured confusion that enables a rich, impure and exciting heterogeneity to flourish.

However modern this city may appear to be, it cannot be understood without examining its past. KL is apparently a city without history, but actually a place where history strangely repeats itself, day by day. The conquest of the jungle through sheer optimism, the triumph of hope over doubt and of the daring over the meek are characteristics of this tropical boomtown, now developing into a hitherto unknown form of postmetropolis.

A city can be like an individual, who, even as an adult, cannot give up habits familiar from his childhood. Kuala Lumpur is such a city with an 'existential history', in which events and people repeat their pasts in unexpected ways. Many seemingly inexplicable phenomena are easier to understand when viewed as variations of events that have once taken place, or personalities that have appeared on the stage at some point during the city's densely packed history. This is surprisingly often the case for a place that actually believes it has no past, only a future.

Reading this account as an allegory will help explain a city that is not as readable as cities where imposing edifices are usually a reflection of the prevailing power structure. Postmodern analysis focuses attention away from the 'big' relationships of national and global power, economy and production and towards the symbolic dimensions of urban life. More than the many towers, the key to understanding the geographical and discursive identities of Kuala Lumpur often lies in the examination of certain towering personalities who, like heroes in the Asian epics, single-handedly change the course of events. One of these is the legendary Yap Ah Loy, another the long-term Prime Minister, Dr Mahathir Mohammed.

The Peninsula of Malaya, the legendary 'Golden Khersonese', has been a perpetual crossroads and meeting place for adventurers, soldiers of fortune, pirates, mad geniuses and romantics. It was home to the earliest *Homo sapiens* in Asia. But leaving aside for the moment those who were hanging around here 40,000 years ago in the Stone Age (and who didn't bother even then to clear up their rubbish) which is now displayed in museums as archaeological remains. In October 2002, Sunday newspaper headlines were still bemoaning the residents' inability to separate and dispose of their refuse. Around 2,000 years ago, the Peninsula saw the development of numerous towns arising from trade with India, Arabia, Indonesia and China. In the seventh and eighth centuries these were powerful sea-going and trading city-states under the influence of the Sumatran Buddhist kingdom of Sri Vijaya. Later, they were governed from Hindu Java, with constant interference from Thailand.

Islam came in very early from Arabia. Marco Polo, traveling on a Frequent Sailor program in the thirteenth century, notes seeing Islamic communities. The coastal town of Melaka (Malacca) gradually became the most important city in Southeast Asia by the middle of the second millennium, showing an unexpectedly long urban tradition in an area commonly associated only with the 'jungle'. During all this time, merchants from North Asia, India and Arabia, tin miners from China and Ceylon, planters, missionaries and soldiers from Portugal, Holland, Japan and Britain brought their cultures, their foods, their religions and their architectures with them, planted them in the humid, tropical air pregnant with the aroma of spices and sudden thunderstorms, and watched them grow into strange forms. One sees a similar process of cultural and architectural assimilation today, in a place that was 'multicultural' centuries before that adjective became fashionable. The cosmopolitan ethic, the interweaving of cultures is too delicate to dispose of in one telling, but to objectively understand the form that the city has taken it is necessary to look at its two main motors: the politics of money and global ambitions, and the communal substratum of a complex ethnicity.

Kuala Lumpur, astonishingly, did not exist before 1857, when a tin-mining settlement built by Chinese laborers emerged at the confluence of two muddy rivers. The city never looked back. Then came many mosquitoes, followed by Hakka merchants from South China, who supplied the brawling, noisy settlement with the necessary goods. Entire wooden palaces were dismantled, moved to and rebuilt in the new town, a precursor of the architectural imports of today, when skyscrapers from the USA or Hong Kong are reproduced here by the dozen. Thus it could be described in parts as 'Xerox City'. Even the illegal 'squatter settlements' one sees now in the interstices of the city, housing several hundred thousand migrants from rural areas or from the islands of Indonesia, resemble the pioneer settlements of the first miners 150 years ago, if you ignore today's omnipresent satellite dishes.

Ramesh Kumar Biswas Kuala Lumpur: an Allegorical Postmetropolis   **63**

figure 1 Photo from the Kuala Lumpur Tower at night

Immigrants from China first entered Malaya to extract tin from the rich earth, and later formed the majority of the business community. The Malays, mostly descendants of Indonesian migrants, were occupied in rural or cultural activities. Those from the Indian subcontinent were brought in by the British, as manual labor to work on the rubber plantations, as educated 'babus' (clerks), or, at Independence in 1957, as doctors, engineers, accountants and lawyers to take the place of departing British staff.

The Malay Sultans of the nineteenth century, in their cozy capital in the port town of Klang, did not want to interfere with the seemingly unsavory activities in the mining settlement. They nominated a Chinese administrator, a kind of sheriff of the Wild East, the so-called 'Kapitan China', who to all intents ruled the urban area politically and commercially. The local sultans let the Chinese immigrants get on with the job of making money, and collected their percentage, an arrangement that continues in one form or another to this day. Thus the roles played by the different ethnic groups in the building of the city did not change dramatically until the New Economic Policy was introduced 100 years later, in 1969.

The Kapitan China did not have an easy life in the mid-nineteenth century. He had to control an unruly Chinese population of fortune-seekers from different regions and dialect groups, organized in conflicting secret societies and clans. The most famous of these sheriffs was a young Hakka-Chinese called Yap Ah Loy. This fascinating personality played a crucial role in the rise of Kuala Lumpur. He got stuck here by chance – as many others did over the centuries. In his role as administrator, he managed to curb crime by applying draconian measures. In typical KL manner, he then proceeded to pursue his numerous business sidelines undisturbed. These included tin-mining, pig-breeding, running gambling clubs and opium dens, brothels and drinking saloons, many of these being activities he had himself previously banned. Yap went bankrupt several times – he once had to flee the town in his striped underpants – but he always returned and made his way back to the top (not unlike many property developers or politicians during the boom-and-bust years of the 1980s and 90s). He had all the qualities of the typical KL wheeler-dealer businessman – not for nothing was he known as 'Mr Kuala Lumpur'. He earned this title in many different ways. KL was then a maze of small lanes, lined with wooden houses roofed with dried palm leaves. After a big (and not entirely accidental) fire in 1884 destroyed the town, he compelled the superstitious Chinese, who had already packed their bundles, to remain and rebuild it with brick walls and tile roofs. How convenient that Yap owned the only brick kiln in town! He multiplied his wealth and his influence several times, but his days were numbered. The British, who had been waiting in the wings for several years on an imperial adventure-holiday, finally decided to drop the prevailing non-interference policy towards the Malay States, and made the Sultan an offer he couldn't refuse. Malaysia became a British colony overnight, KL its capital. Yap Ah Loy was even allowed to retain his position until his death. The Hong Kong and Shanghai Bank tower now stands on the spot where his magnificent villa once stood. How would Yap react if he could see this ugly block today? Probably by rubbing his hands and demanding a commission.

The first British administrator built his fortress on a hill overlooking Chinatown so that he could bestow it with cannon fire if necessary – an attitude which demonstrated a particularly close and trusting relationship with the old city. Until recently this very same hill housed top government offices, where all decisions about major urban projects were made, including a 1980s plan to replace the politically suspect Chinatown with a series of politically neutral office towers (this plan was shelved in the recession of the mid-1980s). Central Market, the former wet market, was turned instead into a highly successful shopping center similar to Covent Garden in London. Chinatown was saved by its proximity to Central Market and has since flourished as a tourist attraction.

Frank Swettenham, the second and best-known British administrator of Kuala Lumpur, had a somewhat more positive attitude towards the city, which he described as "a place of eternal summer, where every living being seems yet inspired to a feverish desire for growth and reproduction as though they were still in the dawn of creation."[1] In the nineteenth century he built the famous 'five-foot-ways' – an urban pattern of rows of shop-houses connected by a five-foot-wide covered arcade, widely adopted as a climatically appropriate, characteristically Asian way of building.

[1] Frank Swettenham, quoted in Ramesh Kumar Biswas, *Malaysia*, Springer Wien New York, Vienna 2003

This peninsula was 'the land in which the winds meet', a reference to the pause in the monsoon winds that forced ships to layover in the Straits of Malacca for months before they could proceed to China or India, Arabia and Europe. Tolerance towards the armies of immigrants, passers-by and rulers appeared to herald a truly multicultural society. A closer look at settlement patterns, labor flows and inter-group relations reveals that the different ethnic groups lived harmoniously but separately, next to each other. Symbolic economies, political alignments and cultural agendas all reflected an inherent resistance to complete integration. The reasons for this are various. The British 'divide and rule' system was implanted deeply, and has proved its longevity. Also, the many immigrant religious and ethnic groups tended to emphasize rather than suppress their differences. Division of labor remained unchanged after Independence: in spite of the Malays forming the majority of the populace, they still ran only 1.5 percent of all firms in 1969. This inequitable sharing of the cake built up resentments that exploded that year.

On 13 May 1969 – a date spoken of even today with a shudder – ethnic-tinged political riots set the city in flames. Heads were impaled on traffic lights as a horrible example. "On this day", writes journalist Karim Raslan, "Malaysia lost its innocence. The Thirteenth of May became a totem, a symbol of everything that could go wrong... Each and every Malaysian saw Hell eye-to-eye on that day, and was willing to do anything to hinder its recurrence."[2]

Everything has been different since then. A strong regime with special powers introduced the New Economic Policy (NEP), a massive positive-discrimination program for Malays at all levels. For a start, most government posts and university places, most jobs in all limited companies, tax holidays for new businesses, interest-free loans and preferred shareholding opportunities at reduced rates were reserved for the Malay Bumiputra ('sons of the soil'). The NEP encouraged them to drop the afternoon nap and switch to the fast lane. Of course, the NEP also referred to the general abolition of poverty as one of its aims, but its policies were clearly directed towards helping the main ethnic group that had been disadvantaged and prevented from participating in economic success. Affirmative action is, after all, a perfectly legitimate tool used in many countries to rectify imbalances, as long as care is taken to limit its duration and to avoid personal injustice. Today many bright young Western-educated Malay business people and professionals are succeeding on their own terms, but even the government recently complained that too many people use the positive discrimination legislation as a 'crutch'.

The new economic order was the price for ethnic peace, but what effect did it have on the city? The tens of new banks and corporations that were founded or privatized under the NEP each had to put up their own tower. The Urban Development Authority (UDA), founded to boost general morale as well as to implement the NEP, and staffed by highly professional experts, developed into a powerful urban planning influence, often more powerful than City Hall itself. All major projects had to be passed by the UDA, which appropriated a compulsory percentage for resale to Bumiputra investors. Protests against the indiscriminate destruction of historic substance or greenery were not well received. While most people got their piece of the cake (economic benefits were spread widely among the whole populace, unlike the situation in Indonesia or Africa) they were

[2] Karim Raslan, *Malaysia in Transition*, Singapore: Times Books International, 1994

Kuala Lumpur: an Allegorical Postmetropolis **Ramesh Kumar Biswas**

figure 2 Photo from the Kuala
Lumpur Tower by day

discouraged from expressing opinions about the development of the city as a whole. Kuala Lumpur, which until that point had constantly exchanged its building substance but not its basic street network, began to change radically from the top down.

The blessing and the curse of Kuala Lumpur, as the capital of a rich country with major natural and human resources, has been its rapid, almost constant economic growth for 150 years, interrupted only by World War II and the recessions of the mid-1980s and the late 1990s. The city has been a permanent building site as long as anyone can remember; like a predatory animal it hunts, roars and swallows anything in its path. Familiar buildings are demolished overnight – Malaysian property developers love to work at night, especially if permissions have not yet been granted. Entire streets or parks disappear in the course of weeks or months to be replaced by overwhelming new building complexes. History and conservation are the first victims of a forward-looking, 'can do' dynamism, where each force in the city is trying to assert itself, regardless of the common good.

Some of the more superficial Western studies of Asian city growth to emerge in recent years ignore the complexity of the transfer of goods, favors and services as well as deep-rooted linguistic-psychological structures in nominally modernizing societies. Thus they are baffled by much: for example, why do people accept the destruction of their heritage with such equanimity?

Ramesh Kumar Biswas Kuala Lumpur: an Allegorical Postmetropolis

figure 3 Kuala Lumpur skyline

Part of the answer is that Asians are brought up in a paternalistic system to do what they are told, and tend to accept the wisdom of their elders or their bosses without contradiction. They are also more tolerant of change and renewal – or more fatalistic, depending upon your viewpoint. Asia has long been influenced by the old ethos of China and India, by the idea of constant change symbolized by the I-Ching, by the concept of cycles of creation and destruction embodied in the theory of reincarnation, or by the agricultural, cyclical view of time determined by the passage of the seasons. Acceptance of radical renewals is supported by the highly symbolic content of material things. A new glass skyscraper for a bank is perceived to a certain degree as the same entity (the same bank) as the old stone building it replaces; therefore there is no feeling of loss.

Kuala Lumpur is a new Asian city type whose flexible, hybrid and fluid shape is dictated by more than material welfare and globalization because it cannot really shake off its cultural identities. The promise of the city – the modernization of the mind – has not been completely fulfilled, and that gives KL its identity. Its growth resembles that of cities of the New World at the end of the nineteenth century, but that kind of mechanical urban planning never had a chance in KL. Structure plans galore can be found at the back of cupboards in City Hall, one of whose top officials confided to me, "In the 90s, the city was changing so fast based on decisions from above that we had no time for plans. All we could do was to look out of the window and take photographs." Though aspects of KL's development have been harshly criticized for their lack of coherence, they are accepted by residents as *faits accomplis*, even with a certain tenderness. KL's inhabitants are secretly proud of the phalanx of shining new towers pointing to the sky, towards a shining future.

Most new office towers in Southeast Asian cities are occupied only on their lower floors and the penthouse, leaving the intervening 20 to 40 floors vacant. In the upside-down Alice-in-Wonderland world of speculative property investment, these tall air-storage towers make sense: they are a means of converting profits from commodity trade, privatized services and currency speculation into fixed assets, which can then be used as collateral for further loans for industrial or infrastructural investment. As long as property prices rose, the increased value of a building as potential sale capital or collateral for new loans made it profitable, even if it was largely unoccupied. Some buildings openly function as tax write-offs. The NEP firms and agencies also have to have a city-center presence, advertised by their logos on their towers, even if they only occupy a few floors. The regional Asian business sector of Hong Kong and Japan also invests in vast shopping centers, hotels and high-rise housing projects.

There is a third motive: prestige. Napoleon was not the only 'vertically challenged' person who needed to prove that he was capable of great deeds; certain young cities feel the urge too, especially if they want to overcome setbacks in their past. To make up for the real and perceived humiliations of colonial and neo-colonial times, everything in KL now has to be bigger and better than in the West. It does not count for much in this value system if a building reflects, reacts to or develops the indigenous style, climate or culture (in any case, the few attempts to paste superficial local features on high-rises have turned out to look like gigantic cases of gangrene). Everything has to be in the style of the best of the West, but, if possible, even more grandiose. The image of a metropolis with the obligatory high-rise skyline has to be put across effectively to international investors (who are mostly simple-minded folk) if they are to be attracted in sufficient numbers to fill the empty skyscrapers. KL is full of projects loaded with superlatives. The race started many years ago with the erection of the 175m-high flagpole (you heard right, flagpole). It may well be true that the national flag holds a special cementing role in the mythology of young, multi-ethnic nations such as Malaysia and the USA, whose flags even look similar, but as soon it was realized that the intimidatingly high North Korean flagpole on its border with South Korea was even taller, a new symbol had to be found for KL. No time was wasted: the Petronas Twin Towers were born.

The strategy of erecting prestige projects with the attendant rhetoric to make a city well known has been used often in the West, from the monuments of ancient Greece to the nineteenth century's World Expositions. It became a deliberate policy of the Prime Minister, who took the urban development of the city into his own hands and still has the last word on any large-scale project. This strategy was admired by many and has obviously succeeded, confounding the handful of skeptics. For instance, there is hardly anyone with access to a satellite dish anywhere who has not heard of the world's tallest twin towers. Their statistics are overwhelming: 88 stories and 450 m of shim-

figure 4 Petronas Twin Towers

mering stainless steel and glass, 180,000 square m of floor space per office tower, two-story elevators and highly computerized operations being only some of the character-istics of a building that dominates views of the Klang Valley for tens of kilometers. 'Rockets', 'giant tiffin carriers', 'corn on the cob', 'Christmas trees' and other affectionate nicknames show that they have been wholeheartedly adopted by the population. In spite of the rumors surrounding the project - was one of the towers leaning during construction or merely 'deviating', as a construction company boss described it to me? - the citizens of KL are obviously proud that the International High-Rise Building Commission officially declared their twins to be taller than Chicago's Sears Tower. After all, it is much nicer to lay claim to the tallest towers in the world than to have merely the second-tallest flagpole. And they are, one would agree, quite simply the most stun-ning towers anywhere, by day or by night.

Kuala Lumpur is still searching for its place on the globe. The symbolic and representa-tional strategies to assert itself in a competitive world, to ensure social mobilization (and mobility) have expanded the scope of new *grands projets* to include the informa-tion and the leisure industries. KL's mega-airport, conceived by Kisho Kurokawa to be a symbiosis of nature and technology, is not merely situated within a rainforest. It also has a token, but highly effective bit of decorative rain forest in an atrium within it, intended to symbolize the tropical country around. A forest within an airport within a forest; an airport that ultimately demonstrates the dominance of technology over nature; an airport that occupies an area far greater than the main city itself; an airport that is a clearing-house for more passengers every year than KL itself houses, most of whom will never visit the city; and an airport that confirms the assumption that it makes a vital contribution to the image of the city it serves. To take a contrasting exam-ple: Singapore's airport, regularly evaluated as the best in the world, is an appropriate representation of that city - sterile, perfect, unexciting and tedious. KL airport and the Twin Towers have long replaced KL's old British-built neo-oriental railway station as symbols of the city on calendars or T-shirts. They are identifiable icons of economic power and the will to succeed, but more than that, they have achieved a cult status normally reserved for places of historic or religious importance.

The visitor to KL may well complain that it is the daily traffic jam in this vast 'parking lot of the East' that is more typical of the city. But the fact is that successful prestige projects as well as undeniably inadequate infrastructure, absent public amenities or fre-quent environmental disasters all reflect the reality of KL. It is nevertheless education-al to observe how these status symbols are appropriated by the public mind; how an intensely local, Malaysian everyday life evolves in the spaces between the high-tech, implanted structures.

Color, Contrast, Brightness, Volume - all the knobs have been turned up to the maxi-mum. What Ken Yeang has dubbed 'Karaoke Architecture' is clearly visible all over the 'tiger economies' throughout Southeast Asia. In karaoke, how well you can sing is not important, what matters is that you do it with verve and gusto. But how does KL differ from other Southeast Asian cities?, A lot of the architecture is obviously better than

that of Bangkok, Jakarta or Manila. The last few traces of the sleepy little town of barely two decades ago are marked to vanish completely by the self-imposed deadline of
2020. It is ultimately fascinating to watch Kuala Lumpur growing, in spite of severe
infrastructure deficits, environmental sins and the earnest recommendation of most
guidebooks to 'give it just a quick day or two before heading for the beach'. Even a skep-
tic cannot help but be infected by its prevalent optimism and its perpetual motion. It is
definitely a friendly place, not arrogant about its remarkable achievements. Bizarre and
questionable though some of the developments may be, they possess a bubbling life
and dynamism that many a smug, self-satisfied European city could benefit from. There
are those who love finding something weird around every corner; they liken it to *rojak*,
a delicious Malaysian salad of vegetables, prawns, fish, chilies, fruit and nuts – if you
can stretch your culinary imagination to picture such a strange creation.

The *rojak* effect goes beyond the many colorful buildings. KL is turning into a movie
with lots of heroes and villains to identify with. This inherent variety and multipolarity
is developing further into a new kind of urban entity. It is guiding the emergence of a
rhizomatic Asian 'postmetropolis' over the entire Klang Valley, similar to what geogra-
pher Edward Soja sees happening in LA[3] yet with its own distinct character.

What is emerging is the sucking-away of power from the traditional center and its dispersal into a widely spread, fragmented agglomeration, full of functional nodes and
new towns such as the national administrative capital in Putra Jaya and the 50-km-
long Multimedia Super Corridor centered on Cyber Jaya (literally: Cybertown) that takes
Silicon Valley conceptually a step further. The conscious development of an entire urban
agglomeration along a virtual IT core is a radically high-tech version of previous
attempts by other cities to establish themselves as trade fair or entertainment centers.
Various specialist universities, some of them privately financed by telecommunications
or utility companies, add to the picture, while industry or service points and other functionally faceless entities complete it. A capillary structure replaces a concentric one.
Anonymous warehouses form the new urban mass in between patches of tropical rainforest, ghost towns containing whirring servers being worked by people in other parts
of town. The new securities exchange complex is not only mostly occupied by computers and robots, it is also mostly operated by them. Even formerly sleepy suburban satellites such as Petaling Jaya are now bustling mixed-use beehives with traffic jams, crime,
divorce, drugs, teenage vagrancy, five-star hotels and pizza takeaways – everything, in
fact, that a classic city has, except its appearance.

Multiple allegiances and secret double lives are common. The transformation of urban
style also marks life in the margins. In Bukit Bintang, an old commercial quarter now lined
by mega-malls, the overlapping lives of KL are visible. Parts of Bukit Bintang that by day
are used as parking lots change in the evenings into street markets and food squares.
Raucous music and the aroma from freshly stirred woks hang thick in air illuminated by
naked light bulbs. Night-shift workers, lawyers and truck drivers, stranded night-birds and
insomniacs gather to eat and drink until the early hours of the morning, when the stands
are dismantled, the rubbish removed before dawn and nothing is left to bear witness to

3] Edward Soja,
Postmetropolis, Oxford:
Blackwell, 2002

the activities of the night before. Ephemerality reigns and no trace remains of the shadow life that will return as soon as night descends.

Public space is, after an interval of neglect, coming into its own again. For too long, street life had almost disappeared from the major thoroughfares. It is now returning, albeit in a way that reflects the new diasporic, transnational KL rather than the traditional city.

Next to the traditional night-time food stalls night scenes have sprung up out of the blue. Bintang Walk, a private investor's initiative, built with the support of the powers-that-be, was realized within an incredibly short few weeks. The pavements around the big commercial boxes have been turned into tree-lined boulevards enlivened by jazz bands, fountains and lasers and lined with new cafés and bars, *über*-cool by any international standards. Here the young and the beautiful are out in full force, parading and commuting between bars all night long. City Hall is objecting to its expansion into neighboring streets, because it violates so many traditional by-laws. But there were some things that even Yap Ah Loy in his time couldn't control. A city often develops a mind of its own. The new colors, tongues and flavors of KL are out here next to the old, enjoying the good life, mixing and growing. Architecture and fashions from the 70s and the new millennium mingle so casually that it is difficult to decide which are original and which retro. It's an exciting, eclectic *mélange*, somewhere between *rojak*, paella and karaoke, typically KL, typically Euro-Asian, very metropolitan.

Number of inhabitants [p]	3,392,000
Area [km²]	892
Density [p/km²]	3,803
Population urbanized (national) [2003]	88%

The Voids of Berlin
Andreas Huyssen

Part I

Eight years after the fall of the Wall, seven years after the unification of East and West Germany and just a couple of years before the final transfer of the national government from Bonn to the city on the Spree, Berlin is a city text frantically being written and rewritten. As Berlin leaves behind its heroic and propagandistic role as flashpoint of the Cold War and struggles to imagine itself as the new capital of a reunited nation, the city has become something like a prism through which we can focus issues of contemporary urbanism and architecture, national identity and statehood, historical memory and forgetting. Architecture has always been deeply invested in the shaping of political and national identities, and the rebuilding of Berlin as capital of Germany gives us significant clues to the state of the German nation after the fall of the wall and about the ways it projects its future.

As a literary critic I am naturally attracted to the notion of the city as text, of reading a city as a conglomeration of signs. Mindful of Italo Calvino's marvelously suggestive *Invisible Cities*, we know how real and imaginary spaces commingle in the mind to shape our notions of specific cities. No matter where we begin our discussion of the city of signs - whether with Victor Hugo's reading Paris in *Notre Dame de Paris* as a book written in stone, with Alfred Döblin's attempt, in *Berlin Alexanderplatz*, to create a montage of multiple city discourses jostling against each other like passers-by on a crowded sidewalk, with Walter Benjamin's notion of the *flâneur* reading urban objects in commemorative meditation, with Robert Venturi's upbeat emphasis on architecture as image, meaning, and communication, with Roland Barthes' city semiotics of the *Empire of Signs*, with Pynchon's TV-screen city or with Baudrillard's aesthetic transfiguration of an immaterial New York - a few things should be remembered: the trope of the city as book or as text has existed as long as we have had a modern city literature. There is nothing particularly novel or postmodern about it. On the other hand, one may want to ask why this notion of the city as sign and text assumed such critical mass in the architectural discourse of the 1970s and 1980s, arguably the high point of an architectural obsession with semiotics, rhetorics and codings which underwrote much of the debate about architectural postmodernism. Whatever the explanation may be – and no doubt, there is no single, simple answer to this question – it seems clear that today this interest in the city as sign, as text, is waning in much architectural discourse and practice, both of which have by and large turned against an earlier fascination with literary and linguistic models, no doubt at least partially as a result of the new image graphing technologies offered by ever more powerful computers.

The notion of the city as sign, however, is as pertinent as before, even though perhaps more now in a pictorial and imagistic rather than a textual sense. But this shift from script to image comes with a significant reversal. Put bluntly, the discourse of the city as text in the 1970s was primarily a critical discourse involving architects, literary critics, theorists, and philosophers bent on exploring and creating the new vocabularies of urban space after modernism. The current discourse of the city as image is one of 'city fathers', developers and politicians trying to increase revenue from mass tourism, conventions and office or commercial rental. Central to this new kind of urban politics are aesthetic spaces for cultural consumption, megastores and blockbuster museum events, Festspiele and spectacles of all kinds, all intended to lure that new species of the city-tourist, the urban vacationer or even the metropolitan marathoner who have replaced the older leisurely *flâneur*. The *flâneur*, even though something of an outsider in his city, was always figured as a dweller rather than as a traveler on the move. But today it is the tourist rather than the *flâneur* to whom the new city culture wants to appeal, just as it fears the tourist's unwanted counterpart, the displaced migrant.

There is a clear downside to this new notion of the city as sign and image in our global culture, nowhere as visible to me as in a recent front page article in the *New York Times* in which the paper's art critic celebrated the newly Disneyfied and theme-parked Times Square as the ultimate expression of a commercial billboard culture that has now, in this critic's skewed view, become indistinguishable from real art.[1] One can only hope that the transformation of Times Square from a haven for hustlers, prostitutes and junkies into a pop art installation will not presage the wholesale transformation of Manhattan into a museum, a process already far advanced in some older European cities.

This brings me back to Berlin, a city justly famous for its glorious museum collections, but, due mainly to its decenteredness and vast extension, much less liable to turn into an urban museum space such as the centers of Rome, Paris or even London have become in recent decades. Thus it is no big surprise to me that after an upsurge in the early 1990s, tourism to Berlin is significantly down. This slump may of course have something to do with the fact that Berlin is currently the most energized site for new urban construction anywhere in the Western world: enormously exciting for people interested in architecture and urban transformation, but for most others mainly an insufferable mess of dirt, noise, and traffic jams. Once all this construction has been completed Berlin will, it is hoped, take its rightful place as a European capital next to its more glamorous competitors. But will it? After all, Berlin is in significant ways different from other West European capitals, in terms of its history as capital and as industrial center as well as in terms of its building substance. And the fact that the city is now caught between the pressures of this new urban image politics and the more general crisis of architectural developments in the last years of the twentieth century makes any such hope appear simply misplaced, if not deluded. Indeed, I do think that Berlin is the place to study how this new emphasis on the city as cultural sign, combined with its role as capital and the pressures of large-scale developments, prevents creative alternatives and thus represents a false start into the twenty-first century. Berlin may be well on the way to squandering a unique chance.

Part II

There is perhaps no other major Western city that bears the marks of twentieth-century history as intensely and self-consciously as Berlin. This city text has been written, erased, and rewritten throughout this violent century, and its legibility relies as much on visible markers of built space as on images and memories repressed and ruptured by traumatic events. Part palimpsest, part *Wunderblock*, Berlin now finds itself in a frenzy

[1] Michael Kimmelman, 'That lashing Crazy Quilt of Signs? :'s Art', *New York Times*, 31 December, 1996, p. 1

figure 1 Philip Johnson Haus

of future projections and, in line with the general memorial obsessions of the 1990s, in the midst of equally intense debates about how to negotiate its Nazi and communist pasts, now that the safe dichotomies of the Cold War have vanished. The city is obsessed with architectural and planning issues, a debate that functions like a prism on the pitfalls of urban development at this turn of the century. All of this in the midst of a government and corporation-run building boom of truly monumental proportions. The goal is nothing less than to create the capital of the twenty-first century, but this vision finds itself persistently haunted by the past.

Berlin as text remains first and foremost historical text, marked as much, if not more, by absences as by the visible presence of its past, from prominent ruins such as the Gedächtniskirche at the end of the famous Kurfürstendamm to World War II bullet and shrapnel marks on many of its buildings. It was in the months after the collapse of the East German State that our sensibility for the past of this city was perhaps most acute, a city which for so long had stood in the dead eye of the storm of twentieth-century European politics. Empire, war and revolution, democracy, fascism, Stalinism, and the Cold War all were played out here. Indelibly etched into our memory is the idea of Berlin as the capital site of a discontinuous, ruptured history, of the collapse of four successive German states; Berlin as ground of literary expressionism and the revolt against the old order; Berlin as epicenter of the vibrant cultural avant-gardism of Weimar and its elimination by Nazism; Berlin as command center of world war and the Holocaust, and, finally, Berlin as symbolic space of the East-West confrontation of the nuclear age with American and Soviet tanks staring each other down at Checkpoint Charlie, which is now

The Voids of Berlin **Andreas Huyssen**

being turned into an American business center watched over, temporarily, by the towering photographic cut-out figure of Philip Johnson and a shrunk, gilded Statue of
Liberty placed atop the former East German watchtower.

If, at that confusing and exhilarating time after the fall of the Wall, Berlin seemed saturated with memories, the years since have also taught us multiple lessons about the
politics of willful forgetting: the imposed and often petty renaming of streets in East
Berlin, which were given back their presocialist (and often decidedly anti-socialist) cast,
the dismantling of monuments to socialism, the absurd debate about the tearing down
of the GDR's Palace of the Republic to make room for a rebuilding of the Hohenzollern
palace, and so forth. This was not just tinkering with the communist city text. It was a
strategy of power and humiliation, a final burst of Cold War ideology, pursued via a politics of signs, much of it wholly unnecessary and with predictable political fallout in an
East German population which felt increasingly deprived of its life history and of its
memories of four decades of separate development. Even though not all of the plans to
dismantle monuments and to rename streets came to fruition, the damage was done.
GDR nostalgia and an upsurge for the revamped communist party (PDS) were the
inevitable political results, even among many in the younger generation who had been
active in the opposition to the state in the 1980s.

Forgetting is equally privileged in an official ad campaign of 1996, literally written all
over the city: BERLIN WIRD (BERLIN BECOMES). But 'becomes' what? Instead of a proper object, we get a verbal void. Indeed, this phrasing may reflect wise precaution, for in

the current chaos of public planning, backdoor scheming, and contradictory politicking, with many architectural developments (Spreeinsel and Alexanderplatz among them) still hanging in the air and their feasibility and financing insecure, nobody seems to know exactly what Berlin will become. But the optimistic subtext of the ellipsis is quite clear, and radically opposed to Karl Scheffler's 1910 lament that it is the tragic destiny of Berlin "forever to become and never to be".[2] Too much of the current construction and planning actually lacks the very dynamism and energy of turn-of-the-century Berlin that Scheffler, ever the cultural pessimist, lamented. As much of central Berlin in the mid-1990s is a gigantic construction site, a hole in the ground, a void, there are indeed ample reasons to emphasize the void rather than to celebrate Berlin's current state of becoming.

Part III

The notion of Berlin as a void is more than a metaphor, and it is not just a transitory condition. It does carry its historical connotations. As early as 1935, the Marxist philosopher Ernst Bloch, in his *Erbschaft dieser Zeit*, described life in Weimar Berlin as functions in a void.[3] He then referred to the vacuum left by the collapse of an earlier, nineteenth-century bourgeois culture, which had found its spatial expression in the heavy ornamental stone architecture of Berlin's unique apartment buildings, the pejoratively called *Mietkasernen* (rent barracks), with their multiple wings in the back, the so-called *Hinterhäuser* enclosing inner courtyards accessible from the street only through tunnel-like archways. The post-World War I vacuum was filled by a functionalist and, to Bloch, insubstantial culture of distraction: Weimar modernism, the movie palaces, the six-day bicycle races, the new modernist architecture, the glitz and glamour of the so-called 'stabilization phase' before the 1929 crash. Bloch's phrasing "functions in the void" also articulated the insight that in the age of monopoly capitalism built city space could no longer command the representative functions of an earlier age. As Brecht put it in those same years, when he discussed the need for a new, post-mimetic realism: reality itself had become functional, thus requiring entirely new modes of representation.[4]

A little over a decade later, it was left to fascism to transform Berlin into the literal void that was the landscape of ruins in 1945. Especially in the center of Berlin, British and American bombers had joined forces with Albert Speer's wrecking crews to create the tabula rasa for Germania, the renamed capital of a victorious Reich. And the creation of voids did not stop then; it continued through the 1950s, when, under the heading of *Sanierung*, entire quarters of the old Berlin were razed to the ground to make room for the simplistic versions of modern architecture and planning characteristic of the times. The major construction project of the postwar period, the Wall, needed another void, that of the no man's land and the minefields that wound their way through the very center of the city and held its Western part in a tight embrace.

During the Cold War, West Berlin always appeared on East European maps as a void, the hole in the East European cheese, just as weather maps on West German television

2] Karl Scheffler, *Berlin—Ein Stadtschicksal*, Berlin: Fannei und Walz, 1989 reprint, p. 219

3] Ernst Bloch, *Erbschaft dieser Zeit*, Frankfurt am Main: Suhrkamp, 1973, pp. 212–228. Of course, Bloch's phrasing 'Funktionen im Hohlraum" (literally: functions in a hollow space) suggests a bounded void which, after all, is appropriate whenever one discusses a void in a spatial or temporal sense

4] See Bertolt Brecht, 'Against Georg Lukács', trans. Stuart Hood, in Ernst Bloch et al., *Aesthetics and Politics*, London: W.W. Norton & Co. Inc, 1977, pp. 68–85

The Voids of Berlin **Andreas Huyssen**

Figure 3 Wall area

for a long time represented the GDR as an absence, a blank space surrounding the Frontstadt Berlin, the capitalist cheese in the real existing void.

When the Wall came down, Berlin added another chapter to its narrative of voids, a chapter which brought back shadows of the past and spooky revenants. For a couple of years, the very center of Berlin, the threshold between the eastern and the western part of the city, was a 17-acre wasteland that extended from the Brandenburg Gate down to Potsdamer Platz and Leipziger Platz, a wide stretch of dirt, grass and remnants of former pavement under a big sky that seemed even bigger given the absence of any high-rise skyline so characteristic of other parts of this city. Berliners called it affectionately their "wonderful city steppes", their "prairie of history."[5] It was a haunting space, crisscrossed by a maze of footpaths going nowhere. One slight elevation marked the remnants of the bunker of Hitler's SS guard which, after having been reopened once the Wall came down, was soon sealed shut again by the city authorities to avoid making it into a site of neo-Nazi pilgrimage. Walking across this space, which had been mined no man's land framed by the wall and which now served occasionally as staging site for rock concerts and other transitory cultural attractions, I could not help remembering that this tabula rasa had once been the site of Hitler's *Reichskanzlei* and the proposed

[5] As quoted by Francesca Rogier, 'Growing Pains: From the Opening of the Wall to the Wrapping of the Reichstag', *Assemblage*, Vol. 29, 1996, p. 50

figure 4 Albert Speer, North–South axis

site of Speer's megalomaniac North–South axis with the Great Hall in the North and Hitler's triumphal arch in the south, the power center of the empire of a thousand years, all to be completed by 1950.

In the summer of 1991, when most of the Wall had already been removed, auctioned off, or sold to tourists in bits and pieces, the area was studded with the steel reinforcing rods left behind by the *Mauerspechte*, the wall peckers who had removed most of the masonry, and decorated with colorful triangular paper leaves that were blowing and rustling in the wind: they powerfully marked the void as second Nature and as memorial.

The Voids of Berlin **Andreas Huyssen**

Figure 5 Installation in the void

The installation increased the uncanny feeling: a void saturated with invisible history, with memories of architecture both built and unbuilt. It gave rise to the desire to leave it as it was: the memorial as empty page right in the center of the reunified city, the center that had always been the very threshold between the eastern and western parts of the city, and the space that now, in yet another layer of signification, seemed to be called upon to represent the invisible 'wall in the head' that still separated East and West Germans and that was anticipated by Peter Schneider long before the actual Wall came down.[6]

Since then, the rebuilding of this empty center of Berlin has become a major focus of all discussions about the Berlin of tomorrow. With the new government quarter in the bend of the River Spree next to the Reichstag in the North and the corporate developments at Potsdamer and Leipziger Platz at the southern end of this space, Berlin will indeed gain a new center of corporate and governmental power.

But how important should the city center be for the cities of the future? After all, the city as center and the centered city are themselves in question today. Bernard Tschumi puts it well where he asks "how can architecture whose historical role was to generate the appearance of stable images (monuments, order, etc.) deal with today's culture of the disappearance of unstable images (twenty-four-image-per-second cinema, video, and computer-generated images?"[7] For some Web-surfers and virtual city *flâneur*s, the built city itself has become obsolete. Others, however, like Saskia Sassen, the New York urbanist, or Dieter Hoffmann-Axthelm, a well-known Berlin architectural critic, have argued persuasively that it is precisely the growth of global telecommunications and the potential dispersal of population and resources that have created a new logic for concentration in what Sassen calls the global city.[8] Indeed, the city as center is far from becoming obsolete. But as center, the city is increasingly affected and structured by our

[6] Peter Schneider, *Der Mauerspringer*, Darmstadt, Lucktehand, 1982, p. 102

[7] Bernard Tschumi, *Event Cities*, Cambridge, Mass.: MIT Press, 1994, p. 367

[8] Saskia Sassen, *The Global City: New York, London, Tokyo*, New Jersey, N.J.: Princeton University Press, 1991

figure 6 Potsdamer Platz around 1930

culture of media images. In the move from the city as regional or national center of production to the city as international center of communications, media and services, the very image of the city becomes central to its success in a globally competitive world. From New York's new Times Square with its culture industry giants Disney and Bertelsmann and its ecstasies of flashing commercial signage to Berlin's new Potsdamer Platz with Sony, Mercedes and Brown Boveri, visibility equals success.

Not surprisingly, then, the major concern with developing and rebuilding key sites in the heart of Berlin seems to be image rather than usage, attractiveness for tourists and official visitors rather than heterogeneous living space for Berlin's inhabitants, erasure of memory rather than its imaginative preservation. The new architecture is to enhance the desired image of Berlin as capital and global metropolis of the twenty-first century, as a hub between Eastern and Western Europe and as a center of corporate presence, however limited that presence may in the end turn out to be. But ironically, the concern with Berlin's image, foremost in the minds of politicians who desire nothing so much as to increase Berlin's ability to attract corporations and tourists, clashes with what I would describe as the fear of an architecture of images.

Part IV

This tension has produced a very sharp debate in which the battle lines are firmly drawn between the defenders of a national tradition and the advocates of a contemporary high-tech global architecture. The traditionalists champion a local and national concept of urban culture that and they call it 'critical reconstruction.'[9] Its representatives, such as Hans Stimmann, the city's director of building from 1991 to 1996, and Victor Lampugnani, former Director of Frankfurt's Museum of Architecture, call for a new simplicity which seems to aim at a mix of Schinkel's classicism and Peter Behrens's once

[9] Some of the key contributions to the debate about critical reconstruction are collected in G. Kähler (ed.), *Einfach schwierig: Eine deutsche Architekturdebatte*, Basel: Birckhäuser Verlag, 1995

The Voids of Berlin **Andreas Huyssen**

daring modernism, with Tessenow as a moderate modernist thrown in to secure an anti-avant-gardist and anti-Weimar politics of traditionalism. Berlin must be Berlin, they say. Identity is at stake. But this desired identity is symptomatically dominated by pre-World War I architecture, the *Mietkaserne* and the once again popular notion of the traditional neighborhood, affectionately called the *Kiez*. In the late 1970s, the *Kiez* emerged as counterculture in run-down quarters close to the Wall, such as Kreuzberg, where squatters occupied and restored decaying housing stock. In the 1980s, it was embraced by the city's mainstream preservation efforts. Now, it dictates key parameters of the new architectural conservatism. Forgotten are the architectural and planning experiments of the 1920s, the great Berlin estates of Martin Wagner and Bruno Taut. Forgotten – or rather, repressed – is the architecture of the Nazi period (of which Berlin, after all, still harbors significant examples, from the Olympic Stadium to Goering's aviation ministry near Leipziger Platz). Ignored and to be quickly forgotten is the architecture of the GDR, which many would like to commit in its entirety to the wrecking-ball, from the Stalinallee all the way to satellite housing projects like Marzahn or Hohenschönhausen. What we have instead is a strange mix of an originally leftist *Kiez* romanticism and a nineteenth-century vision of the neighborhood divided into small parcels, as if such structures could provide a blueprint for the rebuilding of the city as a whole. But this is precisely what bureaucrats like Stimmann and theorists like Hoffmann-Axthelm have in mind with critical reconstruction. Prescriptions such as city block building, traditional façades with classically-proportioned window openings, a uniform height of 22m (the ritualistically invoked *Traufhöhe*), and building in stone are vociferously defended against all evidence that such traditionalism is wholly imaginary. Building in stone, indeed, at a time when the most stone you'd get is a thin stone veneer covering the concrete skeleton underneath.

There is not much of interest to say about the other, the corporate, side of the debate. There we have international high tech, façade ecstasy, preference for mostly banal high-rises, and floods of computer-generated imagery to convince us that we need to go with the future. But this dichotomy of Stone Age vs. cyber age is misleading: the fight is over image and image alone on both sides of the issue. The new nationally coded simplicity is just as image-driven as the image ecstasies of the high-tech camp, except that it posits banal images of a national past against equally banal images of a global future. The real Berlin of today, its conflicts and aspirations, remains a void in a debate that lacks imagination and vision.

Take Hans Stimmann and Victor Lampugnani. Lampugnani disapproves of "easy pictures ... superficial sensation ... tormented lightness ... wild growth ... nosy new interpretation."[10] Stimman in turn protests that 'learning from Las Vegas' is out of place in a central European city, a programmatic statement as much directed against postmodernism in architecture as it is quite blatantly anti-American in the tradition of conservative German *Kulturkritik*.[11] But this attack on a 25-year-old founding text of postmodern architecture and its reputed image politics are strangely out of place and out of time. Las Vegas postmodernism has been defunct for some time, and nobody has ever suggested that Berlin should become casino city. The hidden object of Stimmann's

[10] As quoted in Dagmar Richter, 'Spazieren in Berlin', *Assemblage*, Vol. 29, 1996, p. 80

[11] Hans Stimmann, 'Conclusion: From Building Boom to Building Type', in Annegret Burg, *Downtown Berlin: Building the Metropolitan Mix/Berlin Mitte: Die Entstehung einer urbanen Architektur*, Hans Stimmann (ed.) trans. Ingrid Taylor, Christian Caryl, and Robin Benson, Basel: Birkhäuser Verlag, 1995

figure 7 Potsdamer Platz
construction site with
Info Box

moralizing protest is Weimar Berlin. For Berlin in the 1920s, we must remember, defined
its modernity as quintessentially 'American'. Berlin was a 'Chicago on the Spree', and as
such different from older European capitals and different also from the Berlin of the
Wilhelmine Empire. The embrace of America was an embrace of pragmatic technological modernity, functionalism, mass culture, and democracy. America then offered
images of the new, but memories of the Weimar architecture produced by Mendelsohn,
Gropius and the Bauhaus, Bruno Taut, Martin Wagner, Hannes Meyer and Mies van der
Rohe simply do not figure in the current debates about architecture in Berlin. In their
anti-modernism, the conservatives themselves have gone postmodern. Small wonder
then that Stimmann's preference for 'critical reconstruction' is itself primarily concerned with image and advertising: the image of built space creating a sense of traditional identity for Berlin whose voids must be filled, and the more intangible, yet economically decisive international image of the city in an age of global service economies,
urban tourism, cultural competition, and new concentrations of wealth and power. But
the desired image is decidedly pre-1914. The critical reconstructionists fantasize about
a second *Gründerzeit* analogous to the founding years of the Second Reich after the
Franco-Prussian war. Never mind that the gold rush of the first *Gründerzeit* quickly collapsed with the crash of 1873 and the beginning of a long-term depression.

The issue in central Berlin, to use Venturi, Scott Brown and Izenour's by now classical postmodern terms from *Learning from Las Vegas* in this very different context, is about how
best to decorate the corporate and governmental sheds to better attract international

The Voids of Berlin **Andreas Huyssen**

attention: not the city as multiply-coded text to be filled with life by its dwellers and its readers, but the city as image and design in the service of displaying power and profit. This underlying goal has paradigmatically come to fruition in a project on Leipziger Platz called Info Box, a huge red box on black stilts with window fronts several stories high and with an open-air roof terrace providing panoramic views.

This Info Box, attracting some 5,000 visitors per day, was built in 1995 as a temporary installation to serve as a viewing site onto the construction wasteland studded with building cranes that surrounds it. With its multi-media walls, sound-rooms, and inter-active computers, it serves as an exhibition and advertising site for the corporate developments by Mercedes, Sony and the A+T Investment Group on Leipziger and Potsdamer Platz. As cyber *flâneur* in 'Virtual Berlin 2002,' you can enjoy a fly-through via a computer simulation of the new Potsdamer and Leipziger Platz developments or arrive by ICE at the future Lehrter Bahnhof. You can watch the construction site on a wraparound amphitheatrical screen inside, listening to an animated Disneyfied Berlin sparrow deliver the proud narrative cast in that typically street-smart, slightly lower-class Berlin intonation. Or you can admire plaster casts of the major architects – the cult of the master-builder is well and alive as simulacrum, all the more so as architects have become mere appendages in today's world of urban development. More image box than Info Box, this space offers the ultimate paradigm of the many *Schaustellen* (viewing and spectacle sites), which the city mounted in the summer of 1996 at its major *Baustellen* (construction sites). Berlin as a whole advertised itself as *Schaustelle* with the slogan *Bühnen, Bauten, Boulevards* (stages, buildings, boulevards) and mounted a cultural program including over 200 guided tours of construction sites, 800 hours of music, acrobatics, and pantomime on nine open-air stages throughout the summer. From void, then, to *mise-en-scène* and to image, images in the void: *Berlin wird...* Berlin becomes image.

Is it only perverse to compare the gaze from the Info Box terrace onto the construction wasteland of Potsdamer Platz to that other gaze we all remember, the gaze from the primitive elevated wooden (later metal) platform erected near the Wall West of Potsdamer Platz to allow Western visitors to take a long look eastwards across the death strip as emblem of communist totalitarianism? It would only be perverse if one were to simply equate the two sites. And yet, the memory of that other viewing platform will not go away as it shares with the Info Box a certain obnoxious triumphalism: the political triumphalism of the Free World in the Cold War now having been replaced by the triumphalism of the free market in the age of corporate globalization.

Perhaps the box and the screen *are* our future. After all, the recently completed developments on Friedrichstrasse, that major commercial artery crossing Unter den Linden, look frighteningly similar to their former computer simulations, with one major difference: what appeared airy, sometimes even elegant, and generously spacious in the simulations, now looks oppressively monumental, massive, and forbidding, especially when experienced under the leaden Berlin skies in mid-winter. Call it the revenge of the real.

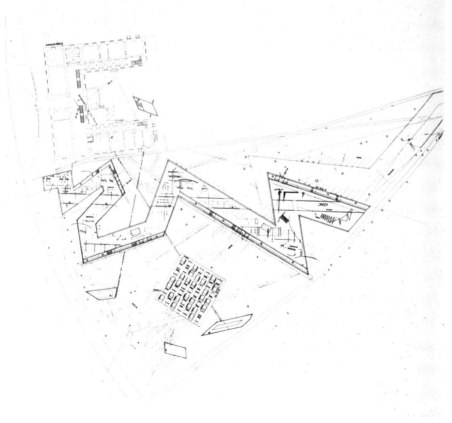

figure 8 Berlin Museum with the Jewish Museum, model.

figure 9 Libeskind Museum, ground plan.

The Voids of Berlin **Andreas Huyssen**

In addition, some of the new fancy malls on Friedrichstraße, meant to compete with the KaDeWe (*Kaufhaus des Westens*) and the shopping area on and near Kurfürstendamm, are already going belly-up, and Berlin already has surplus office space for rental as more is being built day by day. Hence my fear for the future of Potsdamer and Leipziger Platz: just as the Info Box immobilizes the *flâneur* facing the screen, the tight corporate structures (despite their gesturing toward public spaces and piazzas) will encage and confine their visitors, rather than recreate the open, mobile, and multiply-coded urban culture that once characterized this pivotal traffic hub between the eastern and western parts of the city. There is good reason to doubt whether Helmut Jahn's happy plastic tent hovering above the central plaza of the Sony development will make up for the loss of urban life that these developments will inevitably entail.

Part V

Looking at the forces and pressures that currently shape the new Berlin, one may well fear that the ensemble of architectural solutions proposed may represent the worst start into the twenty-first century one could imagine for this city. Many of the major construction projects, it seems, have been designed against the city rather than for it. Some of them look like corporate spaceships reminiscent of the conclusion of *Close Encounters of the Third Kind*. The trouble is: they are here to stay. The void in the center of Berlin will have been filled. But memories of that haunting space from the months and years after the Wall came down will linger. The one architect who understood the nature of this empty space in the center of Berlin was Daniel Libeskind, who, in 1992, made the following proposal:

> Rilke once said that everything is already there. We only must see it and protect it. We must develop a feel for places, streets, and houses which need our support. Take the open area at the Potsdamer Platz. I suggest a wilderness, one kilometer long, within which everything can stay as it is. The street simply ends in the bushes. Wonderful. After all, this area is the result of today's divine natural law: nobody wanted it, nobody planned it, and yet it is firmly implanted in all our minds. And there in our minds, this image of the Potsdamer Platz void will remain for decades. Something like that cannot be easily erased, even if the whole area will be developed.[12]

Of course, what Libeskind describes tongue-in-cheek as "today's divine natural law" is nothing but the pressure of history that created this void called Potsdamer Platz in the first place: the saturation bombings of 1944–5 which left little of the old Potsdamer Platz structures standing, the building of the Wall in 1961 which required a further clearing of the area, the tearing down of the Wall in 1989 which made this whole area between the Brandenburg Gate and Potsdamer Platz into that prairie of history which Berliners quickly embraced. It was a void filled with history and memory, all of which will be erased (I'm less sanguine about the power of memory than Libeskind) by the new construction.

12] 'Daniel Libeskind mit Daniel Libeskind: Potsdamer Platz', 1992, in Daniel Libeskind, *Radix–Matrix: Architekturen und Schriften*, Munich and New York: Prestel, 1994, p. 149

In light of Libeskind's own architectural project, however, which is crucially an architecture of memory, even his suggestion of leaving the void as it was in the early 1990s was not just romantic and impractical. For Libeskind gave architectural form to another void that haunts Berlin, the historical void left by the Nazi destruction of Berlin's thriving Jewish life and culture. A discussion of Daniel Libeskind's museum project, arguably the single most interesting building currently going up in Berlin, is appropriate here not only because it gives a different inflection to the notion of Berlin as void in relation to memory and to history, but more importantly because, however indirectly, it raises the issue of German national identity and the identity of Berlin. While all the other major building sites in Berlin today are inevitably haunted by the past, only Libeskind's building attempts to articulate memory and our relationship to it in its very spatial organization.

Part VI

In 1989, just a few months before the Wall cracked, Daniel Libeskind surprisingly won a competition to build the expansion of the Berlin Museum with the Jewish Museum, as it is awkwardly—and yet appropriately—called.

The Berlin Museum was founded in 1962 as a local history museum for the Western part of the divided city, clearly a reaction to the building of the Wall which had made the former local history museum, the Märkisches Museum, inaccessible. Since the mid-1970s, the Berlin Museum has had a Jewish section which documents the role of German Jewry in the history of Berlin. With the new expansion, the museum was to consist of three parts: general history of Berlin from 1870 to today, Jewish history in Berlin, and an in-between space dedicated to the theme 'Jews in Society', which would articulate the relations and crossovers between the other two components. Libeskind's proposal was as architecturally daring as it was conceptually persuasive, and even though multiple resistances—political, aesthetic and economic—had to be overcome, the museum is being built and it is to be finished in the fall of 1997.

The expansion sits next to the old Berlin Museum, a baroque palace which used to house the Berlin Chamber Court before it became a museum in 1962. The old and the new parts are apparently disconnected, and the only entrance to the expansion building is underground from the old building. Libeskind's structure has often been described as zigzag, as lightning, or, since it is to house a Jewish collection, as a fractured Star of David. He himself has called it "Between the Lines."

The ambiguity between an architecturally spatial and a literary meaning (one reads between the lines) is intended, and it suggests the conceptual core of the project. The basic structure of the building is found in the relation between two lines, one straight but broken into pieces, divided into fragments, the other multiply bent, contorted, but potentially going on ad infinitum. Architecturally, this longitudinal axis translates into a thin slice of empty space that crosses the path of the zigzag structure at each intersection and that reaches from the bottom of the building to the top. It is sealed to the exhibition halls of the museum. It cannot be entered, but it is accessible to view from

Figure 10 Void in Libeskind Museum

the small bridges that cross it at every level of the building: it is a view into an abyss extending downward and upward at the same time. Libeskind calls it "the void."

This fractured and multiply interrupted void functions like a spine to the building. It is both conceptual and literal. And clearly, it signifies: as void it signifies absence, the absence of Berlin's Jews most of whom perished in the Holocaust.[13] As fractured void it signifies history, a broken history without continuity: the history of Jews in Germany, of German Jews and therefore also the history of Germany itself, which cannot be thought as separate from Jewish history in Germany. Thus, in line with the original demand of the competition, the void provides that in-between space between Berlin's history and Jewish history in Berlin, inseparable as they are, except that it does it in a form radically different from what was originally imagined by the competition. By leaving this in-between space void, the museum's architecture forecloses the possibility of re-harmonizing German-Jewish history along the discredited models of symbiosis or assimilation. But it also forecloses the opposite view that sees the Holocaust as the inevitable telos of German history. Jewish life in Germany has been fundamentally altered by the Holocaust, but it has not stopped. The void thus becomes a space nurturing memory and reflection for Jews and for Germans. Its very presence points to an absence that can never be overcome, a rupture that cannot be healed, and it can certainly not be filled with museum stuff. Its fundamental epistemological negativity cannot be absorbed into the narratives that will be told by the objects and installations in the galleries of the museum. The void will always be there in the minds of the spectators crossing the bridges that traverse it as they move through the exhibition space. The spectators themselves will move constantly between the lines. Organized around a void without images, Libeskind's architecture has become script. His building itself writes the discontinuous narrative that is Berlin, inscribes it physically into the very movement of the museum visitor, and yet opens a space for remembrance to be articulated and read between the lines.

Of course, the voids I have been juxtaposing are of a fundamentally different nature. One is an open urban space resulting from war, destruction, and a series of subsequent historical events; the other is an architectural space, consciously constructed and self-reflexive to the core. Both spaces nurture memory, but whose memory? The very notion of the void will have different meaning for Jews than it will for Germans. There is a danger of romanticizing or naturalizing the voided center of Berlin just as Libeskind's building may ultimately not avoid the reproach of aetheticizing or monumentalizing the void architecturally.[14] But then the very articulation of this museum space demonstrates the architect's awareness of the dangers of monumentality: huge as the expansion is, the spectator can never see or experience it as a whole. Both the void inside and the building as perceived from the outside elude the totalizing gaze upon which monumental effects are predicated. Spatial monumentality is undercut in the inevitably temporal apprehension of the building. Such anti-monumental monumentality, with which the museum memorializes both the Holocaust and Jewish life in Berlin, stands in sharp contrast to the unselfconscious monumentality of the official, government-sponsored Holocaust Monument that is to be built at the northern end of that highly

13] For a gentle, though to me ultimately unpersuasive, critique of Libeskind's void as being too determined by history, meaning, and experience, see Jacques Derrida, 'Jacques Derrida zu "Between the Lines"', in Libeskind, op. cit., p. 115–117.

14] This is implied by Derrida, for whom a void that represents is no longer proper void

Figure 11 Reichstag under renovation

5] At the time of writing, it is not clear which of the many proposals for the Monument to the Murdered Jews of Europe is going to be accepted. A competition in 1995 with a total of 27 entries ended in a public outcry over the winning entry, a slanted concrete slab the size of two football fields with millions of victims' names carved in stone. Even Helmut Kohl did not like it, though surely for the wrong reasons

6] I am only talking here about the building as architecture. Its museum and curatorial functions are still too much in flux for us to comment with any degree of certainty about the ways in which the exhibition spaces will be used or even who will have ultimate curatorial control over the expansion space.

charged space between the Brandenburg Gate and Leipziger Platz.[15] For those who for good reasons question the ability of traditional monuments to keep memory alive as public or collective memory, Libeskind's expansion of the Berlin Museum may be a better memorial to German and Jewish history, the history of the living and of the dead, than any official funereal Holocaust monument could possibly be.[16]

As architecture, then, Libeskind's museum is the only project in the current Berlin building boom that explicitly articulates issues of national and local history in ways pertinent to post-unification Germany. In its spatial emphasis on the radical ruptures, discontinuities, and fractures of German and German-Jewish history, it stands in opposition to the critical reconstructionists' attempts to create a seamless continuity with a pre-1914 national past that would erase memories of Weimar, Nazi, and GDR architecture in the process. As an architecture of memory, it also opposes the post-nationalism of global corporate architecture à la Potsdamer and Leipziger Platz, an architecture of development that has neither memory nor sense of place to begin with. As unintentional manifesto, the museum points to the conceptual emptiness that currently exists between a nostalgic pre-1914 understanding of the city and its post-2002 entropic corporate malling. The history of Berlin as void is not over yet, but then perhaps a city as vast and vibrant as Berlin will manage to incorporate its latest white elephants at Potsdamer and Leipziger Platz into the larger urban fabric. If Paris is able to live with Sacré Coeur, who is to say that Berlin cannot stomach Sony Corp. Once the current image frenzy is over, the Info Box dismantled, and the critical reconstruction-

Andreas Huyssen The Voids of Berlin

ists forgotten, the notion of the capital as a montage of many historical forms and spaces will reassert itself, and the commitment to the necessarily palimpsestic texture of urban space may even lead to new, not yet imaginable forms of architecture.

Coda: seven years later (2004)

When the German Reichstag, renovated and crowned with a stunning glass cupola by Sir Norman Foster, was inaugurated with a plenary session of parliament on April 19, 1999, Berlin had officially reclaimed its status as capital of a united Germany and the Berlin Republic was participating as a member of NATO in the war in Kosovo. Indeed, the new united Germany is new in ways hardly imagined in the early 1990s when the triumphalists of national sovereignty dreamed about a self-confident nation (*selbstbe-wusste Nation*) that would finally overcome its past, while the detractors of national unification painted the horrific picture of a Fourth Reich. Today, Germany is neither. Two weeks after German troops moved into Kosovo, the German parliament affirmed the Berlin Republic's commitment to commemorate the Holocaust. The much debated, though still controversial Memorial to the Murdered Jews of Europe designed by Peter Eisenman will be built in the very heart of Berlin just south of the Brandenburg Gate. Only time will tell whether the Memorial will nurture commemoration or foster oblivion, but the decision to go ahead with the project is politically significant, even though the decision itself was reached in 1999 with a sense of exhaustion after a 12-year long debate.[17]

If memories of the past and an evolving present have mixed in unforeseeable ways in the recent politics of the Berlin Republic, then the same can be said about the architectural reconstruction of Berlin as capital. At a time when many building projects are coming to fruition, the assessment of the new Berlin has become more fluid and ambiguous than it was five years ago. The stifling architectural debate then pitted the traditionalists of 'critical reconstruction' against the triumphalists of postmodern high tech, and both faced the radical skeptics who diagnosed a total lack of any persuasive urban or architectural vision on either side of that debate. Today the boundaries that separated the various factions seem blurred. Critical reconstruction, with its restrictive regulations and its ideology of building in stone, has never become a Procrustean bed for the new Berlin architecture, as some had feared. Some high-tech and postmodern projects have been absorbed rather well into the city fabric. And even though there may still not be anything resembling a cohesive urban vision, a decentered network of new building sites and changing neighborhoods is emerging that is increasingly being accepted by the public and that has begun to shape the image of Berlin as a part creative, part timid mix of old and new.

The rebuilt Reichstag may serve as an emblem for this mix of the creative and the timid at this time. Its façade and shell are the only residues left from Wilhelmine times: stone walls as much as 3 m thick, pompous columns, a lot of monumental stone permeated by historical reminiscences. The inside of the building has been totally ripped out and pragmatically, though coldly, refurbished in muted materials and colors, but the graffiti left by Soviet soldiers in 1945 are still visible and highlighted on several walls. The

17] For more on the German role in the Kosovo war in comparison to German reactions to the Gulf War in 1991 see Andreas Huyssen, 'After the War: Berlin as Palimpsest', in my forthcoming *Present Pasts: Urban Palimpsests and the Politics of Memory*, Stanford University Press

The Voids of Berlin **Andreas Huyssen**

only real architectural attraction is the Reichstag's cupola, destroyed by arson in the first year of Nazi rule, and redesigned by Norman Foster as a gigantic glass dome, oddly reminiscent of a beehive or an oversize space egg.

The doubled winding ramps on the inside are accessible to the public, providing panoramic views of the surrounding city and setting the open interior space with its light-reflecting mirroring central cone into slow motion for the walking spectator, a veritable *flâneur dans l'air*. But it is especially the illuminated dome at night that has been embraced by the media and the public as a symbol of the new Berlin. Foster's overall renovation may not satisfy on purely aesthetic grounds, but it successfully embodies the tensions between the unloved imperial past (the building's outside shell), a bureaucratic functional present of the German republic (the plenary hall for the Bundestag), and the desire to have a flashy image of democratic transparency marking Berlin's reclaimed status as capital.

Talk of the voids of Berlin seems less pertinent today than it was in the early or mid-1990s. Indeed, the urban tabula rasa fantasies of the early 1990s have faded fast. Enthusiasm about building the new Berlin from scratch is giving way to a more pragmatic outlook. Not metaphors of the void, but emptiness is at stake at a time when so many new office and apartment buildings are still looking for occupants. At the federal level, financial calculations have forced a scaling-back of many plans, mandating reutilization rather than destruction of several major fascist buildings in the heart of Berlin (including Goering's Aviation Ministry and the Reichsbank). Overblown images of a new global Berlin as capital of the twenty-first century have made way for a more modest reality.

Berlin is now past the point when the debate focused primarily on the vast corporate construction site at Potsdamer and Leipziger Platz. Gigantic developments by Daimler-Benz and Sony loomed large as threats to the urban fabric as a whole. The malling of Potsdamer Platz, that mythic traffic hub of the Weimar Republic, Germany's Piccadilly Circus and

figure 13 Reichstag cupola, interior perspective

Times Square rolled into one, seemed a foregone conclusion and a symbol of all bad things to come. Potsdamer Platz has indeed been malled, and the architectural results are, as predicted, appalling. Its relationship to the neighboring Kulturforum with the Staatsbibliothek, the Philharmonie (both by Scharoun) and the Neue Nationalgalerie (Mies van der Rohe) is ill-defined. The new Potsdamer Platz will never match the myth of the square as emblem of Weimar modernity. As imaginary center of a metropolis, the narrative of Potsdamer Platz expires in its arcades, a drab two-story shopping mall stuffed with mini-boutiques and fast-food units at either side of the open floor-to-ceiling space in the middle, which more closely resembles the inside of a prison than a consumer paradise.

And yet Potsdamer Platz in its new incarnation has received a surprisingly positive press, and the public seems to accept it with open arms. To some, the city's insistence on maintaining the old street plans for the Potsdamer Platz area has turned out to be a blessing

The Voids of Berlin **Andreas Huyssen**

in disguise. For the narrow streets, alleys, and piazzas allow for a certain intensity of street life, as long as one forgets that it is the street life of the late twentieth century: that of the pedestrian shopping mall. Others feel that the corporate and commercial buildings are different enough in size, material and design at least to suggest a real urban space. If it is a mall, to them it is also still Potsdamer Platz. Much will depend on how these buildings will age and how attractive Potsdamer Platz will remain as a public space once its current novelty has worn off. I remain skeptical, but Potsdamer Platz today may well embody the structural irreconcilability between contemporary consumer society and older notions of public space.

At any rate, the Potsdamer Platz development, the big white elephant of Berlin reconstruction, has been joined by other architectural attractions. There now is a web of sites of very different size and function that fleshes out the architectural landscape of the new Berlin: the new Pariser Platz just east of the Brandenburg Gate, entryway into classical Berlin; the Hackesche Höfe, an imaginative reutilization of one of the most fabled multiple inner courtyards of the old Berlin; the Aldo Rossi complex of apartment buildings and offices at Schützenstrasse with its southern German-style courtyards and colorful and varied façades that loosen up the block building prescriptions of critical reconstruction; the fast-paced renovations at Prenzlauer Berg, in the old Jewish quarter known as Scheunenviertel, and in other neighborhoods of East Berlin.

Architecturally neglected in most discussions are of course those socialist mass housing projects (*Plattenbau*) in East Berlin familiar from similar examples all over Eastern Europe. And yet it would be quite challenging to imagine ways of integrating housing projects such as Marzahn, Hohenschönhausen and especially Hellersdorf into the new urban fabric, now that they have lost their grounding in socialist notions of collective living. Whether they will stand as ruins of socialism and urban decay or whether they can be modified in some creative form, only time will tell. The larger question here is to what extent the socialist city text will remain part of the fast-changing palimpsest that is Berlin. Daniel Libeskind's plan for Alexanderplatz pointed creatively in that direction, but it never had a chance to be realized.

A mix of the old and the new, the creative and the timid - that does not seem such a bad recipe for a city that has never had the luster of London or the aura of Paris. Building on its historical de-centeredness as architectural urban space and maintaining the city as a palimpsest of many different times and histories may actually be preferable to the notion of a centered Berlin which would inevitably revive the ghosts of the past, not just in the minds of Germans, but in the imagination of Germany's neighbors to the East and West. Berlin as palimpsest implies voids, illegibilities and erasures, but it also offers a richness of traces and memories, restorations and new contructions that will mark the city as lived space. Bernhard Schlink, author of the best-selling novel *The Reader*, is certainly right in suggesting that Berlin still lacks a physical and psychological center. I see this as an advantage, and in that sense the title for the architectural sightseeing tours organized by the city in the summers of the late 1990s may not be inappropriate after all: *Berlin - offene Stadt* (Berlin - open city).

Number of inhabitants [p]	17,810,000
Area [km²]	4,355
Density [p/km²]	4,090
Population urbanized (national) [2003]	28%

Mumbai: Millennial Identities
Jim Masselos

A decade ago, in December 1992 and through January 1993, Mumbai was racked with severe riots and massive numbers of killings. It was not the only place where this happened - throughout India extensive rioting had similarly followed the destruction of an ancient Muslim mosque, the Babri Masjid at Ayodhya, by Hindu nationalists and religious fundamentalists. But the rioting in Mumbai seemed greater in extent, depth, duration and intensity than that which took place elsewhere in the country. It was perhaps even qualitatively different; even if it were not, the shock of the destruction seemed all the greater in an urban conglomerate that had prided itself on its cosmopolitan mixtures of ethnicities, religions and cultural constituents.

Having been a chance observer of the January rioting in the city I analyzed the experience in a couple of interlinked articles, written soon afterwards.[1] I tried to understand what had happened through noting what I had seen and heard – or learned from friends and acquaintances at the time. Though the English-language newspapers produced excellent coverage which was both detailed and accurate, fuller evidence of what had happened only emerged later as the Srikrishna commission of inquiry revealed information about the various incidents that cumulatively had formed the riots. The greater detail now available has not provided any alternate compelling reading of what happened, although the involvement of the city-based populist Shiv Sena political organization has become more sharply defined.[2]

Apart from the riots themselves, I was interested in seeing what the riots revealed about the city itself and about how it had changed as India had moved out from colonial status under British rule into Independence from August 1947. In the decades afterwards it had so expanded that by the 1990s it was one of the largest cities in the world, a megalopolis with a population that had grown exponentially in the final decades of the century.[3] If the 1992/93 riots in Bombay were different from those elsewhere in the country then even a cursory glance at Bombay's massive size pointed through such difference to an importance in other key matters which had made possible the underlying structures of space and economy necessary for growth. I was thus interested in considering the implications of the riots insofar as they reflected on what kind of a place Bombay had become. (The city was not to get its new name till later in the decade.)

From then it was an obvious step to contextualize Bombay within postmodern theory and to classify it as a postmodern city, especially given the equivalent attention that had earlier been given to Los Angeles following its traumatic riots and the similar ways they had cut across demarcations of class and ethnicity. Bombay met many of the criteria for postmodern ascription: size, globalizing economy, central location in the national economy, social fragmentation and spatial demarcation, stark contrasts in wealth, the forceful expression of subjugated narratives and so on. I therefore used the notion to explain the riotings and to assess their range and social depth, just as I used it to try to understand current urban life and to locate Bombay within an urban pattern that was then becoming increasingly apparent around the world.

[1] Jim Masselos, 'Postmodern Bombay: fractured discourses', in Sophie Watson and Kathie Gibson (eds), *Postmodern Cities and Spaces*, Oxford: Basil Blackwell, 1994, pp. 199–215; Jim Masselos, 'The Bombay Riots of January 1993: The Politics of Urban Conflagration', in *South Asia*, Special Issue 1994, pp. 79–96 and reprinted in John McGuire, Peter Reeves and Howard Brasted (eds), *Politics of Violence. From Ayodhya to Behramapada*, New Delhi: Sage Publications, 1996, pp. 111–26

[2] See, for example, Thomas Blom Hansen, *Violence in Urban India. Identity Politics, 'Mumbai,' and the Postcolonial City*, Delhi: Permanent Black, 2001, pp. 132–147

[3] In 1980 Mumbai was the 15th largest urban agglomeration in the world in terms of population; in 1995 it was fifth and in 2010 it is estimated it will be third. See Sujata Patel, 'Bombay and Mumbai: identities, politics and populism', in Sujata Patel and Jim Masselos (eds), *Bombay/Mumbai: the city in transition*, Delhi: Oxford University Press, 2003, p. 29 fn. 50

Mumbai: Millennial Identities **Jim Masselos**

A decade on from those explorations the critical issues about the city are less the riots and what they revealed about urban structures and more about what the city has become and where it is going. Does the city's trajectory parallel equivalent developments elsewhere? Do its distinguishing characteristics place it alongside other cities?

Postcolonial identities

Ostensibly Bombay enters the millennium in a new guise, behind a different official name, Mumbai. The name itself is not in the least new but has been current in Marathi and Gujarati, the languages of the city's two major ethnic groups, since the city was established, in 1661. In particular the renaming of the city represented a populist attempt by the state government of the day, the Shiv Sena, to assert the city's links with its Marathi-speaking hinterland, a sentiment perforce accepted by most parties involved with the city. The renaming affirmed the interposition of Mumbai within the Marathi-speaking region and its coterminous state, Maharashtra, and thus assigned its primary identity as its geographical surroundings and the hinterland which it abuts.[4]

As a nomenclature delinking present realities from past memories it had other resonances – around ideas of postcolonial freedom. In this sense it continued the processes behind urban renamings which had begun in the years immediately after Independence, when patriotic Indian names replaced the British names of many main streets. Successively less important streets were given new names over the years, some of which were accepted into current parlance while others remain unused and unknown except on maps, official correspondence and street signs. Other reminders of Raj domination survived longer. Statues of monarchs, governors, governors general and other imperial worthies lasted 18 years after Independence, until 1965, when overnight they were dramatically removed from their dominating positions around the city and reinstalled in the grounds of a museum. By then freedom fighters and other Indian

[4] See also Sujata Patel's discussion on this issue in Patel and Masselos (eds), op. cit., pp. 3–5

figure 2 Statue of Albert Edward, Prince of Wales, and later King Edward VII, unveiled in 1879 and moved in 1965 to Jijmata Bhonsle Udyan (Victoria Gardens)

celebrities already had their places around the city, some of their statues having been installed well before Independence, in the second half of the nineteenth century and later in the 1920s and 1930s. Many more were added after Independence.[5]

If such earlier renamings and removals asserted notions of national pride and denied a past of colonial subordination, the renamings of the 1990s embedded a further element – the political realities of regional pride. Thus in the closing years of the twentieth century two institutions that had kept their colonial names, VT (the Victoria Terminus railway station) and the Prince of Wales Museum, were given new ones. The name was the same for both – that of the great seventeenth-century Maharashtrian king and military leader, Shivaji, who had fought the might of the Mughal Empire and who, by the twentieth century, was honored as the founder of modern Maharashtra. Most recently, the state government, a coalition of the Congress party and the Nationalist Congress party, determined the date of Shivaji's birth, a matter about which there had been no unanimity previously, and proclaimed its future public observance.[6] Equally potent throughout the city is the image of Shivaji himself, usually depicted as a proud warrior astride a powerful horse, and potently present in a large and magnificent statue confronting the Gateway of India, a grand relic of the Raj built to commemorate the entry of the King-emperor, George V, into India in 1911 but not opened till the 1920s.[7]

The naming of Mumbai operated within the same context of historical pride for a past that excluded the British interregnum and privileged the idea of an overarching Indian past. But added to past time was a further element – territoriality – so that Mumbai was emotionally incorporated within something of which it had never formed part, the space of Shivaji's state and of its successor eighteenth-century Maratha confederation. Mumbai has thus been absorbed into its surroundings, and the history of those surroundings. In its renaming was asserted city identity, itself a complex interweaving of

5] See my paper, 'Solid identities: the statuary of memory', presented at the 14th Biennial Asian Studies Association of Australia Biennial Conference, Hobart, July 2002

6] 19 February. See Neeta Pradhan's 'infomercial', 'We are Number 1', *India Today International*, 30 July 2001, p. 52

7] Indian Science Congress *Bombay-Poona*, Poona: The Aryabhushan Press, 1934, p. 32

Figure 3 The original site for the Prince of Wales statue, an area still known as Kalaghoda or 'black horse'. The University Clock Tower is in the background

overlapping layers of meanings, ranging from postcolonial delinking and national identification through to regional patriotism.

While the name attempts to ensure that Mumbai is contextualized within the state of which it is the capital, and has regional characterization, the point has not been universally accepted within the city even some years after its official imposition. The old and new names often coexist and are used simultaneously, particularly when English is being used and more so by city elites. Past custom, habit and practice – and in some cases preference – have meant that the 'Bombay' usage has often been retained, as indeed has at a mass level the usage of 'Victoria Terminus' or 'VT' rather than 'CST' or 'Chhatrapati Shivaji Terminus'.

Nevertheless, there has been political advantage in pursuing the renaming option. The city-based party, the Shiv Sena, has fought to represent Marathis in the city and to ensure that Maharashtrian identity and interests are not drowned in a large cosmopolitan megalopolis. From its inauguration in the mid-1960s under the leadership of Bal Thackeray, the Sena has aggressively asserted Marathi rights and used the symbol of Shivaji in its political struggles. It has spoken directly to working-class and middle-class Marathis who have felt that they have been deprived of their rightful position in the city. In the last two decades of the century, the Sena targeted outsiders and in particular those who were not Hindu: some of its members were involved in the attacks on Muslims during the 1992/93 riots. The Sena has forged alliances with the India-wide Hindu nationalist party, the BJP, and has at various times been in a ruling coalition at the state and municipal level along with the BJP.

The use of regional pride is thus of political advantage and has populist value for the Sena. So too for the other leading group in city politics, the Congress party and its offshoot, the Nationalist Congress party. Both of these have important political bases in the Maharashtrian countryside and both need to maintain their positions within the city. For them, too, it is necessary to try and tap the regional feeling that has populist support in the city, as much to counteract the Sena as for the specifics of the attitudes themselves, though Congress has by no means been as successful. Control of the city's municipal corporation and the state government has alternated between the two clusters of parties over the final decades of the century, neither having axiomatic support or assured access to electoral victory.[8]

The force of the ballot box as well as the emotional connotations of postcolonial identities coincided to bring Mumbai within regional parameters. So too has the structure of governance. Mumbai lies administratively within Maharashtra, and its fortunes are largely controlled by the state government. Overall planning and development put Mumbai under the control of the state government and determined its identity as a capital city and the capital city of a state of which it is politically, administratively and 'historically' part. It is thus distinguished from other cities in India and articulates the characteristics of its region. At the beginning of the new century, then, Mumbai has apparently been embedded within its region in ways in which other great cities elsewhere in the world are not located within their surroundings.

The space of the present
Despite all this the city ambiguously retains a character of its own. In many ways it remains as distinctive an entity at the beginning of the twenty-first century as it was earlier. The ambiguity of being within and apart simultaneously is evident even in something as basic as its geography.

Mumbai was once seven low-lying islands which were joined together to become what in the nineteenth century was known as the Town and Island of Bombay. Directly to its north was Salsette Island, adjoining parts of which became an outlying suburban area. The city's center was, paradoxically, at the southernmost part of the seven islands, as far as possible from the mainland. It was there that the British East India Company erected a castle and then a surrounding fort that looked across the harbor to the mainland and protected the Company's trading concerns from hostile neighbors. The city then expanded in successive waves to the north and as far as it could eastward to the Arabian Sea shoreline.

By the mid-twentieth century the city, already heavily and densely populated, occupied an elongated island on a north-south axis. Northwards from the original Fort area with its administrative, commercial and business orientations were more residential areas, major markets, workshops and railway stations, which linked an expansive hinterland to the harbor and enabled the city-as-entrepôt to function. Further north were the cotton mill areas that had from the late nineteenth century made Bombay one of the world's great cloth manufacturers. Then there were more residential areas, markets and light industry, artisan and other small-scale activity. Access to the mainland was through Salsette Island, which at the time, apart from a suburban fringe, was a ring of

[8] For an analysis of the municipal elections at the beginning of 2002, see my 'Routines and routinization: moving towards municipal elections in Mumbai, 2001–2', in *South Asia*, New Series, Vol. XXV, No.3, December 2002, pp. 61–82.

Mumbai: Millennial Identities **Jim Masselos**

rural and forest land setting the city apart from the neighboring hinterland. In the course of development in its built-up area, Bombay had moved administratively from being a city-state to a capital city[9] but, given its unique location as a promontory jutting southward from the mainland, it was still spatially distinct from the mainland of which it was the capital – and mentally separate.

By the end of the twentieth century Mumbai's relationship with its surroundings had changed, not only emotionally – as has been suggested in the preceding section - but also physically. On the one hand, the original center of the city at the southernmost part of the island retained its importance, less proportionately to the city as a whole in terms of housing and residence, and more as the place for work and employment. Even the physical appearance of this part of the city had not altered dramatically since Independence – with a few exceptions the late nineteenth- and early twentieth-century skyline and ground plan were, in 2004, much as they had been half a century earlier. This was partly because the continued operation of rent controls introduced during World War II and afterwards had served to inhibit urban change. The controls made it almost impossible for landlords to evict tenants or increase rents. The result was that buildings retained the same occupants or their descendants and that landlords could not afford improvements, renovations or any kind of redevelopment. Only on land reclaimed from the Arabian Sea, like that at Veer Nariman Point or Cuffe Parade, did new high-rise buildings appear, mimicking the office towers of other major cities.

[9] See my 'Changing definitions of Bombay: city state to capital city', in Indu Banga ed.), Ports and their Hinterlands in India (1700-1950), New Delhi: Urban History Association of India, Jehru Memorial Museum and Library, and Indian Institute of Advanced Studies series, Manohar Books, 1992, pp. 273–316

[10] See, for example, Marg Publications, Max Mueller Bhavan Bombay and Urban Design Research Institute, Buildings of the Kala Ghoda Art District, Mumbai: Urban Design Research Institute, 2000; Urban Design Research Institute Bombay First, Ballard Estate A Corporate District. A Proposal for Upgrading and Managing the Area, Mumbai: Urban Design Research Institute, 2000; Horniman Circle Association, Restoring a Banking District, Mumbai: Urban Design Research Institute, 1999; Rahul Mehrotra and Sharada Dwivedi, Banganga Sacred Tank, Mumbai: Eminence, 1996

The Raj character of the city center with its imposing nineteenth century Indo-Gothic buildings and colonnaded streets thus largely survived untouched by developers, even if they increasingly showed the ravages of time and neglect. When rent controls were finally eased in the final years of the twentieth century and it seemed as if major destruction of the old parts of the town could follow, significant lobby groups and in particular heritage organizations like INTACHS and the Urban Design Research Institute urged the retention, preservation, renovation and reuse of the old buildings and old parts of the town. Mumbai was hence likely to retain its Bombay appearance – at least in the Fort area and other special precincts.[10]

Elsewhere, change in the built environment did occur and the cityscape acquired contemporary buildings of variable architectural merit. In the most elite part of the city, the Malabar and Cumballa Hills locality, virtually all of the elegant nineteenth-century bungalows owned and occupied by the city's wealthy magnates were replaced by large, soaring apartment blocks. In the mill areas, following the death of the industry in the 1980s, the massive amounts of land the mills once occupied were to be gradually redeveloped in a process that still continues and is still contested by heritage and citizen lobbies on the one side and on the other by developers, with the city's 'mafia' having their own ideas on how to profit from the rebuilding and rehousing. Some buildings have been completed, but it remains to be seen whether the precinct will retain a distinctive character and follow the pattern of what has happened elsewhere as world cities recycle redundant industrial areas by converting them to new uses.

figure 4 Postmodern
apartment building rising
above 19th century
residences in Colaba

The city had spread further to the north by the end of the last century, to sprawl over
the once quiet suburban areas of Bandra and beyond.[11] From Bandra to Kurla a city
development plan ensured the appearance of another commercial and financial district.
Beyond both, directly to the north and north-west, residential blocks shot up. In the
process Thane and Kalyan, once towns on the outskirts of Bombay, were absorbed into
Mumbai. It was here that the city clearly crossed over onto the mainland and from here
a strip development of commuter suburbs followed the railway line out onto the
Konkan plain and into the Maharashtra heartlands. On the other side of the harbor a
new planned city for two million people had also risen, one in which residential areas
and business activities were to operate in planned harmony. The planning behind New

[11] For an analysis of recent
developments see Rahul
Mehrotra, 'Evolution,
Involution, and the City's
Future: A perspective on
Bombay's urban form' in
Pauline Rohatgi, Pheroza
Godrej and Rahul Mehrotra
(eds), *Bombay to Mumbai.
Changing Perspectives*,
Mumbai: Marg, 1997, pp.
258–277

Mumbai: Millennial Identities **Jim Masselos**

Bombay had been aimed at reducing urban congestion from the old parts of the town, but it had mainly prevented the city from being overwhelmed by what would otherwise have been uncontrollable growth.[12]

The figures for growth in the late 1980s give an indication of what was happening. While on the original Island there was no growth in population between 1983 and 1987, Thane grew by 138.8 percent; Kalyan, less dramatically, by 30.8 percent and Navi Mumbai (New Bombay) by 48.3 percent.[13] Further growth continued thereafter, especially a strip development following the expressway through the Konkan plain and up into the Western Ghats (mountains) to Pune, Maharashtra's second city. The expressway has become and defines a silicon corridor linking the three cities (Mumbai, Navi Mumbai and Pune), a corridor for high-tech industry or, in state government parlance, a Knowledge Corridor. As a consequence the government claims that Mumbai/Navi Mumbai have become the nation's hub for IT and IT-enabled services, e-commerce and dotcoms,[14] and by implication outrank the more prominently promoted Hyderabad and Bangalore as the nation's major technology center.

All these developments give Mumbai a unique form. It is as if, to use American examples, Mumbai combines, at the one and same time, the tightly packed island of New York city along with the silicon corridor of San Francisco and Palo Alto, to which is added part of the spread of Los Angeles – all joined to one of the largest of planned cities anywhere, in the form of Navi Mumbai. Mumbai has not only the sprawl of other world megalopolises in its spread eastward, out into the Konkan plain; at the same time it has the tight density of other great cities, although its center is nowhere near its geographic heart but at its furthest point from the rest of the city.

To confound understanding of its morphology, Mumbai is technically the Mumbai Metropolitan Region, defined in 1974 as covering 4,355 sq km of land - which included almost 1,000 villages and 19 urban centers. Of this, only 575.48 sq km was built up in 1987.[15] The Mumbai region thus includes a great proportion of land that is not in the least urban, though as the years pass, more of it is re-inhabited as urban settlement and loses its rural character. Thus in terms of the relationship of the city with its surroundings what has happened is that the city has moved out of its island confines and onto the mainland, absorbing some of that hinterland. But it has also imposed its urban presence on those countryside environs which it has not settled. The city has both links with, and an effect on, land that was once separate from the city, and in a variety of ways it has imposed its own needs upon the land. Rather than relating to its hinterland and expressing its ethos, it is as if Mumbai has been colonizing its rural neighborhood and imposing its own urban ethos on what it comes into contact with, thus affecting the lifestyle of all around it. This great urban conglomerate is its own being, whatever characteristics people and groups within the city want to impose on it.

But does this agglomerate, with its different kinds of urban forms occupying space contained within the larger metropolitan region, have any identity of its own, or is it rather a series of different entities, separate enclaves within the region? The fact that

[12] See Charles Correa, 'New Bombay: Marg as an urban catalyst' in Rohatgi, Godrej and Mehrotra (eds), op. cit., p. 312–331

[13] Bombay Metropolitan Region Development Authority, Draft Regional Plan for Bombay Metropolitan Region 1966–2011, Bandra East), Bombay Metropolitan Region Development Authority, 1995, p. 58

[14] 'Maharashtra is Number 1 in IT Too', in Pradhan, op. cit., p. 44

[15] Bombay Metropolitan Region Development Authority, op. cit., p. 42–44, 58

something like 16 major authorities which subdivide into 33 sub-authorities have specific regional jurisdiction within the Metropolitan Region[16] would seem to support a notion of fragmentation. That there is one agency which has overall responsibility for planning, the Mumbai Metropolitan Region Development Authority, suggests otherwise, as does the fact that a single body, the Brihanmumbai Municipal Corporation, has sway over what is now often referred to as 'Greater Mumbai' (the original Bombay Island and the built-up parts of Salsette Island) and hence over most of the city's population. CIDCO (The City and Industrial Development Corporation of Maharashtra) has specific responsibility for Navi Mumbai – and for other urban developments elsewhere in the state. The effect of the congruence of a limited number of major authorities is to give the urban region an overall coherence that might otherwise seem unlikely.

The effective city, as I have further discussed elsewhere,[17] was a linear city defined by a transport backbone which kept far-flung parts of the city together and enabled people to move along the length and, less frequently, the breadth of the city. Despite massive overcrowding, Mumbai was well served by its suburban trains and by its bus system. In the 1990s just over half of the city's population of around 10 million people traveled each day on either a train or a bus,[18] while in 2002 the trains alone carried 6.4 million passengers daily – which, with the bus journeys, accounted for 88 percent of daily commuter journeys.[19] These journeys took place in 3,380 buses and 162 suburban trains, which ran over 200km of track, constituting what is claimed to be the world's largest suburban network.[20]

figure 5 Updating the municipal infrastructure: pipes ready to be laid along the retail area of Colaba Causeway

16] Ibid., p. 63

17] 'Defining moments/defining events: commonalities of urban life' in Patel and Masselos (eds), op. cit., pp. 31–49

18] Bombay Metropolitan Region Development Authority, op. cit., p. 26 and Times of India, 14 July 1994, p. 5

19] Mumbai Metropolitan Region Development Authority, 'MUTP. Mumbai urban Transport Project'. Online. Available <www.mmrdamumbai.org/mutp2.htm>, accessed 19 September 2002

20] 'Mumbai's Transport. Simply the BEST', in India Today International, 19 Augus 2002, p. 49

Mumbai: Millennial Identities **Jim Masselos**

What happens on the trains and buses during the rush hour has been described as "a unidirectional lemming-like frenzy".[21] If so, it is sustained over considerable distances. The estimate, again for the early 1990s, was that the average journey on a suburban train was slightly above 22 km and the average bus journey 4.67 km.[22] Individual journeys could of course be longer, and it is not uncommon in Mumbai for people to travel a couple of hours or more to get to work in the morning. Given that such a large proportion of the population daily traverses so much of the city space, the railways are important in developing and defining the city, and bringing the disparate conglomerate into a single focus. Moreover, since there are only two main railway lines, running for much of the time parallel to one another on north-south axes until one line diverges towards the north-east, the sense of the city that the railways mediate is a linear one. The linear map of the two railway lines becomes the extenuated map of the city and an expression of the way it is linked as a single entity.

Urban disparities

Mumbai has other identities. Its self-image, as projected by those who have been successful, is that it is a powerhouse of energy, that it is the city of success *par excellence*, the financial and commercial center. It produces 40 percent of India's revenue and is "undeniably the financial capital of the country", as Maharashtra's Chief Minister is proud to proclaim.[23] On most measures of economic achievement, Mumbai is equally far ahead of any other city or even region within India. It is a major generator of national wealth and productivity: more stock exchange and bank transactions happen in Mumbai than elsewhere, its factories produce over a third of the nation's goods and it is the center of major industries and innovative technology.[24]

It was quick to adapt to the new economic circumstances created when India decided to liberalize the economy in 1991, to encourage foreign investment and collaboration and move into the global economy in every way possible. The result has been that money has flowed into the city via foreign collaboration and foreign investment and that Indian entrepreneurs and major companies have benefited, despite the occasional hiccup, from the burst of energy that followed liberalization.

Mumbai's image combines two dreams – gold and glamour, wealth and allure, commerce and culture. It is, according to one of the country's leading Hindi film producers, Subash Ghai, "the cultural and financial melting pot of the country. A combination of Lakshmi and Saraswati."[25] The reference is to the goddess of wealth and the goddess of learning and culture. The presence of Lakshmi is evident in the city's financial eminence, while that of Saraswati may be in its educational institutions and its high culture; but the reference is probably more pertinent in terms of Mumbai being the center of the nation's popular culture as created through the Hindi cinema, the largest film industry anywhere. Bombay/Mumbai is India's Hollywood, hence Bollywood (but not yet Mollywood). The aura of Mumbai is mediated through its films, the glamour of its stars and the lifestyle they display. Their style links with the equally lavish life of the rich, those magnates from old families and the nouveau riche. All combine to present a Mumbai that is far from the reality of what is happening on the ground in the city itself.

[1] Ibid.

[2] Bombay Metropolitan Region Development Authority, op. cit., p. 386

[3] Interview with Vilasrao Deshmukh, c. July 2001, in Pradhan, op. cit., p. 38

[4] For a summary of Mumbai's pre-eminent economic role in the early 1990s see my 'The Bombay Riots of January 1993' in McGuire, Reeves and Brasted (eds), op. cit., pp. 123–124

[5] Interview in Pradhan, op. cit., p. 42

figure 6 Second-hand market
in the Chor Bazaar locality

On the streets live more than half of the city's inhabitants, at least six million of them. The figures are, by the very nature of what they attempt to record, essentially tentative. Even among the pavement-dwellers there is a kind of hierarchy. Newer arrivals live literally on the pavements, encamped there amid their meager possessions. People who have been in Mumbai longer, earlier arrivals, may be more settled. They live in shanties, shelters made from makeshift materials, recycled plastic, bits of timber and whatever else comes to hand. There are numerous colonies of such shanties – slums (zopadpatties) spread throughout most of the city. The zopadpatties have an ecological development of their own: those occupied by the earliest arrivals may well have electricity (and even TV satellite dishes), bitumened or concreted narrow paths through the huts, a few taps around the colony, but no sewerage facilities. Their huts may be of more permanent material – even brick and tiles, and they occupy land that has a high value; even if the landowners of the property on which they are squatting gain no benefit, others do. There are slum 'landlords' who exact 'rent' from slum residents, while the inhabitants themselves may be able to trade their occupancy to others for large sums as 'key money'. The huts are a valuable resource; during the 1992/3 riots, for example, many were burnt by gangs said to be employed by developers or others trying to get control over the space they occupied.

Slums are everywhere in the city – in rich as well as in poorer working-class neighborhoods. Though householders often object to the presence of slums, a symbiotic relationship may develop between them. Householders may draw on the pool of local slum-dwellers for servants or rely on them to perform basic tasks and provide services. Slum-dwellers may be a locality's hawkers and traders, its dhobis (washer men and women) or those who stitch or repair clothing; they may be the workers in the local markets, or shoeshine boys. Larger slums may be noted for their productive energy as the location for significant economic activity. Among such is Dharavi, often described as India's largest slum: in the nineteenth century, while it was still well away from major areas of habitation, it was where the tanneries were located. Since then it has been surrounded by suburbs but retains a spatial identity of its own. The slum has continued to produce and tool leather, but a range of cottage industries make a variety of other goods, including even surgical catgut.

The overlapping of social classes in Mumbai is evident not only in the contrast between the housing of the rich and the poor but in almost every other aspect of city living. Sudha and Lalit Deshpande have demonstrated that there has been some improvement in the incomes and living standards of the poor and the working classes over the past three decades and hence there has been some general flow-on of benefits from the city's engines of prosperity.[26] In this sense Mumbai's promises of opportunity and employment have not been empty, though their fulfillment has been limited for most people. The improvement has not made the poor rich, or even most of them comfortably affluent, unlike their middle-class compatriots. Nor, despite continuing efforts on the part of municipal and government agencies – and of an activist and dedicated NGO sector, have their living conditions notably improved. Overall, conditions in slums continue to be bad, whatever the improvements made in some of them. Nor have other benefits of big city living flowed equally to all inhabitants. As Neha Madhiwala has shown, access to medical facilities is limited in the slum areas, as indeed it is in the extended and more recently developed outer regions of the city.[27] Much the same applies to many other matters of daily concern, such as education, childcare, recreational facilities and environmental pollution. As in so many other matters, the rich have more ready and more convenient access to medical facilities than the working class and the poor.

[26] See their 'Work, wages and well-being: 1950s and 1990s' in Patel and Masselos eds), op. cit., pp. 53–80

[27] See her 'Hospitals and city health' in Patel and Masselos eds), op. cit., pp. 111–133. Most of the other papers in this volume, including those by Swaminathan, Harini Narayan and P.K. Das, also bear strongly on the general point about the lack of facilities accessible or available to the city's under classes

figure 7 Clothes drying in residences above the second-hand market

The escalation of economic inequality merges into an escalation of social inequality. The polarity of social discrimination derived from notions of caste superiority is reinforced by the poor economic status of those who are lowest in ascribed caste position. Though legislation operates to prevent discrimination and to provide for reserved positions in education and government employment, the position of Dalits (the former untouchables) remains difficult. This is despite the religious conversion of many to Buddhism, a self pride movement, political activism, increasingly wide education and a powerful literary upsurge which has expanded the boundaries of Dalit existence in unmistakable terms and in the process changed the parameters of Marathi literature. Outbreaks of overt discrimination still occur from time to time – for example, the desecration of statues of the extraordinary Dalit leader, Dr Babasaheb Ambedkar, installed in Dalit slums.[28]

Other polarities were still evident in the city at the beginning of the new millennium. In particular, the polarities of religious difference so evident during the 1992/3 riots remained, though without the massive violence of those times, and were reinforced by institutions and events in and out of the city. The Shiv Sena retained its politics of division and drew on an India-wide discourse of antagonism promoted by the BJP, currently the dominant political party at the center, and by its associated organizations and others of similar inclination. Terrorist-style bombings in Mumbai a couple of months after the riots of 1993 led to several hundred deaths and damage to major city institutions including the stock exchange, Air India offices, and a five-star hotel. Interpreted as retribution against the city for the attacks on Muslims during the riots, responsibility has

[28] See for example the *Times of India*, 4 February 2000, p. 1., for an account of such an incident at Powai

Mumbai: Millennial Identities **Jim Masselos**

been placed on a Mumbai Muslim underworld boss operating from outside India with the suspected connivance of a Pakistani secret service agency. Later, at the beginning of the new century, the attack on the World Trade Center in New York on 11 September 2001 had its impact on Muslims in Mumbai. Their position was already badly affected by the confrontations in Kashmir between India and Pakistan and by the situation in the state of Jammu and Kashmir – all of which ensured that the city's Muslim population remained under suspicion, the object of continued intolerance.

Mumbai, then, is a city in which disparities and social fragmentation are more than evident. They are facts of daily life, unmistakable and highly visible. On almost any axis of analysis divisions can be seen to be present and to have an effect upon the city and its people. On the other hand, they are more often than not contained and restrained by the matters of daily life and by the necessities of survival and of earning a living, and by the routines of life in the city. For those in Mumbai there is a sense of distinctiveness and of a composite identity, and of being part of deep-seated changes that are occurring as the city moves further into the twenty-first century. It will be a different place as it rethinks itself and repositions itself, in terms not only of its unique geography and morphology and its continued phenomenal growth, but also of the blend of social and economic elements that will continue to drive the city's changing shape and character. It is possible to adopt an interpretive perspective of increasing urban chaos, dislocation and fragmentation for the city – to see it along lines guided by apocalyptic visions of future cities, dystopias, of the kind present in *Blade Runner* or the novels of William Gibson. The converse is a more plausible and more likely future for Mumbai: the maintenance of an urban entity that copes or just manages to cope, and does perhaps manage to achieve the end of providing an environment for work, and a space for living that enables personal dignity to be maintained, and for an inhabitant's quality of life to be just better than it might otherwise have been. That is, after all, the dream that Mumbai sends out and it is the message that people receive and in which they believe – whatever the specific experiences encountered in a city which retains an overall unity and an identity of its own, whatever the emotive values which may attach to it and however they are interpreted.

Richard Sennett
Capitalism and the City

My theme is the relationship of capitalism and the city. The conditions of capitalism are very different today than they were a century ago, when the formal discipline of urban studies began. In my view, we have yet to catch up as scholars with these changes in reality.

Urban virtues

Let me begin, with a certain amount of trepidation, by stating flatly what is the human worth of living in a city, what is its cultural value. I think there are in fact two urban virtues which made it worthwhile to live even in badly-run, or crime-infested, dirty or decaying urban places.

The first has to do with sociability. A city is a place where people can learn to live with strangers. The practice of modern democracy demands that citizens learn how to enter into the experience and interests of unfamiliar lives. Society gains when people's experience is not limited just to those who resemble them in class, race, or ways of life. Sameness stultifies the mind, diversity stimulates and expands it.

Cities are places where learning to live with strangers can happen directly, bodily, physically, on the ground. The size, density, and diversity of urban populations makes this sensate contact possible – but not inevitable. One of the key issues in urban life, and in urban studies, is how to make the complexities a city contains actually interact. If contact occurs, and people can make a life with those who are not like themselves, then city dwellers become cosmopolitans.

The second urban virtue has to do with subjectivity, and it derives directly from the first. The experience of urban life can teach people how to live with multiplicity within themselves. The experience of complexity is not just an external event; it reflects back on individuals' sense of themselves. People can develop multiple images of their own identities, knowing that who they are shifts, depending upon who they are with. More, complex social systems tend to be open-ended rather than tightly closed; they are incomplete ways of living which can reflect back into the subjective realm, as lessons about the unresolvable and necessarily incomplete character of experience – lessons in human limits.

In principle, of course, a farmer could have as complicated an inner life as a city dweller. All that cities do, and it is a lot, is furnish the concrete materials for developing that consciousness. Walking in a dense crowd is, if you like, a kind of evidence for what might lie in one's own head. Again, this is a possibility rather than an inevitability; the specific conditions of a particular city might prompt people to shut out that evidence, treat the crowded street as a space of fear rather than a space of self-knowledge.

For me, the writings of the French philosopher Emmanuel Levinas, though he is no urbanist, have formed a bridge between these two urban virtues: Levinas asserts that, when a person's experience is so complex as to become multiply-defined or open-ended, he or she has need of others, others whom he or she does not know. He calls this "the neighborliness of strangers,"[1] and the phrase aptly captures the aspiration we ought to have in designing cities.

This *confession de foi* sets the stage for my own theme, which is not quite so spiritual. The virtues of urban sociability and subjectivity were played out a century ago, when urban studies began, in terms of a dialectic between rigidity and strangeness. Today they are played out in terms of a dialectic between flexibility and indifference. My argument is that a great change in capitalism has transformed the context of urban cultural values, a contrast between then and now I will try to make more objective and precise.

Rigidity and strangeness

To understand this duality, we need to recall that, though cities are as ancient as human civilization, the discipline of urban studies is only a century old. It took root first in sociology and geography, then spread to economics, political science, and more recently anthropology. In sociology, we owe to German writers such as Weber and Simmel the first modern analyses of cities; this 'Berlin school' at the turn of the century inspired in some of its American students a desire to work more collaboratively, and they did so at the University of Chicago from the 1910s to the 1940s.

Both the Berlin and Chicago Schools took form in an age of bureaucratic stabilization. Nineteenth-century capitalism was frequently anarchic and disorganized, but unwillingly so. In Germany, the Bismarckian era saw an effort to remedy these crises through consolidating the relations between the state and private enterprise; government was to supply the rule the free market lacked. In the USA the massive formation of monopolies by Rockefeller, Gould, and Carnegie similarly sought to escape the competitive eruptions of the market. The "search for order," as the historian Robert Wiebe put it, bred enterprises on an ever-larger scale, and with ever more internally complex bureaucratic structures. In turn, this arduous history affected cities, and what urbanists could say about them.

For the moment, I want to delay discussing how that happened, and focus on its opposite, the other side of the urban dialectic, the importance accorded to strangers and strangeness. This was Georg Simmel's subject par excellence. In a letter he wrote to a friend about Potsdamer Platz in Berlin he evoked the cacophony of languages he heard, the strange costumes of the people in the great square. As he would later write, "the urbanite is a stranger." By this he meant to describe – in modern jargon – a condition of alterity rather than of difference: not a fixed classificatory scheme of

[1] Emmanuel Levinas, *Totality and Infinity: An Essay on Exteriority,* Trans. Alphons Lingis Pittsburgh, PA: Duqueske University Press, 1969

identity but rather the unknown other, marked by strangeness. Alterity is a provoker, a force of anxiety, since you don't know what the other will do, how he or she might behave. And each of us bears this power to provoke unease in a crowd.

The power of strangeness makes sense in the conditions of Simmel's time. Berlin was in the midst of rural-to-urban migration, and these migrants came not just from Prussia but from Poland, Hungary and the Balkans, speaking languages other than German, the rural cultures they brought with them not at all of a piece. As important, at this stage of capitalism, there was as yet no culture of mass consumption which unified people as social subjects in the city: the consolidation of production preceded the standardization of consumption, so that desire, taste, and life styles were discontinuous and puzzling. We could as easily cite parallel material phenomena in New York in 1900, the complex world of immigrants on the lower East Side squeezing hard south against Wall Street, north against the bourgeois, WASP residential neighborhood around Washington Square. Alterity was the material condition of urban culture.

Strangeness as alterity is a force which Simmel celebrated in cities. Like Joyce or Proust, Simmel believed the stranger is the bearer of a new freedom. I will give you an American example of what he meant. When Willa Cather finally arrived in New York's Greenwich Village in 1906, she, who had been haunted in small-town America that her lesbianism would be discovered, wrote to a friend, "at last, in this indecipherable place, I can breathe." Simmel's own labors aimed at specifying just how, on crowded streets and squares, the freedom of strangeness, the freedom of alterity, played itself out. In public, the urbanite dons an impassive mask, acts cool and indifferent to others on the street; in private, however, he or she is aroused by these strange contacts, disturbed and reactive, certainties are shaken in the presence of others: subjective life seethes behind the protective mask.

In itself, this is a highly Romantic view of the city, but it acquires weight precisely because the subjective stimulation of strangeness is depicted in exactly the same places ruled by the emerging forces of bureaucratic rigidity. Bureaucratic rigidity was of course the great theme of Max Weber, Simmel's colleague and protector. In the Berlin of their time, you would only have to look at the insurance companies, banks, and railroad corporations housed in structures meant to resemble Egyptian temples or Renaissance palaces to see the realization of the desire for economic stability in stone.

We owe to Simmel's student Robert Park, and to Park's student Louis Wirth, an analysis of how the organizational consolidation of capitalization could be related to the territory of a city, rather than just to its architecture. Though Park remained loyal to Simmel's insights into urban subjectivity, which the young American rephrased as the "moral order" of the city, when Park returned to Chicago he had to take up the other side of the coin. Both Park and Wirth sought to depict an ecological division of land based on the division of labor in modern capitalism. The most interesting maps the Chicago School produced of the city were maps of where different functions occurred

Capitalism and the City **Richard Sennett**

in the city; you can find them, for instance, in a book with a resoundingly dull title, *One Hundred Years of Chicago Land Values*, written by Homer Hoyt.[2] This data on the functional articulation of urban space Louis Wirth tied directly to the phenomenon of bureaucratization.

How then to relate the ecology of city to the figure of the stranger and the freedom of alterity? How, as Park put it, are the city as a "place on the map" and a "moral order" the same place? The Chicago urbanists responded by imagining the urbanite as a permanent, internal migrant traveling through the city's ecology. Wirth, for instance, depicted the city as a mosaic of different roles in different places - what he called "segmented roles" – but he argued that the subject transcends each of his or her roles in space. The idea of a subject superior to his or her surroundings is familiar to us in the writings of Wirth's contemporary Walter Benjamin – specifically in Benjamin's figure the flâneur. Less arty, Wirth was interested in the examples of second generation immigrants in Chicago and the city's nascent black bourgeoisie. Both groups seemed to him at once located in an ever-more defined urban ecology and mobile across fixed territories. In their lack of a single definition, in their multiple identities, lay their freedom.

The dialectic between strangeness and rigidity defined the mental compass, if you like, of modern urban studies when it first began. Like any serious version of culture, it both embodied and addressed contradictions. In the visual realm, for instance, the urban design of this time sought both to flee the anxiety of strangeness of the city yet preserve the freedom of the urbanite. This is the great drama in Daniel Burnham's plan of 1909 for Chicago, at once an attempt to impose a rigidly functional order on the city yet in each of the city's zones to mix the different classes and immigrant groups in the city. German and Viennese city planners were at once attracted by the healthy qualities of the Garden City movement of Ebenezer Howard in Britain and repelled by its infantile simplicities.

Today, many of the material conditions which formed the first era of urban studies a century ago still continue: the flood of immigrants into cities, for example. And we continue – as indeed we should – to think of alterity as a social condition which holds out the promise of subjective freedom, freedom from arbitrary definition and identification. But the larger conditions of capitalism have taken a new turn, and this change in political economy has altered both the nature of the city itself and the intellectual tools we need to understand our own times.

Flexibility and indifference

When we talk about a new stage in capitalism, we are really pointing at two phenomena. One is the globalization of labor and capital flows. The other consists of a transformation in production, that is, a change in institutions and bureaucracies so that people can work more flexibly and less rigidly.

[2] Homer Hoyt *One Hundred Years of Land Values in Chicago: The Relationship of the Growth of Chicago to the Rise of its Land Values, 1830–1933* New York: Arno Press, [1933] 1970

The word 'new' instantly arouses suspicion, because it belongs to the realm of advertising. Labor migration and multinational finance are long-established in the capitalist economy, but in the last generation they have been reformulated. Banks no longer trade within national constraints; labor migrants have found new international routes. Changes in workplaces have similarly not been conjured out of thin air. Anarcosyndicalists have long argued for less rigid workplaces, an argument which by a rich irony modern capitalists have taken to heart.

Because the bureaucratic revolution which had made capitalism flexible is less in the news than globalization, let me start with this part of the story. Max Weber's description of rational bureaucracy was founded on an analogy between military and business organization. His image for both was the bureaucratic triangle; the more the rational division of labor progressed, the more slots opened up unequally; the need for different kinds of soldiers or workers expanded far more rapidly than the need for more generals or bosses. The chain of command within this triangle operated on the principle that each niche had a distinctive function; efficiency dictated that there be as little duplication as possible. The general can thus strategically control platoons far from his command post, the corporation executive determine how the assembly line or back office functions.[3]

In industrial production, Weber's triangle became embodied in the phenomenon of Fordism, a kind of military micro-management of a worker's time and effort which a few experts could dictate from the top. It was graphically illustrated by the General Motors' Willow Run auto plant in America, a mile-long, quarter-mile-wide edifice in which raw iron and glass entered, as it were, at one end and a finished car exited at the other. Only a strict, controlling work regime could coordinate production on this giant scale. In the white-collar world, the strict controls of corporations like IBM in the 1960s mirrored this industrial process.

A generation ago businesses began to revolt against the Weberian triangle. They sought to 'delayer' organizations, to remove levels of bureaucracy, making use of new information technologies in place of bureaucrats. They sought to destroy the practice of fixed-function work, substituting instead teams which work short-term on specific tasks – teams which are shuffled when the organization embarks on new projects. Just as these techniques enabled businesses to respond externally to new market opportunities, the organizations sought to create internal markets. In this new business strategy, teams compete against one another, trying to respond as effectively and quickly as possible to goals set by the top. Internal markets mean that the old Weberian logic of efficiency is overthrown; instead of each person doing his or her own particular bit in a defined chain of command, you have duplication of function, many different teams compete to do the same task fastest, best.

All these practices are meant to make corporations flexible, able to change quickly within, in response to rapidly changing conditions without. The apologists for this new world of work claim it is more democratic than the military-style organization of the

[3] Max Weber, *Theory of Economic and Social Organization*. Trans. A.M. Henderson and T. Parsons Glencoe, Ill.: Free Press, 1947

Capitalism and the City **Richard Sennett**

past. But in reality that is not the case. In place of the Weberian triangle, an image of the new realm of power might be a circle with a dot in the center. At the center, a small number of managers rules, makes decisions, sets tasks, judges results; the information revolution has given it more instantaneous control over the corporation's workings than in the old system, where orders often modulated and evolved as they passed down the chain of command. The teams working on the periphery of the circle are left free to respond to output targets set by the center, free to devise means of executing tasks in competition with one another, but not free to decide what those tasks are. In the Weberian triangle of bureaucracy, rewards came for doing one's job as best one can; in the dotted circle, they come to teams winning over other teams – which the economist Robert Frank calls winner-take-all organization; sheer effort no longer produces reward. This bureaucratic reformulation, Frank argues, contributes to the great inequalities of pay and perks in flexible organizations, a material reality of inequality entirely at odds with work-place democracy.

To understand the effect of this new form of organization on the urban places in which people live, we have to specify one further characteristic of flexibility: its time dimension. The mantra of the flexible workplace is 'no long term'. The short-term dimensions of time are evident in the replacement of clear career paths within fixed organizations by jobs – jobs which consist of specific and limited tasks; when the task ends, often the job is over. In the high-tech sector in Silicon Valley, the average length of employment is now about eight months; the re-engineering of corporations often leads to abrupt, involuntary job change; in the shifting world of flexible work – as in advertising, the media, and financial services – voluntary job change follows an erratic path, people tending to make lateral, ambiguous moves. Finally, within a given corporation, the emphasis on tying teams to tasks means that people are constantly changing their working associates – modern management theory argues the 'shelf life' of a team ought to be at most a year.

These changes in institutional time, I want to make clear, do not dominate the workplace at present, no more than global finance is the dominant mode of finance. Rather, they represent a leading edge of change, an aspiration of what businesses ought to become: no one is going to start a new organization based on the principle of permanent jobs. Just as the space of power in the flexible organization is not democratic, so the time dimension of these institutions promotes neither loyalty nor fraternity. Business leaders who were once enthusiasts for constant corporation reinvention are beginning, as it were, to sober up. It is hard to feel committed to a corporation which has no defined character, hard to act loyally to an unstable institution which shows no loyalties to you. Lack of commitment translates into poor productivity, and to an unwillingness to keep a corporation's secrets.

The lack of fraternity bred by 'no-long term' is rather more subtle. Task-work puts people under enormous stress; on losing teams recrimination tends to mark the final stages of working together. Again, trust of an informal sort takes time to develop; you have to get to know people, which team break-ups short circuit. And the experience of being only temporarily in an organization prompts people to keep loose, not to get involved, since you are going to exit soon. Practically, this lack of mutual engagement is one of the reasons it is so hard for labor unions to organize workers in flexible industries or businesses like Silicon Valley; the sense of fraternity as a shared fate, a durable set of common interests, has been weakened. Socially, the short-term regime produces a paradox: people work intensely, under great pressure, but their relations to others remain curiously superficial. This is not a world in which getting deeply involved with other people makes much sense, in the long run.

My argument is precisely that flexible capitalism has the same effects on the city as in the workplace itself. Just as flexible production produces more superficial, short-term relations at work, this capitalism creates a regime of superficial and disengaged relations in the city. This dialectic of flexibility and indifference is a challenge both to those who live in cities and those who study them.

The dialectic of flexibility and indifference appears in three forms. The first is expressed in physical attachment to the city; the second expressed in the standardization of the urban environment; the third in relations between family and urban work.

The issue of physical attachment to place is perhaps the most self-evident of the three. Rates of geographic mobility are very high for flexible workers. Service temp-workers are a good example – and temp-work is the single fastest-growing sector of the labor market. Temp-work nurses are for instance eight times more likely to move house in any two-year period than single-employer nurses; main-frame servicemen are 11 times more likely than their single-employer mates. Lack of fixed work means less attachment to place.

In the higher reaches of the economy, executives in the past frequently moved as much as in the present, but the movements were different in kind; they remained within the groove of a company, and the company defined their 'place', the turf of their lives, no matter where they were on the map. It is just that institutional thread which the new workplace breaks. Some urbanists, like Sharon Zukin, have argued, intriguingly, that for this elite certain zones in the modern city – gentrified, filled with sleek restaurants and specialized services – have replaced the corporation as an anchor; this new elite has become more attached to their style of life in the city than their jobs. That argument looks a little different, however, if we consider the other effects of the flexible realm on cities.

Standardization of the environment results from the economy of impermanence, and standardization begets indifference. I can make this dictum clear, perhaps, by describing a personal experience. A few years ago I took the head of a large, new economy corporation on a tour of New York's Chanin Building, an art deco palace with elaborate offices and splendid public spaces. "It would never suit us," the executive remarked, "people might become too attached to their offices, they might think they belong here."

Capitalism and the City **Richard Sennett**

The flexible office is meant not to be a place where you nestle in. The office architecture of flexible firms requires a physical environment which can be quickly reconfigured - at the extreme, the 'office' becomes just a computer terminal. The neutrality of new buildings also results from their global currency as investment units; for someone in Manila easily to buy or sell 100,000 sq ft of office space in London, the space itself needs the uniformity, the transparency, of money. This is why the style elements of new economy buildings become what Ada Louise Huxtable calls "skin architecture," the surface of the building dolled-up with design, its innards ever more neutral, standard, and capable of instant refiguration.

Another phenomenon in the modern city reinforces "skin architecture". That is the standardization of public consumption – a global network of shops selling the same commodities in the same kinds of spaces whether they are located in Manila, Mexico City, or London. This standardization forms a stark contrast to the conditions of Simmel's Berlin. There, a century ago, though institutional coherence was the economy's aim, consumption remained erratic in form and mostly small-scaled in the city's economy. Today, institutional coherence is coming apart, but the consumable results of production and services are becoming more uniform.

It is hard to become attached to a particular Gap or Banana Republic; standardization begets indifference. Put another way: the problem of institutional loyalties in the workplace, now beginning to sober up managers once blindly enthusiastic about endless corporate re-engineering, finds its parallel in the urban public realm of consumption; attachment and engagement with specific places is dispelled under the aegis of this new regime. Benjamin's image of the flâneur gets a new meaning in a world of Starbucks and Niketowns: no longer is the urban flâneur someone who can discover – at least in the new public realm – the strange, the unexpected, or the arousing. Alterity is missing. Equally, the accumulation of shared history, and so of collective memory diminishes in these neutral public spaces. The space of public consumption attacks local meanings in the same way the new work-place attacks 'ingrown', shared histories among workers.

This is, visually, one way to interpret the relation between flexibility and indifference. I don't mean to invoke clichés of urban 'alienation' or argue that the impulse to seek stimulus in the city has died. Rather, the visual economy of modern capitalism has put up new barriers to the experience of complexity on the city's streets.

Socially, the coupling of flexibility and indifference produces a conflictlessness visible to the eye. High-pressure, flexible work profoundly disorients family life. The phenomena of 'latch-key childhood', of adult stress, or of geographic uprooting - so often cited in the press – do not quite get at the heart of this disorientation. It is rather that the codes of conduct which rule the modern work world would shatter families if taken home from the office: don't commit, don't get involved, think short-term. The assertion of 'family values' by the public and by politicians has a more than right-wing resonance; it is a reaction, often inchoate but strongly felt, of the threats to family solidarity in the new economy; Christopher Lasch's image of the family as a "haven in a heartless world" takes on a particular urgency when work becomes at once more unpredictable and more demanding of adult time. One result of this conflict, by now well-documented on middle-aged employees, is that adults withdraw from civic participation in the struggle to solidify and organize family life; the civic becomes yet another demand on time and energies in short supply at home.

I introduce this third element because 'indifference' can seem only moralistic and pejorative. Withdrawal from the civic realm, neglect of it, can be something to which people are driven by the contrary demands of family and work.

In sum, when a society's organizational, bureaucratic forms alter, both the experience of time and space alters. This conjoined alteration in the time of labor and the space of cities is what we are living through today, expressed in geographic impermanence, the effects of impermanence on standardization in the public realm, and conflicts between work and family, office and home.

I want to say less about the effects of globalization on cities, since they are the subject of many other critiques. I only wish to take up the issue posed by Sharon Zukin, about the peculiar home the new global elite has made for itself in cities like New York, London, and Chicago. Here we would do better to focus on politics than on lofts and trendy restaurants. This is an economic elite avoiding the urban political realm. It wants to operate in the city but not rule it; it composes a regime of power without responsibility.

Let me give an example. In Wirth's Chicago, in 1925, political and economic power were coextensive: presidents of the city's top 80 corporations sat on 142 hospital boards, composed 70 percent of trustees of colleges and universities. Political machines were deeply linked to business; tax revenues from 18 national corporations in Chicago formed 23 percent of the city's municipal budget. By contrast, in New York now – with London, the world's most globalized city – political and economic power are not coextensive in this way. Big players in the global economy located in the city are absent from civic enterprises – hospitals, libraries, universities and schools; few CEO's of global firms in New York, for instance, are trustees of its educational institutions, none sits on the boards of its hospitals (as of 1999). The network of the bourgeois 'great and the good' is no more international in London, despite the fact that the City of London is Europe's financial capital.

The reason for this change is that the global economy is not rooted in the city in the sense of depending on control of the city as a whole. It is instead an island economy, literally so within the island of Manhattan in New York, architecturally so in places like Canary Wharf in London, which resemble the imperial compounds of an earlier era. As John Mollenkopf and Manuel Castells have shown, this global wealth does not trickle down, leech out, very far beyond the global enclave – which is why Mollenkopf and Castells speak of global cities as "dual cities."

Capitalism and the City **Richard Sennett**

Indeed, the politics of the global enclave cultivates a kind of indifference vis-à-vis the city which Marcel Proust, in an entirely different context, calls the 'passive beloved' phenomenon. Threatening to leave, go anywhere in the world, the global firm is given enormous tax breaks to stay, a profitable seduction made possible by the firm appearing indifferent to the places where it touches down.

In other words, globalization poses a problem of citizenship in cities as well as nations. I remarked that the conflicting demands of family and work are now diminishing civic participation. But here is another, less sympathetic form of civic indifference, particularly urgent at the top of global organizations. Cities can't tap into the wealth of these corporations, and the corporations take little responsibility for their own presence in the city. The threat of absence, of leaving, makes possible this avoidance of responsibility; we lack correspondingly the political mechanisms to make unstable, flexible institutions contribute fairly for the privileges they enjoy in the city.

For all these reasons, I want to argue that the dialectics of flexibility and indifference pose three new dilemmas for cities: a dilemma of citizenship; of arousal in the public realm, since the impermanence/standardization connection leaves people indifferent to public places; and finally the dilemma of sheer, durable attachment to the city.

The political economy of a century ago posed the problem of how to cut free from rigidity. The city embodied that rigidity in its ecology, but paradoxically, in the newness and rawness of the urban population, the very concentration of strangers seemed also to promise an escape from rigidity, from Weber's iron cage: a promise of freedom. We now have cities of globally mobile corporations, flexible workers, a dynamic capitalism bent on erasing routine. Paradoxically, in the city, this restless economy produces political disengagements, a standardization of the physical realm, new pressures to withdraw into the private sphere.

The fate of the urban virtues

I would like to conclude by asking what this new kind of city life implies about the two ethical values for which the city durably stands.

About the sociability of living with strangers: the mark of the civic realm now is mutual accommodation through dissociation. That means the truce of letting one another alone, the peace of mutual indifference. In the language of cultural studies, identity has taken the place of alterity in urban life. This is one reason why, on the positive side, the modern city is like an accordion easily able to expand to accommodate new waves of migrants; the pockets of difference are sealed. On the negative side, mutual accommodation through dissociation spells the end of citizenship practices which require understanding of divergent interests, as well as marking a loss of simple human curiosity about the 'other'.

About subjectivity: personal experience of the incomplete seems achieved by this new capitalist time. Flexible time is serial, rather than cumulative; the spaces of flexible time are unmarked, neutral. But there is no Levinasian bridge, no sense that because sometime seems missing in my own life, I should turn outward to others, toward the "neighborliness of strangers."

This very problem of capitalist time, however, suggests something about the art of making better cities today. We want to overlay different activities in the same space, as for example, family activity in working space. The incompleteness of capitalist time returns us to the issue which marked the very emergence of the industrial city, a city which broke apart the domus – that spatial relation which had before the coming of industrial capitalism combined family, work, ceremonial public spaces, and more informal social spaces. Today, we need to repair the collectivity of space to combat the serial time of modern labor.

The art of making a city is not, I believe, like rocket science. Almost none of the good city-builders of the past possessed a comprehensive theory of the city; but equally, they did more than just represent the existing economic and political conditions of their times. They sought to interpret and so to transmute the material conditions of the political economy through the expressive medium of walls and windows, volumes and perspectives – an art which concentrated on details, compounded specific dis-coveries about space into an urban whole. The art of urban design is a craft-work.

Today's capitalism imposes on us a specific task: creating complexity and mutual attachment in a city which tends to difference rather than alterity, a city in which peo-ple withdraw behind the walls of difference. We need to discover the craft-work which answers to this particular challenge.

Erik Swyngedouw
Exit 'post' – the making of 'glocal' urban modernities

> How to capture and give form to the fleeting, the ephemeral, and the endan-
> gered? ... The experience of the urban environment provides the answer. It is
> after all, in the Metropolis, that one become accustomed to, and esteems, the
> transient. [1]

Cities are – and have always been – highly differentiated spaces expressive of het
erogeneity, diversity of activity, excitement and pleasure. They have been the hotbeds
for the formulation of and experimentation with new philosophies, politics and socia
practices. Ever since Plato's 'Republic', cities have been identified with sites of civic
activity and of creative encounters as well as of the intrigues of bureaucracies and
the power games of elites.[2] They are arenas for the pursuit of un-oppressed activities
and desires, but also ones replete with systematic power, danger, oppression, domi
nation and exclusion. Mediating the tensions between these dialectical twins o
emancipation and disempowerment has of course been the bread and butter of urbar
planners, designers and architects since the earliest days of urbanization. Yet the cit
– and in particular the modern city – does not invite easy taming. In recent decades
parameters of urban life have shifted in new directions and moved rapidly out of the
straightjacket in which modernist urban design and managerial urban practices had
tried to capture it. The domain of the urban began to flow beyond the limits imposed
by the master planners' sketch pads, while its internal ordering collapsed as a whirl
wind of social, cultural, economic, political, aesthetic and ideological change blew
away the last vestiges of a presumably moribund urban order.[3] The urban multiplex
has become, more than ever before, a fragmented kaleidoscope of apparently dis
jointed spaces and places, a collage and patchwork of images, signs, functions and
activities that are nevertheless globally connected in myriad ways. The whirlwind o
recent changes that engulfed the urban has been heralded by many as constituting a
radical break with modernity, announcing the dawn of a postmodern era. A smal
library of books has attempted to identify the contours of these assumed new times
'ephemerality', 'fragmentation', 'disorder', 'uniqueness', 'collage', 'deconstruction'
'particularity', 'image', 'speed', 'time/space compression', 'open-endedness', 'nonto
talitarian', 'aestheticized', 'vernacular' are just some of the verbal gimmickry that has
been identified with postmodernity.

This contribution asserts, first, that this alleged transition to a postmodern urbanity sig
nals rather a dramatic reassertion of the forces of modernity. The prefix 'Post-' that has
accompanied much of urban and cultural debates over the past two decades gleefull
ignored the relentless and accelerating reassertion of the contradictory movements o
modernity. Together with David Harvey in *The Condition of Post-Modernity*,[4] I would like

Graeme Gilloch, *Myth &
Metropolis – Walter Benjamin
nd the City*, Cambridge: Polity
ess, 1996, p. 178

Plato, *The Republic*, London:
ordsworth Edition Ltd., 1997

See Erik Swyngedouw
he Specter of the Phoenix –
eflections on the contempo-
ry urban condition', in
Bosma and H. Hellinga (eds)
astering the City I,
otterdam: NAi Publishers;
he Hague: EFL Publications;
ew York: Distributed Art
ublishers, 1997, pp. 104–121

to argue – contra the advocates of the 'postmodern turn' – that the last two decades have seen, if anything, the reassertion – with a vengeance – of the process of modernization, whose contradictory dynamics were wrestling free from the cocoon in which the managed capitalism and the planned modernity of the postwar era had tried to contain them; dynamics that work through spatially in new, complex and contradictory configurations.

In a second part, attention will turn to the new conditions and fissures that infuse contemporary urbanization. Differentiation and fragmentation at all levels have become the corollary of internationalization, globalization and the creeping imposition of a total(izing) commodity culture. The commodity as a heterogeneous and perpetually changing and expanding spectacle "has attained the total occupation of social life."[5] The tensions between a set of decidedly local/regional cultures, the growing inter- and intra-regional disparities and the fragmentation, pulverization and proliferation of bodily, local, regional or national identities in a homogenizing global cultural landscape of production and consumption prompted more intense (local) resistances to the imposed cultural norms that revolve increasingly around the tyranny of a spreading market-Stalinism. These local resistances often take global forms as they territorialize in unexpected and often deeply disturbing ways. The radical transformation of New York City's urban fabric on 11 September 2001 is a frightful reminder of how 'local' resistance against the tyranny of particular forms of modernization becomes globally urbanized.

The increasing local differentiation, combined with global integration, has proliferated all manner of fissures, ruptures and tensions: class, gender, sexual, ethnic and other relations are woven together or broken down in complex, often disempowering and sometimes emancipatory ways. Group affinities are replaced by a politics of identity in which the body has become a central locus of struggle. The body as a discursive and material construction becomes the site on which power is exercised, but also the place from where resistance and struggle emanates: women, gays and lesbians, workers, ethnic minorities, unemployed, migrants, refugees, suicide bombers, urban social movements, youth subcultures, cultural movements, the homeless, green activists, postmaterialists and post-socialists attempt to reconstruct a sense of identity and self-consciousness and demand an unoppressive space for the expression of their desires, identities and life-worlds; identities that have become multiple and rhizomatic.[6]

These localized bodies are entering a maelstrom of instantaneous global encounters, mediated by a digital technological maze that William Gibson in *Neuromancer* defined as 'cyberspace'. The possible urbanity associated with this multiple-identity-based and inherently unstable body is still in the making and its outcome contested and open, as the future always is. Whether it will lead to the multiplication of the post-human landscapes of Ground Zero, Srebrenica, Baghdad, or the death-camp of Jenin, or to a genuinely humane urban geography of unoppressed and multiple encounters

4] David Harvey, *The Conditio. of Post-Modernity*, Oxford: Blackwell, 1989.

5] See Guy Debord, *The Societ of the Spectacle*, Detroit: Blac and Red Books, 1968 (1979)

6] For an exploration of how the schizophrenia of multiple identities relates to the fuzzy dynamic of capitalist modernization and urbanity, see G. Deleuze and F. Guattari, *A Thousand Plateaus: Capitalism and Schizophrenia*, Minneapolis: University of Minnesota Press, 1987

The Making of 'Glocal' Urban Modernities Erik Swyngedouw

is open for negotiation, struggle and confrontation. The future is always there for the making.

This is the theme we shall turn to in the final section. While urban planning and urban-ization during the postwar period became wrapped up in a Rawlsian view of 'Justice as Fairness' and framed in largely redistributive terms, the mirage of a just, redistrib-utional city and region was shattered as the geopolitics of capital accumulation took a decisive new turn after the cataclysmic transformations of the past two decades. Much of the underlying quest for justice that inspired many urban planning efforts during the twentieth century appealed to a Rousseauist ideal that Michel Foucault described as:

> ... a transparent society, visible and legible in each of its parts, the dream of there no longer existing any zones of darkness, zones established by the priv-ileges of royal power or the prerogative of some corporation, zones of disor-der. It was the dream that each individual, whatever position he occupied, might be able to see the whole of society, that men's hearts should communi-cate, their vision be unobstructed by obstacles and that the opinion of all reign over each.[7]

However, the reinvigorated belief in the enabling powers of the hidden hand of the market and in the trickling-down of wealth by untrammeled market forces shifted the ideological terrain from a collective perspective to one heralding the virtues of indi-vidualism. This 'communitarian' ideal that had been the leitmotiv of many urban utopi-ans, from Owen and Proudhon to Jane Jacobs, also became increasingly seen (by self-styled postmodernist critics) as a potential harbinger of a totalitarianism that excluded the different and repressed – the 'unassimilated Other'. Moreover, the fram-ing of emancipation and the scripting of justice in terms of a body politics at a time when individualized market liberalism reigns supreme, completed a socio-cultural and ideological 'turn' which relegated considerations of social justice to the back burner of urban politics.[8]

[7] Michel Foucault, Power/Knowledge, New York: Pantheon, 1980

[8] See Andrew Merrifeld and Erik Swyngedouw (eds.) The Urbanization of Injustice, New York: New York University Press, 1997

[9] For detailed case studies, see Frank Moulaert, Arantxa Rodriguez, and Erik Swyngedouw (eds), Urbanising Globalisation, Oxford: Oxford University Press, 2003

The future of the city resides, so it seems, in embracing an entrepreneurial stance in which state, architect, urbanist and entrepreneur join forces to construct urban 'growth machines' that permit successful development and a vigorous competitive stance in the spiraling inter-urban competition that governs urban dynamics today. The horrid consequences of this market-led urban development in a context of shrink-ing attention to issues of distribution and socio-economic power come to the fore in pervasive mechanisms of exclusion, social polarization and diminishing citizenship rights.[9] Is the contemporary city there just for us, or should considerations of social justice still matter as the recent market triumphalism begins to show major fractures and fissures? In a context of fragmentation, dissolution and disorder, can there still be a basis to begin to chart an alternative urban trajectory? Is the clarion call for a more just urbanization inevitably caught in a modernist straightjacket that necessarily leads to repression and dominance, or is an enabling and empowering urbanization process still possible to contemplate and to act out in the present time?

Our answer to these questions will be an unqualified yes. This new urbanism will demand a new urban vision that revolves around decidedly pluralist ideals in which the unoppressed expression of desires, dreams, and aspirations can be achieved via a distinct politics of difference; a politics that unashamedly captures utopian desires in a progressive and emancipatory fashion; a politics that is decidedly local, that revels in the "militant particularisms"[10] of distinct localized identities and struggles for empowerment, but also a politics that aspires to universalist inclusions and inserts itself in the contemporary rhizomatic circuits of globally-connected networks. The final decade of last century already announced the rise of a new form of urbanism and urban policy, largely controlled by the totalizing sign of the commodity, but where in the interstices of this commodifying logic lurks with all its vibrant potentiality, the possibility for a truly humane urban form and urban living. The maelstrom of modernization that has infused, driven and shaped our cities is still rushing ahead. The challenge here is to dive headlong into the whirlpool of change and transgress the boundaries imposed by those who call the shots.

The city and the maelstrom of modernization

The 1970s announced the beginning of an era of major upheaval as the cracks in the managed urbanism of the postwar period began to widen. The symptoms of this 'new' urban condition will be outlined in the context of the broader and often contradictory processes that have swept through the world, leaving cities in a state of permanent flux and transformation. Modernist planning and urbanism as a strategy and method of intervention may be under severe attack, but modernization as a decidedly urban-based process of social change is alive and kicking. The contemporary dynamics of modernization, expressed in rapid and unprecedented urban change, are part of wider social, cultural, technological and political-economic transformations. Internal fragmentation and external integration into a global space-economy situate the city as the material and metaphorical nexus from where bodies enter the cyberspace of what Manuel Castells defines as the new 'informational' world.[11] The City of the Spectacle, in which the body participates only as a passive consumer and not as a stage actor, is the city turned into a kaleidoscopic experience in which some call the shots, others lament the end of all certainties and most try to survive in the turmoil unleashed by an unfettered market dominance.

For Henri Lefebvre, the modern city is something akin to a vast and variegated whirlpool, replete with all the ambivalence of a space full of opportunity, playfulness and liberating potential, while being entwined with spaces of oppression, exclusion and marginalization.[12] Ironically, relations of domination and power that infuse urban practices and which are contested and fought against in innumerable ways help create the differentiated public spaces that give cities their sweeping vitality. At the same time, these forms of resistance and subversion of dominant values tend only to perpetuate the conservative imagery of cities as places of chaos, disintegration and

[10] David Harvey, *Justice, Nature, and the Geography of Difference*, Oxford: Blackwell, 1997

[11] Manuel Castells, *The Informational City*, Oxford: Blackwell, 1991

[12] Henri Lefebvre, *La Production de l'Espace*, Paris: Anthropos, 1974; translated as *The Production of Space*, Oxford: Blackwell, 1989; Henri Lefebvre, *La Révolution Urbaine*, Paris: Gallimard, 1972; Henri Lefebvre, *Le Droit à la Ville*, Paris: Anthropos, 1968; see also Henri Lefebvre, *Writings on Cities/Henri Lefebvre*, selected, trans. and intr. by Eleonore Kofman and Elisabeth Lebas, Oxford: Blackwell, 1996

'moral decay, rather than as spaces where the prospects of hope, joy and freedom reside.

Guy Debord's situationist manifesto *Society of the Spectacle* also revolved around the dialectical nexus of the city as the site of freedom and the space of tyranny and exploitation.[13] His political program revolved squarely around recapturing the modern spirit of the urban, especially as an embodiment of *jouissance*; even though his prophetic vision spotted the coming of the 1990s anodyne theme-park urbanism[14] of the late capitalist 'spectacular order', with its war of attrition against the city as a public space. Venice and Florence have long ago surrendered the erotic pleasure of the fleeting and melancholic encounter with the city that still inspired novelists like Thomas Mann or Goethe, to the commodified prostitution of street life. Of course, other cities like Paris or Amsterdam, where Rimbaud, Proust and Jacques Brel still roamed the street and dwelled in the permanent excitement of the turbulence that Baudelaire defined as 'modern' life, have followed suit, as have the burgeoning metropolises of what was once called the 'Third World'. The *jouissance* of the immersion in urban life that inspired entire generations of artists, novelists and poets has been replaced by the quick fix of the organized city tour and the commodified pleasure of a staged flick. The city has turned into the ruination of experience as offered by the spectacle-as-modernization.

The city as ruin: modernization as spectacle
In Spring 2000, Tate Modern opened its doors on London's South Bank and met with immediate critical and public acclaim. Long queues meandered along the landscaped gardens and visitors queued patiently in the drizzling rain to get a glimpse of what the new cosmopolitan cultural elite had staged and celebrated as the cultural icons of and beacons for our times. The Tate Modern is only a stone's throw away from the ill-fated Millennium Dome project at Greenwich. The latter, another bid to recreate the city in the assumed image of what is expected of a cultural spectacle at the turn of the millennium, was situated as an extension of London's showcase Docklands development, which was conceived to be the thriving hub of a globally-networked and competitive city.

In many ways, these two millennial projects embody two widely diverging and contradictory, yet uncannily related, visions and practices of contemporary urbanity: the sort of urbanity that is becoming an all-too-familiar image of cities around the world. The Dome aspired to herald and materially celebrate the enduring significance, politically and culturally speaking, of UK Inc. and was staged as a 'national' experience. Even the choice of its location in Greenwich – the site of the world's meridian – symbolically attests to the national mission that the Dome's advocates imagined. It embodied a economic national project, supported by the state, designed by a national cultural icon and state appointee (Richard Rogers), co-financed by the National Lottery, and portrayed as a showcase to advertise British technological know-how, cultural achievements and vision for the urban future. Of course, it is as much a shrine to corporate power and the fusion of national interest with a privatized liberal economy.

[13] Guy Debord, *La Société du Spectacle*, Paris: Champs Libre (1971(1967))

[14] See M. Sorkin (ed.), *Variations on a Theme Park: The New American City and the End of Public Space*, New York: Noonday Press, 1992

British Telecom, British Airways, Marks & Spencer, Thames Water and a host of other prominent companies, sponsored, officially supplied, or otherwise partnered what was conceived, planned and commercialized as a national flagship project, first by the Conservative Government, but later embraced by Tony Blair as a symbol of the principles and practices of the 'Third Way'.[15] The market-driven and market-led shrine to corporate ethos and national culture, for which your average citizen would pay a considerable entry fee (in the end, grand urban development schemes are these days supposed to profitable), became a grandiose disaster, a ruin before its date of expiry. The ruination of the Dome and the doomed urban vision that underpinned it, signals the failure of spasmodic attempts to re-instill national identity and national pride within the harness of the new cultural and economic orders of the twenty-first century. The hyper-technological Dome was turned into ruin before it even began to embark on its mission to become the national cultural-technological shrine that resonated in tune with the vibrations of the new century.

Tate Modern, in sharp contrast, takes a decidedly different turn and celebrates an urbanism and cultural cosmopolitanism that has taken the ruins of modernity as an aesthetic and material foundation upon which to re-enact a vision and practice of the city in which decay, museum and twenty-first-century urban experience blend together in a decidedly localized, yet uncannily decentered and de-nationalized, global cosmopolitan experience.[16] Housed in the former Bankside power station, which was built as a shrine to national power and modernizing progress in the mid-twentieth century, Tate Modern has now become a lynchpin of the cultural district of the South Bank that epitomizes 'Cool Britannia'. This hub of faded national pride and landmark for London is now turned into a new urban experience, designed by Swiss architects Herzog and de Meuron, originally headed by Swedish curator Lars Nittve, and adjacent to one of the world's largest modernist centers of culture, the South Bank's unashamedly modernist 1950s redevelopment. Barely two months after opening, it had already welcomed its millionth visitor.

Of course, also here, the private sponsors are prominently listed among the benefactors that the Tate foundation thanked, but entry is free. Inside, the new and the ruin are combined as Bill Viola or Damien Hirst mingles with Warhol, Picasso or Monet. The very sense of time as history, progress and continuous building-up of new layers and of geographies of places as distinct historical-cultural entities, is replaced by a celebration of the collage, the juxtaposition of works of art whose temporal and geographical frame of reference is transgressed and subtly disrupted. The displays produce an eerie feeling, with time apparently out of joint and space strangely out of place - a dislocation which creates a unique sense of hybrid, multi-cultural location, identification and remembrance, where past, present and future, the here and distant, blend in ways that pervert received meanings of time and space, transcending the celebration of ruination and decay that for Benjamin constituted part of the essence of the modern experience. Of course, it is easy to forget today that the area's revival has as much to do with the desire of the culture elites to reposition London in the global cultural and economic order as with the very successful struggle that local commu-

[15] The 'Third Way' symbolizes the political agenda and program of Tony Blair's New Labour. Its best-known ideologue is Antony Giddens, *The Third Way*, Cambridge: Polity Press, 1998

[16] For a detailed account of Tate Modern's visionary conceptualization, see Iwona Blazwick and SimonSimon Wilson (eds.) *Tate Modern: The Handbook*, Berkeley: University of California Press, 2000; Rowan Moore, Raymond Ryan, Adrian Hardwick, and Gavin Stamp, *Building Tate Modern*, London: Tate Gallery Publishing, 2000

nity groups and grassroots organizations (notably the Coin Street Community Group) have waged since the 1960s to maintain affordable and decent housing for local people.[17] It is exactly the perseverance of community action that has preserved the area as a lived space and has succeeded in producing a context in which the lived, the everyday and the porosities that define the urban environment are maintained and nurtured.

However, regardless of the deep division in the urban visions articulated by these two emblematic projects, they, of course, share the satanic geographies that choreograph contemporary globalized urbanism. Indeed, neither of them can escape the contradictions that rampage through the city as the political-economic parameters and discursive-ideological apparatuses that have infused everyday life over the past two decades reshape the urbanization process in decisively new, but often deeply disturbing, directions. While the Bankside redevelopment reasserts the position of London on the cultural map of the world by paying homage to a de-nationalized hybrid cosmopolitan culture and rubbing shoulders with those who aspire to or celebrate similar multiple constructions of identity, the inevitability of the reterritorializations upon which such revamped experience is based, thrusts deep cuts in the social, political, economic and cultural fabric of the city. Homelessness is spreading rapidly, social polarization and exclusion have reached dizzying heights, and immigrants die at the ports of entry. It is ironic, if not perverse, how capital as commodities and money are freely floating around the globe, while immeasurable violence is inflicted on capital as laboring people – the neo-liberal utopia's reality. Urban land rents are sky-high and rapidly reconfigure the social geography of the city, while the colonization of everyday life by the commodity has completed its full spectacular and phantasmagoric form.

Despite the election of a London Mayor, the infamous 'Red Ken' Livingstone, the London public is conspicuously absent from the boardrooms and drawing tables where the alternative visions for twenty-first-century London are dreamed up and take shape. London may be a 'cool' (read culturally hybridized, cosmopolitan, and globally and competitively well-positioned and connected) place, but it is a place designed, manicured and financed by a particular global-local ('glocal') elite, and reveled in through the staging of cultural spectacles that try (although by no means always successfully) to subvert, undermine and marginalize the cultures of everyday urban life. Cultural commodities such as museums, exhibits and spectacular events shape an urbanity that is colonized. The reconquest of the city by the commodity and capital (after decades of willful neglect and rampant de-territorialization and emptying-out) has produced a revanchist city[18] that has draped itself in the phantasmagoria of the spectacular commodity. The latter announces, in its turn, no longer the ruination of a particular site, building, or social group, but the ruination of urban culture itself. As Gilloch remarks, "just as the experience of the commodity involves the commodification of experience, so the experience of the ruin is the ruination of experience".[19] In the millennial city, embedded in a neo-liberal utopian dream-cast, spectacle as the commodity-culture has become seemingly total. The ruination of the city

[17] See Guy Baeten, 'Urban Regeneration, Social Exclusion and Shifting Power Geometries on the South Bank, London', *Geographische Zeitschrift*, Vol. 89, nos. 2 and 3, 2001

[18] Neil Smith, *The Revanchist City*, London: Routledge, 1997

[19] Gilloch, op. cit., p 138

is all there is apparently to see and experience. And this is the theme that we shall turn to next.

The city as ruin/urbanization as ruination: reversing the porosity of the interior/exterior

For Walter Benjamin, the ruin epitomizes modernity and the modern city. The kaleidoscopic, mesmerizing, fleeting and perpetually recast materiality and porous experiences that constitute urbanity create the forever new. The commodity, with its emphasis on exchange and exhibition-value, is for Benjamin the material expression of modernity.[20] The maelstrom of modernity in which "everything that is solid melts into air"[21] is nothing more than the eternal recreating of phantasmagoric images devoid of substance and meaning. The inevitable fate of the commodity-form within the cycle of production and consumption is to become old-fashioned, out of date and obsolete, often long before its sell-by date. In its hollowed-out existence, the commodity turns into what it really is, a ruin. The spectacle as commodity represents a process of ruination, of decay and mortification. As David Harvey notes with respect to the commodification of the urban experience:

> Many...cultural institutions – museums and heritage centers, arenas for spectacle, exhibitions and festivals – seem to have as their aim the cultivation of nostalgia, the production of sanitized collective memories, the nurturing of uncritical aesthetic experiences, and the absorption of future possibilities into a non-conflictual arena that is eternally present. The continuous spectacles of commodity culture, including the commodification of the spectacle itself, play their part in fomenting political indifference. It is either stupefied nirvana or totally blasé attitude that is aimed at... [T]he multiple degenerate utopias that surround us do as much to signal the end of history as the collapse of the Berlin Wall ever did.[22]

The contemporary city – this fantastic geographical celebration of progress, change and innovation – has become the space of ruin. The commodified and spectacular museum-city as the heralded booster strategy to revive urban economies represents nothing other than the universalization of the recasting of tumultuous historical reorderings into the ossified ruins of theatrically staged places: time frozen as place, a mere moment of space. When the museum-experience is turned into a pure gazing at the commodified spectacle and the city the generous, but conspiring, prostitute to stage it, the real life of everyday urban experience is replaced by a 3-D reel life of the ever-the-same.

In the contemporary city-as-spectacle, the experience of the ruin-in-museums is radically transformed. While the classically modern museum was a practice of interiorizing what was originally outside/experiential/lived (i.e. turning the public space of the strange encounter, the public meeting and the social process into the crystallized display of the frozen ruined display-moment), in the spectacularized city-museum, the dualities of inside-outside and public-private is turned topsy-turvy as the divisions

[20] For excellent accounts of Benjamin on the city, see among others Gilloch, op. cit. and Susan Buck-Morss, *The Dialectics of Seeing*, Cambridge, Mass.: MIT Press, 1989

[21] From Karl Marx and Friedrich Engels, *The Communist Manifesto*, 1848

[22] David Harvey, *Spaces of Hope*, Edinburgh: Edinburgh University Press, 2000, p. 168

The Making of 'Glocal' Urban Modernities Erik Swyngedouw

between inside-outside and public-private evaporate. Whereas Benjamin could still picture and, on occasion, mock the bourgeois interior or the shopping displays of the arcades as housing the obsolete, the ridiculous, the faded (yet blindly, pompously and arrogantly displaying the ruined artifact as desirable, permanent and enduring - as utopia redeemed), the outside has now become itself part of the interiorized commodified spectacle. While the porosity between inside and outside used to reveal the sense of decay and mortification whenever the interiors were exteriorized again in junk-yards and fleamarkets – that is, the moment when they enter the public again as sublime phantasmagoric allegories – in the spectacularized city, the old is refashioned in the context of the present. As with the city-as-museum, the exteriorized archaeological remnants of bourgeois homes have quickly become part of the city-as-spectacle. The accelerating gentrification of many of the world's inner cities testify to this in their own parochial mediocrity, as much as the more visionary and emblematic Tate Modern, Bilbao's Guggenheim, or Seattle's Rock Museum have been staged as integral parts of the city-as-museum, where the permeability of the inside and the outside has now been rendered total. The city itself has become part of the spectacularized commodity. It is exactly this process of interiorizing the exterior within the phantasmagoric web of the commodity that led Baudrillard to proclaim that the spectacle is all there is to see, gaze at and contemplate; urban life turned into a staged archaeological theme park experience.[23]

However, the assertion of modernity with a vengeance over the past two decades or so, not least because of the tumultuous reordering of the time-space coordinates of everyday life and the perplexing reconfigurations of the choreographies and chronologies of every-day practices – in which the most familiar is staged at the other side of the globe while the most exotic appears around the corner – questions, if not subverts, the hegemony of the city as spectacular museum. In addition, the ruin produces an uncanny feeling – what Freud described as *unheimlich* [24] – a feeling of being strangely out of place. Of course, when the homely, the interior, blends seamlessly with the exterior; when the creative tension between interior and exterior fades away, exposing both as mere phantasmagoric forms, emptied-out receptacles of literally disembodied spaces and experiences; when the erotic, the sensuous, the life-as-play is violently seen and experienced as vacuous, home itself becomes strangely unfamiliar, alienated and a grinding sub-dermal angst starts creeping in. This is of course particularly strong whenever those processes that the spectacle relegated to the invisible spaces of the urban margins (suburbanized ghettos, the ecological catastrophes produced through the relentless demand of cities for energy or materials and their need for ever-larger garbage depositories) or drove underground (skaters, illegal immigrants, sewage pipes, garbage, dirt, hooligans) surface, become part of the gaze in unexpected ways.[25]

It is exactly out of these close encounters with the unfamiliar and the *unheimlichheit* of the 'officialized' urban experience that the possibility (however problematic it might turn out to be) for imagining and practicing a different form of urban experience resides. It is at these moments as well that the hegemonic discourse and practice of

[23] See Sorkin (ed.), op. cit., or Christine Boyer, *The City of Collective Memory*, Cambridge, Mass: MIT Press, 1996

[24] Sigmund Freud, *Art and Literature*, London: Penguin, (1990 (1991))

[25] Maria Kaika and Erik Swyngedouw 'Fetishising the Modern City: The Phantasmagoria of Urban Technological Networks', *International Journal of Urban and Regional Research*, Vol. 24, 2000, pp. 120–138

elite power configurations is threatened; the moments when officially condoned violence and repression (whether in the form of permanent surveillance, CCTV panoptical control, or sheer bodily violence), or the resurgence of traditional values by a New
Right, inevitably surface.

The emergence of the fragmented 'glocal' city

The past two decades have indeed unleashed a profound restructuring process in virtually all aspects of daily life as well as in the broader technological, spatial, social
and political ordering of our cities. At the beginning of the new millennium, city life has
more than ever become the norm for most of the planet's inhabitants. On a world
scale, we are rapidly approaching a situation in which more than half of the world's
population lives in urban settings, many of them in megacities of over 10 million inhabitants.[26] One in six of the world's population is on the move, migrating to often
unknown and usually unwelcoming, if not downright hostile, places. However, the
beginning of the twenty-first century does not display a vision of a humane urban
world of the kind that urban reformers at the beginning of the twentieth century imagined would prevail. Third world cities have become Malthusian battlegrounds in
which a small elite enjoys a luxury beyond imagination, while most others are
engaged in a daily struggle for survival.

A series of rather disturbing tendencies have become magnified at the scale of the
urban. In an environment in which socio-spatial ordering by and for the market has
become the dogma of the day, urban regions have become, more than ever before,
landscapes of power[27] where islands of extreme wealth and social power are interspersed with places of deprivation, exclusion and decline. The accelerating and spatially deeply uneven processes of 'creative destruction' leave some urban communities uprooted and displaced while propelling others on to new commanding heights of
privilege, money and control. The process of 'globalization' that is trumpeted by a new
global elite as announcing a 'new' world order of stability, prosperity and growth, but
vilified by others as the harbinger of irreversible decline is indeed a double-edged
affair. For the privileged – those who are able to benefit from new technologies and
new modes of communications that span the globe – movement, access and mobility,
and the power that comes with the ability to overcome space, have increased.
Meanwhile, there are those at the receiving end of the process – the impoverished,
the aged, the unemployed and the Third World poor – who have increasingly been
imprisoned by it.

New forms of soft and hard technologies have enabled all manner of geopolitical reor-
ganizations. The powerful, for example, are now able to insulate themselves in her-
metically-sealed enclaves, where gated communities and sophisticated modes of
surveillance are the order of the day – in the public spaces controlled by panoptical
CCTV cameras, in the closely surveilled spaces of leisure and mass consumption
malls and in suburban housing estates. Concurrently, the rich and powerful can
decant and steer the poor into clearly demarcated zones in the city, where implicit
and explicit forms of social and bodily control keep them in place.[28] The efficacy of

[26] United Nations Centre for
Human Settlement (HABITAT),
*An Urbanizing World: Global
Report on Human
Settlements*, Oxford: Oxford
University Press, 1996

[27] Sharon Zukin, *Landscapes
of Power*, Berkeley and Los
Angeles: University of
California Press, 1991

[28] See Andrew Merrifield and
Erik Swyngedouw (eds) *The
Urbanization of Injustice*,
London: Lawrence & Wishart;
New York: New York
University Press, 1996

such a 'militarization of urban space' as Mike Davis appropriately calls it,[29] correlates directly with intensifying social polarization and processes of social exclusion and fragmentation. The contradictions of modernization reassert themselves with a vengeance in the reordering of our urban spaces.

'Globalization' emerged as the rhetorical vehicle and analytical device to describe recent important shifts in the economic and political organization of the world economy, soon to be followed by extensions of the concept into the cultural domain. The world economy has allegedly moved from basically a nation-state system to fundamentally and irrevocably new forms of organization that have surpassed the traditional state-based and state-dominated world system.[30] The propagation of this globalization ideology has become like an act of faith. Virtually every government, at every conceivable scale of governance, has taken measures to align their social and economic policy to the 'exigencies' and 'requirements' of this new competitive world (dis)order and the forces of a new 'truly' free-market-based world economy. In the light of the real or imagined threat from owners of presumed (hyper)mobile capital that they might relocate their activities, regional and national states feel increasingly under pressure to assure the restoration of a fertile entrepreneurial culture. Fiscal constraint has to be exercised, social expenditures kept in check, labor markets made more flexible, environmental and social regulation minimized, etc. This, then, is heralded as the golden path that would lead urban and national economies to the desired heaven of global competitiveness and sustained growth. Surely, such territorial production systems are articulated with national, supra-national and global processes. In fact, intensifying competition on an ever-expanding scale is paralleled exactly by the emergence of locally/regionally sensitive production milieus.[31] Yet, these localized or regionalized production complexes are organizationally, and in terms of trade and other networks, highly internationalized and globalized. In fact, the 'forces of globalization' and the 'demands of global competitiveness' prove powerful vehicles for the economic elites to shape local conditions in their desired image: high productivity, low direct and indirect wages and an absentee state.[32]

Companies are becoming simultaneously intensely local and intensely global; they have 'glocalized'.[33] All this is, of course, closely associated with hard and soft technologies that make possible rapid movement from place to place, to 'annihilate space by time'.

Different groups and individuals consequently bear different relationships to the global flows of money, capital, technology and information that all become condensed in urban arenas, which have become ever greater containers of all sorts of capital. The 'bulls' and 'bears' of the urban financial enclaves and their associated business service districts – the smart buildings and office towers, neatly packaged in decorative postmodern architectural jackets – have displaced traditional urban economic activities and have begun to act as pivotal relay centers in organizing and capitalizing on the flows of increasingly stateless global capital. The breakdown of the financial order at a global scale after 1971 unleashed a ballooning speculative flow of capital

[29] Mike Davis, *City of Quartz: Excavating the Future of L.A.*, London: Verso, 1991

[30] Michael Hardt and Antonio Negri, *Empire*, Cambridge, Mass.: Harvard University Press, 2000

[31] Ash Amin (ed.), *Post-Fordism*, Oxford: Blackwell, 1994

[32] See De Groep van Lissabon, *Grenzen aan de Concurrentie*, Brussel: Vrije Universiteit Pers, 1994; K. Ohmae, *The End of the Nation State*, London: HarperCollins, 1995; Daniel Drache and Meric Gertler (eds), *The New Era of Global Competition*, Montreal: McGill-Queens University Press, 1991; Kevin Cox (ed.), *Spaces of Globalization: Reasserting the Power of the Local*, New York: Guilford; London: Longman, 1997, pp. 137–166

[33] Philip Cooke, Frank Moulaert, Erik Swyngedouw, Olivier Weinstein, Peter Wells, *Towards Global Localisation*, London: University College Press, 1992; Erik Swyngedouw, 'Neither Global Nor Local: "Glocalization" and the Politics of Scale', in Cox (ed.), op. cit., 1997, pp. 137–166

from one place to another, whizzed through the digital lines of cybernetic information systems. These 'Spaces of Flows'[34] amount to a daily total turnover of over US$ 2 trillion that is moved from city to city.[35]

The practices of deterritorialization and reterritorialization by transnational corporate capital have intensified the economic restructuring of urban regions. Many have seen a rampant de-industrialization, sometimes followed by a hesitant transformation into a service economy. Global cities like Tokyo, Los Angeles, Hong Kong, Singapore and London have become the central nervous system of these flows: here financial managers and services reign over an economy whose support structure is maintained by a growing army of workers in part-time and insecure jobs. The service sector is not the glittering panacea to cure all socio-economic ills, as some pundits of a high-tech, service-based urban development model would have us believe. While elite business services cater for the financial and other needs of the new urban gentry, most jobs have been created in the dead-end, low-wage segments of personal services, security, catering and retailing, together with a booming 'sweated' industry in the construction, garment and food industries of the world's major cities.[36]

Needless to say, a new breed of city builders - real-estate developers in association with banking interests - have moved in to replace the state and its master planners in shaping the urban fabric. London Docklands has, of course, become the classic example of this new form of urban entrepreneurialism, but Berlin, Paris, Johannesburg, Singapore, Shanghai, Kuala Lumpur and other cities have been thrown into this development frenzy as well. While financial and service capitals flock to or flow through the reconquered city (reconquered, that is, by capital), industrial production moves to the exopolises surrounding the metropolitan areas or expands into the Third World.[37]

The process of commodification of city spaces has taken unprecedented forms. City imaging, city marketing and the packaging of city life as chunks of commodified units for sale to a burgeoning tourist and business services industry has taken root in most of our cities.[38] Beijing, Atlanta, and Athens hustle to become organizers of the Olympic Games. The spectacle of urban life has been transformed into the spectacle of the commodity. Time-space patterns have accelerated at an unprecedented rate: instantaneous production and consumption have reduced the turnover-time of products, commodities and even ideas to a minimum, again accelerating ruination, where even high-tech spaces and commodities outlive their useful shelf-life even before their sell-by date.

The transformation of cities into package holiday sites and tourist theme parks for the leisure industry collides with the permanent free time that characterizes daily life in the job-free zones of many urban and suburban neighborhoods. In the face of the market tyranny that has become the gospel of dominant political, economic and cultural groups, it is not surprising to find that those most disempowered in cities often have had to resort to desperate forms of protest. The satellite cities of Paris and Lyon, for example, so captivatingly displayed in the French film Noir La Haîne, testify to the

34] See Castells, op. cit.

35] Erik Swyngedouw (1996) 'Producing Futures: Global Finance as a Geographical Project', in Peter Daniels and William Lever The Global Economy in Transition, Oxford and London: Longman, pp. 135–163

36] Saskia Sassen, The Global City, Princeton, NJ: Princeton University Press, 1991; Manuel Castells and John Mollenkopf, Dual City, New York: Russell Sage Foundation, 1991

37] Edward Soja, Thirdspace, Oxford: Blackwell, 1996

38] Chris Philo and Gary Kearns (eds), Selling Cities, Oxford: Pergamon Press, 1993

The Making of 'Glocal' Urban Modernities   Erik Swyngedouw

crumbling social cohesion that feeds a rampant racism and to the boiling rancor that can easily blow the lid off a rumbling urban discontent. The street revolts in cities like Brussels, Lyon, Zurich, Bethlehem or London illustrate the fragility of public acquiescence when marginalized citizens confront a deepening economic, political, or cultural crisis. Violence would seem the only effective conduit to communicate the voice of the dispossessed and politically disenfranchised.

Urban regions of the size and dynamics we see these days are globally connected in ways that reach every nook and cranny of the earth. The ecological footprint of the contemporary city extends from the local milieu to global problems. Unhealthily high ozone concentrations in our city centers in summertime, the increase in cases of asthma and other respiratory diseases (tuberculosis is now again endemic in the rat-infested poor Bengali neighborhoods of East London), the proliferation of HIV and AIDS (particularly in African cities) are reshaping urban landscapes and may claim more casualties than even the most pessimist predictions of the human consequences of global warming. Meanwhile, the bursting life of the city can only be sustained at the cost of unsustainable environmental degradation in other parts of the world. While companies in our cities and regions desperately try to instill an image and practice of environmental sensitivity, they continue to ransack the ecologies of less protected spaces in the postcolonial worlds.[39] Shell opened the world's most environmentally friendly refinery in Rotterdam, but persisted in the socio-ecological destruction of the Ogoni homelands in Nigeria.

The mass migration of economic, political and ecological refugees from Africa and elsewhere to the imagineered honey pots of Western Europe and the USA has resulted in a proliferation of urban asylums and refugee prisons, while a growing number of the homeless freeze to death as the privatized urban spaces close their doors against the winter cold. The 'biopolitics'[40] of control have extended to all spheres of life; the body has become a central urban battlefield. As Celeste Olalquiaga attests: "[P]erhaps the most striking account in the struggle over the... body is its very literal manifestation in the fight over territory. In New York City, the value of people has sunk below that of objects, as the growing numbers of homeless people – bodies without homes, dislocated to leave room for real-estate speculation – bear witness. The substitution of use for exchange value is seldom so blatant: families inhabit parks and streets while hundreds of habitable buildings stand by empty, awaiting the best market opportunity to be reopened'.[41] In one of these buildings, Rem Koolhaas, one of the gurus of contemporary urbanism, designed the hyper-cybernetic new Prada shop; a feat that was immediately met with hyperbolic critical acclaim. Indeed, while the bodies of refugees, immigrants, homeless, sweatshop workers - mainly women - and other 'outsiders' are reconfigured, wounded, often molested, under the aegis of authoritarian political or economic control, the new elites cherish the reconfiguration, the cultivation, the culture of the body – the self-conscious construction of cyborg bodies – as the sign of a self-realizing living.

[9] David Harvey, Justice, Nature and the Geography of Difference, Oxford: Blackwell, 1996

[0] See Michael Hardt and Antonio Negri, op. cit.; Michel Foucault, Power/Knowledge, New York: Pantheon, 1980; Gilles Deleuze, Foucault, Paris: Minuit, 1986

[1] Celeste Olalquiaga, Megalopolis–Contemporary Cultural Sensibilities, Minneapolis: University of Minnesota Press, 1992, p. 18

However selective this bleak picture may be, it casts a light on the condition of the urban that is somewhat different from the glossy image most cities try to present. Surely, cities are still very much the pivotal sites where creative action and emancipatory practices emerge and reside. Cities are containers of the world, it is where the world, the global becomes localized and rooted. The most remote things appear just around the corner, the exotic has become our neighbor. The enabling and exhilarating experiences associated with this close encounter with the 'other', the different, opens up the possibility of endless new configurations that are explored in new forms of music, art, design and lifestyles. The process of global integration has reached its azimuth in the contemporary urban environment.

At the same time, however, this global-local condition is wrought with all manners of tension: conflict as well as benevolent chaos, potential creative encounter and enabling social practices. Each of the above processes that summarize the contemporary urban condition hammer home how social, political, cultural, ecological and economic action are inscribed in space and revolve around the meaning and (re)appropriation of space and place. It is exactly these dynamics that force the question of 'justice' back on the agenda of urban theory and practice.

Urban justice(s)

Recapturing the utopian moment

For Iris Marion Young, the terrain of social justice in the city needs to be recaptured, but on terms that are in striking contrast to the Rawlsian redistributional, assimilationist and eventually totalizing principles of justice that dominated before. For Young, a renewed scripting of justice lies in developing a politics of difference and proposing a normative ideal of life that revolves around four themes that are and have always been integral to city life: (1) social differentiation without exclusion, (2) variety, (3) eroticism and (4) publicity.[42] The multiplicity of affinity groups, the overlapping and interweaving relations of participation and non-participation, the public spaces of strange encounters and fleeting passages produce the kaleidoscopic collage that constitutes city life. Freedom, then, Young argues, resides in the possibility of expressing difference and 'otherness' in unoppressive ways. Observed through rose-colored spectacles, modern city life displays the embryonic conditions of this vision of a just urban order; a vision already explored in the musings of Baudelaire, Simmel or Benjamin. Yet the dialectics of urban life produce at the same time the forlorn dystopias where difference becomes expressed and experienced as exclusion, domination or repression.

Indeed, the obstacles to this ideal of a just politics of difference are formidable: corporate power, bureaucratic domination, hidden mechanisms of redistribution and processes of segregation and exclusion rampage through our metropolitan spaces as cities and regions attempt to reposition themselves in the competitive world order. Moreover, as argued above, the footprint of the city has become truly global, as contemporary urban life attaches itself to socio-ecological processes that reach every

[42] Iris Marion Young, *Justice and the Politics of Difference*, Princeton NJ: Princeton University Press, 1989

The Making of 'Glocal' Urban Modernities Erik Swyngedouw

corner of the earth. Considerations of justice, therefore, need to encompass the socio-ecological destruction unleashed in the remotest places on earth just to maintain the coherence of urban life. Consider, for example, how the spiraling energy and resource demands of the contemporary metropolis, necessitate the socio-ecological transformation, if not destruction, of life worlds in other niches of the globe. A humanized and just urbanization therefore requires a global reach that brings to the fore a commitment towards a more socially and ecologically inclusive urban life. This demands a consideration of how transformations in the urban fabric affect peoples and ecologies in distant places as well. The challenges for theory and practice this century revolve around recapturing the spirit of modernization with a reassertion of the need for a just and humanizing urban order that is sensitive to the excluded, to the 'other' that has become our neighbor and to an environmental justice that does more than pay lip-service to possible remedies for deep (environmental) injustices.

In 'Spaces of Hope', Harvey urges us to recapture utopian moments in the envisioning of alternative urban futures.[43] It is not sufficient to revisit the potentials of past utopian thinking, but to embrace the manifold desires and possibilities for imagining, creating and actively producing a freer, more equitable, enabling, inclusive and fulfilling spatiality contra the stale and plainly dehumanizing territorializations of the spectacularized late-capitalist urban order. First, Harvey invites us to return to Karl Marx's historical-geographical materialism to grasp the current uneven and highly differentiated geographies of globalized life. Ironically, in today's unashamedly free-market environment, Marx's analysis of the functioning of a 'pure' capitalist order may be more relevant than ever. The latter-day strategic withdrawal of the state from regulating capital has reasserted the sort of tensions, instabilities and social perversions that Marx so sharply dissected. Any alternative social project, Harvey maintains, also needs to engage with these material conditions as they are shaped by the contemporary late-capitalist political-economic order.

Second, the failings and possibilities of modern utopian thinking need to be considered. Most utopias, whether of a progressive or conservative ilk, are utopias of spatial form. They insist on the fundamental condition that any social process or project requires, inevitably and necessarily, spatialization. This spatialization, of course, also implies irrevocably a certain closure. Hence, utopias of spatial form (from More and Owen to Howard and Le Corbusier) always had the 'urban' as a central metaphor and practice. It is, of course, exactly this spatialization and its inevitable closure that produces the sort of exclusions, marginalizations and systematic silences that have been so central to postmodern critique. In contrast to utopias of spatial form, there are also utopias of process (of time). The classic example here is the Smithian utopia of a free-market-based, neo-liberal globalization that is currently hegemonically presented as offering the best of all possible worlds; a utopia that will eventually deliver heaven in some undefined future. It is this always open-ended process that keeps (at least discursively) everything apparently radically open and the promise of emancipation alive. Yet such utopias of process inevitably also require material spatialization or territorialization (and hence some sort of closure). It is exactly in these concrete

43] David Harvey, *Spaces of Hope*, Edinburgh: Edinburgh University Press, 2000

landscapes produced by a deregulated 'free' market that the truly dystopian and regressive character of the market-as-utopia-of-process becomes manifest, and, as outlined above, particularly so in the urban domain. The omnipresent triumphalist market-led theme-park urbanism, the accelerating social polarization, the bodily and pervasively cruel violence inflicted on migrating or laboring bodies, and the rampant forms of uneven geographical development at all scales prove conclusively that the utopianism of the market-as-process, when territorialized, foregrounds forms of closure that are deeply disempowering and exclusive.

Third, Harvey, therefore, advocates a dialectical utopianism, a spatio-temporal utopia that is ontologically rooted in a process-based conceptualization and practice of social change, but does not avoid the thorny and invariably ambiguous question of the need to territorialize. Utopias of space/time avoid the stale prison-style of spatial form, but do not fall into the devious trap of the neverland of tomorrow's unfulfilled promises delivered by the utopia-of-process.

It is not a surprise, therefore, that Harvey turns to the figure of the 'insurgent architect' as the pivotal metaphorical and material actor in the production of (emancipatory) spaces. As social beings produce space through their social process, the insurgent architect (whether as a professional or as 'ordinary' people producing their own lives) prefigures, in the context of concrete circumstances, a historical-geographical construct that explores and breaks through the margins of the possible. While producing spaces involves – at least for a while – a certain closure, it invariably also constructs possibilities hitherto unheard of or undreamed. Negotiating the cliff between tending to the specific and the local, while aspiring to the universal and the common, spatio-temporal utopias recognize the importance of closure, of choosing, of – if need be – excluding, yet are sensitive to the processual dynamics of emancipatory change. This requires not only the mobilization of enormous creative powers, but also a courage and will (something critical intellectuals seem to have retreated from) to search for the universal in the particular, to laboriously carve out the niches where possibilities for change reside, to enter the troubled waters of forging alliances and to connect the threads that emanate from all those that resist the forces of globalization.

Such projects are necessarily urban, often already embryonically present in some of the streets, corners and public spaces of our cities, where a kaleidoscopic *mélange* of insurgent architects is already actively at work. James Joyce's 'shouts in the street' as the defining adagio of modernity are all around.[44] Recapturing utopia as a process-of-becoming, but one that is already geographically realizable within the interstices of everyday urban practice, constitutes precisely the foundation for transformative urban programs. Enrolling and celebrating the imagination to prefigure possible configurations is of course necessarily connected to the process of producing alternative urban practices. In other words, imagination and practice are integral parts of the process by which alienation through the spectacle can be countered, while at the same time facilitating consciousness to become concrete in the world.

[44] From James Joyce, *Ulysses*, London: Ebury Vintage, 1999

The Making of 'Glocal' Urban Modernities   Erik Swyngedouw

Negotiating the making of authenticity

The latter brings us squarely to what in the current political-theoretical climate is undoubtedly the most controversial and yet centrally important consideration. As much as Baudrillard has questioned the notion of 'authenticity' and rejected the possibility of excavating an 'authentic' condition below the surface of the simulacrum, a string of other influential intellectuals from a diverse range of perspectives, such as Althusser, Derrida, Foucault, Lyotard and Deleuze, has attacked and questioned the very notion of 'alienation'. Both 'alienation' and 'authenticity' are central to emancipatory urban thinking and politics. Postmodernist and post-structuralist philosophy rejects the claim that the subject is endowed with an essential, non-reducible identity that can either be modified or transformed by society (and hence lead to 'alienation') or that is sufficiently robust to withstand or resist alienating forces and, thus, is capable of fighting to maintain or recapture a 'true' or 'authentic' self. Indeed, to the extent that social structures (with Althusser), language (with Derrida), power (with Foucault) or libidinal drives (with Lacan or Deleuze) are the 'subjects' shaping history and, consequently, producing identities, the idea of humans possessing an 'essence', that can be (mis)directed by 'alienating' forces and to which the subject longs to return, is misconceived. It was exactly in the aftermath of the events of 1968 that these ideas began to gain currency and became the super-radical 'post-everything' doctrines of the late capitalist cultural order. The modern utopias became thereby relegated to a set of views that held onto an antiquated Cartesian notion of the subject as possessing an authenticity and essence that could be perverted, and for whom liberation consisted in recapturing the authentic and essential. However, jettisoning the concept of 'alienation' and its roots in historical-geographical materialist processes not only gave way to a politics and history of 'identity without a subject'; it simultaneously perpetuated an inherently conservative and deeply non-dialectical (and primarily categorical or Cartesian, rather than historical) notion of authenticity, essence and alienation. Also here the notion of 'post' needs to be reconquered by a desire for the production of a (pre-)authentic modernity.

Guy Debord's vision of authenticity and essence, in contrast, is indeed one that resides exactly in the politics of resistance and libidinous transformation of the everyday.[45] For him, transformative (urban) praxis is centrally about the realization of consciousness becoming practice. Authenticity and essence are not innate 'things' or 'conditions' that humans intrinsically possess (and arguably once upon a time were united with, but became alienated from as a result of processes of commodification and reification), but authenticity and essence have to be historically, actively and materially created, produced and spatialized. In this sense, authenticity and essence are there to be made, fought for, captured. They are always up for grabs, contested and contestable, forged in the very process of making history – a process that is always necessarily spatialized. It is about, as Debord puts it, the active and imaginative creation of new - and hitherto undreamed of – desires, possibilities and forms of living.

[45] For further discussions of the work of Debord and the Situationist International, see, among others, Elisabeth Sussman, *On the passage of a few people through a rather brief moment in time: The Situationist International 1957–72*, Cambridge, Mass: MIT Press, 1989; Simon Sadler, *The Situationist City*, Cambridge, Mass: The MIT Press, 1998; Ken Knabb (ed.), *Situationist International Anthology*, Berkeley, Calif.: Bureau of Public Secrets, 1995

In his Hegelian Marxism, Debord puts it this way: "The *subject* of history can be none other than the living producing himself, becoming master and possessor of his world which is history, and existing as *consciousness of his game*"[46]. Emancipation, therefore, resides in the actively lived process of consciousness taking control of and over life itself. 'Essence' and 'authenticity' are, consequently, not static and immutable, but fundamentally dynamic and in flux. They do not exist prior to or outside processes of alienation, but reside as a concrete possibility in time, in a future that has already begun. In 1958, Debord summarizes this as follows: "It is a matter of producing ourselves, and not things that enslave us".[47]

It is in this context that alienation thus fundamentally matters. For Debord, alienation is the very real process through which the process of life as conscious practice is turned into non-life, which is where things (commodities, money, the spectacle) rule our life rather than the other way around. Of course, it is exactly the extreme reification that the society of the spectacle produces that turns 'life' into the passive celebration of the commodity(-sign). Alienation then is nothing else than the historical process through which humans become passive consumers of the spectacle rather than active producers of life. Alienation prevents consciousness from becoming master of life and itself. As such, the conditions of the spectacle render the participants mute, turning them into passive spectators and engulfing them to such an extent that the production of an 'authentic' life as an active historical process has become dramatically stalled, if not impossible. Alienation is, for Debord, a condition produced through the spectacle of the commodity, a condition that stands in sharp contrast to the fluidity, flux, movement and conscious pleasurable living associated with the process of becoming 'authentic'. The dialectic of alienation/life for Debord relates to the tension between alienating conditions produced by the spectacle – which severs the link between being and the restless process of becoming as living – and active consciousness, trying to appropriate and master the world in ways that express the manifold and still largely unexplored possibilities of what humans are capable of.

The concrete expressions of the living, spatial practices, that Debord considered to form the germ of a different form of urbanism, reside in the proliferating number of active repossessions and conscious real and symbolic reconstructions of everyday urban spaces and practices of the kind we have seen mushrooming lately in many parts of the world. One of these examples is a group of very loosely organized activists that operate under the banner of 'Reclaim the Streets'. They engage in practices that subvert received meanings and established spatial routines. For example, they might cordon off a busy city street, cover it with sand, install a sound system and organize a 'beach party' in a space that is otherwise colonized by the car and surrendered to the delights of commodified urban displays and hectic shopping. Other examples of spectacular recapture and recolonization of urban space as part of a political strategy of social transformation are the successive occupations of the central streets of cities like Seattle, London, Prague, Nice, Davos, Barcelona, Genoa or Rome by an eclectic coalition of anti-capitalist activists. This happens whenever the great and the good of the world convene to chart the contours of their own utopian paradise, that is a

[46] Debord, *Society of the Spectacle* , Detroit: Black and Red, 1983, thesis 74

[47] *International Situationniste*, 1, June 1998, p. 90

liberalized de-regulated global space that would be interconnected by free-flowing commodities and integrated e-commercial cyber-networks. These activists testify to a situationist practice that imagines and practices another form of urban and global life.[48]

It is people like these activists who are actively creating – however fleetingly – a space that is simultaneously locally embedded and globally connected, in which the participants move as easily from ecological politics to intellectual property rights, from traditional forms of class struggle to defending the cause of the Zapatista movement, from demanding the right to their locality to asserting the right of the Palestinians to their own space. In the process, they move as easily through cyberspace as physically from Seattle to Prague, from Porto Alegre to Genoa.

Perversely, it is precisely at moments like these, when alternative and concrete urban practices (and not mere words or semiotic deconstructions) hit the streets, that the repressive apparatus of state violence is mobilized in full force. Such urban practices are no longer respected by the powers that be (in contrast to the celebrated aestheticized exhibition displays they sponsor or the glossy coffee-table re-editions of past revolutionary movements). The gathered police forces usually outnumber the activists many times over. Italian protesters were denied entry into Switzerland when the Davos meeting took place in early 2001. While commodities and certain people can freely travel the globe, Italian activists were treated as mere criminals who threatened the continuation of the spectacular order. The creation of differential spaces and the actual staging of different forms of urban life seem to be experienced by the elites as a serious threat to their hegemony and to the continuing domination of the spectacle. In Gothenburg and Genoa, the reconquest of the city even met with the state's guns. The last thing the order of the spectacle desires is people becoming conscious of themselves, waking up from the amnesia instilled by the spectacle and taking their lives into their own hands, rather than living life within the simulacrum that cannot do anything else but promise utopia at every turn, only to pervert and frustrate that promise at the next.

In his search for possible humanizing urban worlds, David Harvey concludes that:

> the tensions of heterogeneity cannot and should not be repressed. They must be liberated in socially exciting ways - even if this means more rather than less conflict, including contestation over socially necessary socialization of market processes for collective ends. Diversity and difference, heterogeneity of values, lifestyle oppositions and chaotic migrations are not to be feared as sources of disorder. Cities that cannot accommodate to diversity, to migratory movements, to new lifestyles and to new economic, political, religious and value heterogeneity, will die either through ossification and stagnation or because they will fall apart in violent conflict. Defining a politics that can bridge the multiple heterogeneities ... without repressing difference is one of the biggest challenges of twenty-first century urbanization.[49]

[48] See, for example, Naomi Klein, *No Logo*, London: HarperCollins, 2000

[49] Harvey, op. cit., 1996, p. 438

The politics of emancipation and freedom require a decisively urban program, and the call for a more humane city demands a decidedly urban project; but one that transcends the aestheticized packaging of urban spaces in which so much of our contemporary efforts to remodel the city are located. Ed Soja refers to these spaces as *Thirdspace*:[50] the lived, interstitial space that is worked out through perception and imagination; a space simultaneously real and imagined, material and metaphorical, ordered and disordered. Visionary thinking does not become realized between the covers of scholarly books or in the corridors of fashionable urban museums, but in the active construction of an urbanism that permits and encourages the living of unoppressed and unoppressing desires and in the realization of an urban program that revolves around recapturing the urban as embodiment of *jouissance*. Without the imagination, the dream, and the creative powers of committed architects and urban designers (whether professional or just anyone trying to create a space, their space), nothing is possible. Let's meet there. We have nothing to lose but the boredom of everyday commodified life: *The world already possesses the dream of a time whose consciousness it must now possess in order to actually live it.*[51]

[50] Soja, op. cit., 1996

[51] Debord, op. cit., 1983, thesis 164

Saskia Sassen
Reading the city in a global digital age: between topographic representation and spatialized power projects

Understanding a city or a metropolitan region in terms of its built topography is, perhaps, increasingly inadequate in a global digital era. Topography is crucial in that it captures much of what a city is about, but it does not help us interrogate or go beyond today's dominant accounts about globalization and digitization which evict place and materiality. Yet, as I will argue below, the digital and the global are deeply imbricated with the material and the local, especially in global cities. Although topography is about place and materiality it is not conducive to capture these imbrications and hence the fact that particular components of a city's topography might be spatializations of global power projects and/or may be located on global circuits. Such spatializations and circuits destabilize the meaning of the local or the sited, and thereby the topographic representation of these cities.

My concern in this brief essay is to distinguish between the topographic representation of key aspects of the city and an interpretation of these same aspects in terms of spatialized economic, political and cultural dynamics.[1] This is one analytic path into questions about cities in a global digital age. It brings a particular type of twist to the discussion on urban topography and spatialization, since both globalization and digitization are associated with dispersal and mobility. Topographic representations fail to capture the fact that cities continue to be key sites for the spatialization of power projects, even in a global digital era. Nor do topographic representations allow one to capture the fact that cities are also key sites for the spatializing of a different type of power project, perhaps better thought of as contestatory. Here my argument is that global cities make possible the emergence of new types of political subjects arising out of conditions of, often acute, disadvantage because they can engage those global power projects that spatialize in cities. A topographic representation of poor areas of a city would simply capture the physical conditions of disadvantage: the poor housing, the bad transport infrastructure, the decaying schools, but not of these new politics. However, in order to develop these new analytics we do need much of the detailed knowledge provided by topography.

Spatialized power projects

Cities have long been key sites for the spatialization of power projects – whether political, religious, or economic. There are multiple instances that capture this. For example in the structures and infrastructures for control and management functions of past colonial empires and of current global firms and markets; we can also find it in the segregation of population groups that can consequently be more easily produced as either cheap labor or surplus people; in the choice of particular built forms used for representing and symbolic cleansing of economic power, as in the preference for

[1] These are all complex and multifaceted subjects. It is impossible to do full justice to them or to the literatures they have engendered. I have elaborated on both the subjects and the literatures elsewhere. For the pertinent sources in art- and architecture-related publications, see the series of annual volumes of the *ANY* project, especially the last few volumes, e.g. C. Davidson (ed.), *Anytime*, Cambridge, Mass.: MIT Press, 1999; and C. Davidson (ed.), *Anything*, Cambridge, Mass.: MIT Press, 2000; 'Revisiting the Edge', in P. Noever (ed.), *Micro Space/Global Time*, Los Angeles: MAK Center for Art and Architecture, 2000; S. Sassen, 'Global cities and Global Value Chains'; Electronic Space and Power', in *Documenta*. The Book, Cantz Verlag: Ostfildern-Ruit, 1997; T. Pillon, A. Querrien (eds), *Futur Anterieur, La Ville-Monde Aujourd'hui: Entre Virtualite et Ancrage* , (Special Issue), Vols 30–32, Paris: L'Harmattan, 1995; L. Krause, and P. Petro (eds), *Global Cities: Cinema, Architecture, and Urbanism in a Digital Age*, New Brunswick, NJ and London: Rutgers University Press, 2003

'Greek temples' to house stock markets; in what today we refer to as high-income residential and commercial gentrification to accommodate the expanding elite professional classes, with the inevitable displacement of lower income households and firms; and we can see it in the large-scale destruction of natural environments to implant particular forms of urbanization marked by spread rather than density and linked to specific real-estate development interests such as the uncontrolled strip-development and suburbanization we see in the Los Angeles region.

Yet the particular dynamics and capacities captured by the terms 'globalization' and 'digitization' signal the possibility of a major transformation in this dynamic of spatialization. The dominant interpretation posits that digitization entails an absolute disembedding from the material world. Key concepts in the dominant account about the global economy – globalization, information economy, and telematics – all suggest that place no longer matters. Moreover, they suggest that the type of place represented by major cities may have become obsolete from the perspective of the economy, particularly for the leading industries that are the most advanced users of telematics.

These are accounts that privilege the fact of instantaneous global transmission over the concentrations of built infrastructure that make transmission possible; that privilege information outputs over the work of producing those outputs, from specialists to secretaries; and that privilege the new transnational corporate culture over the multiplicity of cultural environments, including reterritorialized immigrant cultures, within which many of the 'other' jobs of the global information economy take place.[2]

One consequence of this representation of the global information economy as placeless would be that there is no longer a spatialization of power projects today as there was in the past: power supposedly has dispersed geographically and gone partly digital. It is this proposition that I have contested in much of my work, arguing that this dispersal is only part of the story and that we see in fact new types of spatializations of power.[3]

Mine is a particular kind of reading of digitization and globalization. It seeks to detect the imbrications of the digital and non-digital domains and thereby to insert the city in mappings of the digital, both actual and rhetorical – mappings from which the city is easily excluded. And it is a reading that seeks to detect when and under what conditions the global economy hits the ground and localizes in concrete built environments. The risk in this type of effort, it seems to me, lies in generalizing, using metaphors and figurative language – in brief, to hover above it all. We need to go digging.[4]

How do we reintroduce place in economic analysis? And secondly, how do we construct a new narrative about economic globalization and digitization, one which includes, rather than evicts, all the spatial, economic and cultural elements that are part of the global economy as it is constituted in cities? A topographic reading would introduce place yet, in the end, not do much better than these dominant accounts

[2] The eviction of these activities and workers from the dominant representation of the global information economy, has the effect of excluding the variety of cultural contexts within which they exist, a cultural diversity that is as much a presence in processes of globalization as the new international corporate culture. For a strong analysis on these issues in the context of global city see M. Samers, 'The immigration and the Global City Hypothesis: Towards and Alternative Research Agenda', *International Journal of Urban and Regional Research*, 26 (2) (June), Oxford: Blackwell, 2002, pp. 389–402

[3] See Saskia Sassen, *The Global City*, Princeton, NJ: Princeton University Press, 2001 (new updated edn)

[4] Several scholars have produced important elements for this type of perspective which negotiates different scales, e.g. P.J. Taylor, 'World cities and territorial states under conditions of contemporary globalization', *Political Geography*, Vol. 19 (1), January, Amsterdam: Elsevier, 2000, pp. 5–32; N. Brenner, 'Global cities, glocal states: Global city formation and state territorial restructuring in contemporary Europe', *Review of International Political Economy*, Vol. 5 (2), 1998, pp. 1–37; R. Simmonds G. Hack, *Global City Regions. Their Emerging Forms*, London and New York: E&FN Spon/Taylor & Francis, 2000

about globalization and digitization. It would fail to capture the fact that global dynamics might inhabit localized built environments.

Analytic borderlands

For me as a political economist, addressing these issues has meant working in several systems of representation and constructing spaces of intersection. There are analytic moments when two systems of representation intersect. Such analytic moments are easily experienced as spaces of silence, of absence. One challenge is to see what happens in those spaces, what operations (analytic, of power, of meaning) take place there.

One version of these spaces of intersection is what I have called analytic borderlands. Why borderlands? Because they are spaces that are constituted in terms of discontinuities and usually conceived of as mutually exclusive. In constituting them as analytic borderlands, discontinuities are given a terrain rather than reduced to a dividing line. Much of my work on economic globalization and cities has focused on these discontinuities and has sought to reconstitute their articulation analytically as borderlands rather than as dividing lines.[5]

Methodologically, the construction of these analytic borderlands pivots on what I call circuits for the distribution and installation of economic operations. I focus on circuits that cut across what is generally seen as two or more discontinuous 'systems', or institutional orders, or dynamics. These circuits may be internal to a city's economy or be, perhaps at the other extreme, global; in the latter case, a given city is but one site on a circuit that may contain a few or many other such cities.

Internal circuits allow me to follow economic activities into terrains that escape the increasingly narrow borders of mainstream representations of 'the' urban economy and to negotiate the crossing of discontinuous spaces. For instance, it allows me to locate various components of the informal economy (whether in New York or Paris or Mumbai) on circuits that connect it to what are considered advanced industries such as finance, design or fashion. A topographic representation would capture the enormous discontinuity between the places and built environments of the informal economy and the financial or design district in a city, and fail to capture their complex economic interactions and dependencies.

International and transnational circuits allow me to detect the particular networks that connect specific activities in one city with specific activities in cities in other countries. In my research I unpack the global economy into a variety of often highly specialized cross-border circuits. For instance, if one focuses on futures markets, cities such as London and Frankfurt are joined by Sao Paulo and Kuala Lumpur; if one looks at the gold market, all except London drop out, and Zurich, Johannesburg and Sydney appear.[6] Continuing along these lines, Los Angeles, for example, is located on a variety of global circuits (including binational circuits with Mexico) which are quite different from those of New York or Chicago. This brings to the fore a second important

[5] This produces a terrain within which these discontinuities can be reconstituted in terms of economic operations whose properties are not merely a function of the spaces on each side (i.e., a reduction to the condition of dividing line) but also, and most centrally, of the discontinuity itself, the argument being that discontinuities are an integral part, a component, of the economic system

[6] See, e.g. R.M. Harvey, *Global Cities of Gold*, dissertation research in progress, Department of Sociology, University of Chicago

issue: we can think of these cities or urban regions as criss-crossed by these circuits and as partial (only partial!) amalgamations of these various circuits. Topographic representations would fail to capture much of this spatialization of global economic circuits, except, perhaps, for certain aspects of the distribution/transport routes.

Sited materialities and global span

It seems to me that the difficulty analysts and commentators have had in specifying or understanding the impact of digitization on cities – indeed, on multiple configurations – essentially results from two analytic flaws. One of these (especially evident in the USA) confines interpretation to a technological reading of the technical capabilities of digital technology. This is fine for engineers. But when one is trying to understand the impacts of a technology, such a reading becomes problematic. A purely technological reading of technical capabilities of digital technology inevitably leads one to a place that is a non-place, where we can announce with certainty the neutralizing of many of the configurations marked by physicality and place-boundedness, including the urban.[7]

The second flaw, I would argue, is a continuing reliance on analytical categorizations that were developed under other spatial and historical conditions, that is, conditions preceding the current digital era. Thus the tendency is to conceive of the digital as simply and exclusively digital and the non-digital (whether represented in terms of the physical/material or the actual, all problematic though common conceptions) as simply and exclusively that, non-digital. These either/or categorizations filter out the possibility of mediating conditions, thereby precluding a more complex reading of the impact of digitization on material and place-bound conditions.

One such alternative categorization captures imbrications. Let me illustrate this using the case of finance. Finance is certainly a highly digitized activity; yet it cannot simply be thought of as exclusively digital. To have electronic financial markets and digitized financial instruments requires enormous amounts of material, not to mention human talent (which has its own type of physicality). This material includes conventional infrastructure, buildings, airports and so on. Much of this material is, then, inflected by the digital. Obversely, much of what takes place in cyberspace is deeply inflected by the cultures, the material practices, the imaginaries, that take place outside cyberspace. Much, though not all, of what we think of when it comes to cyberspace would lack any meaning or referents if we were to exclude the world outside cyberspace. In brief, digital space and digitization are not exclusive conditions that stand outside the non-digital. Digital space is embedded in the larger societal, cultural, subjective, economic, imaginary structurations of lived experience and the systems within which we exist and operate.[8]

The complex imbrication between the digital (as well as the global) and the non-digital brings with it a destabilizing of older hierarchies of scale and often dramatic rescalings. As the national scale loses significance along with the loss of key components of the national state's formal authority over the national scale, other scales gain strategic

7] Another consequence of this type of reading is to assume that a new technology will *ipso facto* replace all older technologies that are less efficient, or slower, at executing the tasks the new technology is best at. We know that historically this is not the case. For a variety of critical examinations of the tendency towards technological determinism in much of the social sciences today, see J. Wajcman, 'Information technologies and the social sciences', *Current Sociology* (special issue), Vol. 50 (3), Summer, 2002

8] See S. Sassen, 'Digital networks and power', in M. Featherstone and S. Lash (eds), *Spaces of Culture: City, Nation, World*, London: Sage, 1999, pp. 49–63

importance. Most especially among these are subnational scales such as the global city, and supranational scales such as global markets or regional trading zones.[9]

Older hierarchies of scale (emerging in the historical context of the ascendance of the nation-state) which continue to operate, are typically organized in terms of institutional size: from the international, down to the national, the regional, the urban, the local. Today's rescaling cuts across institutional size and, through policies such as deregulation and privatization, cuts across the institutional encasements of territory produced by the formation of nation-states. This does not mean that the old hierarchies disappear, but rather that rescalings emerge alongside the old ones, and that they can often trump the latter.

These transformations, which entail complex imbrications of the digital and non-digital and between the global and the non-global, can be captured in a variety of instances. For example, much of what we might still experience as the 'local' (an office building or a house or an institution right there in our neighborhood or downtown) actually is something I would rather think of as a 'microenvironment with global span', insofar as it is deeply internetworked. Such a microenvironment is in many senses a localized entity, something that can be experienced as local, immediate, proximate and hence captured in topographic representations. It is a sited materiality.

But it is also part of global digital networks which give it immediate far-flung span. To continue to think of this as simply local is not very useful or adequate. More importantly, the juxtaposition between the condition of being a sited materiality and having global span, captures the imbrication of the digital and the non-digital and illustrates the inadequacy of a purely technological reading of the technical capacities of digitization. A technological reading would exclude the notion that place-boundedness is part of the condition of being an entity with global span. And it illustrates the inadequacy of a purely topographical reading.

A second example is the bundle of conditions and dynamics that marks the model of the global city. Just to single out one key dynamic: the more globalized and digitized the operations of firms and markets, the more their central management and coordination functions (and the requisite material structures) become strategic. It is precisely because of digitization that simultaneous worldwide dispersal of operations (whether factories, offices, or service outlets) and system integration can be achieved. And it is precisely this combination that raises the importance of central functions. Global cities are strategic sites for the combination of resources necessary for the production of these central functions.[10]

Much of what is liquefied and circulates in digital networks and is marked by hypermobility, remains physical in some of its components. Take, for example, the case of real estate. Financial services firms have invented instruments that liquefy real estate, thereby facilitating investment and circulation of these instruments in global markets. Yet part of what constitutes real estate remains very physical. At the same time,

[9] P.J. Taylor, 'World cities and territorial states under conditions of contemporary globalization', Political Geography, Vol. 19 (5), 2000, pp. 5—32

[10] These economic global city functions are to be distinguished from political global city functions, which might include the politics of contestation by formal and informal political actors enabled by these economic functions. This particular form of political global city functions is, then, in a dialectical relation (both enabled and in opposition) to the economic functions. See S. Sassen, 'New Frontiers Facing Urban Sociology', British Journal of Sociology (special millennial issue), January/March, Vol. 51 (1), 2000, pp. 143—159; A. Bartlett, Politics Remade: Modernization and the New Political Culture in England, unpublished thesis, Department of Sociology, University of Chicago, 2001; S. Sassen. 'The Repositioning of Citizenship: Emergent Subjects and Spaces for Politics.' Berkeley Journal of Sociology: A Critical Review, Vol. 46, 2002, pp. 4—26; A. Drainville, Contesting Globalization: Space and Place in the World Economy, London: Routledge, 2004

however, that which remains physical has been transformed by the fact that it is represented by highly liquid instruments that can circulate in global markets. It may look the same, it may involve the same bricks and mortar, it may be new or old, but it is a transformed entity. We have difficulty capturing this multi-valence through our conventional categories: if it is physical, it is physical; and if it is digital, it is digital. In fact, the partial representation of real estate through liquid financial instruments produces a complex imbrication of the material and the dematerialized moments of that which we continue to call 'real estate'. And it is precisely because of the digital capabilities of the economic sectors represented in global cities that the massive concentrations of material resources in these cities exist and keep expanding.

Hypermobility and dematerialization are usually seen as mere functions of the new technologies. This understanding erases the fact that it takes multiple material conditions to achieve this outcome and that it takes social networks, not only digital ones.[11] Once we recognize that the hypermobility of the instrument, or the dematerialization of the actual piece of real estate, had to be *produced*, we introduce the imbrication of the material and the non-material. It takes capital fixity to produce capital mobility, that is to say, state-of-the-art built environments, conventional infrastructure – from highways to airports and railways – and well-housed talent. These are all, at least partly, place-bound conditions, even though the nature of their place-boundedness is going to be different from what it was 100 years ago, when place-boundedness was much closer to pure immobility. Today it is a place-boundednesss that is inflected, inscribed, by the hypermobility of some of its components, products and outcomes. Both capital fixity and mobility are located in a temporal frame where speed is ascendant and consequential. This type of capital fixity cannot be fully captured in a description of its material and locational features, i.e. in a topographical reading. Conceptualizing digitization and globalization along these lines creates operational and rhetorical openings for recognizing the ongoing importance of the material world even in the case of some of the most dematerialized activities.

The spatialities of the center

Information technologies have not eliminated the importance of massive concentrations of material resources but have, rather, reconfigured the interaction of capital fixity and hypermobility. The complex management of this interaction has given some cities a new competitive advantage. The vast new economic topography that is being implemented through electronic space is one moment, one fragment, of an even vaster economic chain that is in large part embedded in non-electronic spaces. There is today no fully virtualized firm or economic sector. Even finance, the most digitized, dematerialized and globalized of all activities, has a topography that weaves back and forth between actual and digital space. To different extents in different types of sectors and different types of firms, a firm's tasks are now distributed across these two kinds of spaces; further, the actual configurations are subject to considerable transformation, as tasks are computerized or standardized, markets are further globalized, and so on.

11] See, e.g. L. Garcia, 'The architecture of global networking technologies' in: S. Sassen, (ed.), *Global Networks/Linked Cities*, London and New York: Routledge, 2002; J. Rutherford, *A Tale of Two Global Cities: Comparing the Territorialities of Telecommunications Developments in Paris and London*, Aldershot, UK and Burlington, Vermont: Ashgate 2004

12] Several of the organizing hypotheses in the global city model concern the conditions for the continuity of centrality in advanced economic systems in the face of major new organizational forms and technologies that maximize the possibility for geographic dispersal. See new Introduction in the updated edition of Sassen, op. cit., 2001. For a variety of perspectives see, e.g. J. Landrieu, N. May, T. Spector and P. Veltz (eds), *La Ville Eclatée*, La Tour d'Aigues: Editiones de l'Aube, 1998; I. Salomon, 'Telecommunications, cities and technological opportunism', *The Annals of Regional Science*, Vol. 30, 1996, pp. 75–90; M. Abrahamson, Global Cities, New York and Oxford: Oxford University Press, 2004; Rutherford, op. cit.; F. Ascher, *Metapolis ou L'Avenir des Villes*, Paris: Editions Odile Jacob, 1995; E.W. Soja, *Postmetropolis: Critical Studies of Cities and Regions*, Oxford: Blackwell, 2000; Ronan Paddison; (ed.), "Introduction", *Handbook of Urban Studies*, London: Sage, 2001

13] P. Cicollela and I. Mignaqui, 'The spatial reorganization of Buenos Aires', in S. Sassen (ed.) op. cit., 2002; Rutherford, op. cit.

[4] E.g. P. Marcuse,
. van Kempen, *Globalizing
ities. A New Spatial Order*,
xford: Blackwell, 2000;
utherford, op. cit.; A. Orum,
. Xianming, *Urban Places*,
alden, Ma: Blackwell, 2002;
ee the papers on GaWC:
ttp://www.lboro.ac.uk/GaWC

[5] This regional grid of nodes
epresents, in my analysis, a
econstitution of the concept
f region. Further, it should
ot be confused with the
uburbanization of economic
ctivity. I conceive of it as a
pace of centrality partly
ocated in older socio-eco-
omic geographies, such as
hat of the suburb or the
arger metropolitan region,
et as distinct precisely
ecause it is a space of cen-
rality. Far from neutralizing
jeography, the regional grid
s likely to be embedded in
conventional forms of communication infrastructure,
notably rapid rail and highways connecting to airports.
ronically perhaps, conven-
ional infrastructure is likely
o maximize the economic
penefits derived from telematics. I think this is an important issue that has been lost
somewhat in discussions
about the neutralization of
geography through telemat-
cs. For an exception see
M. Peraldi, E. Perrin (eds)
*Reseaux Productifs et
Territoires Urbains*, Toulouse:
Presses Universitaires du
Mirail, 1996; Landrieu et al.,
op. cit.; Rutherford, op.cit.;
Salamon, op. cit.

[16] E.g. Yue-man Yeung,
*Globalization and Networked
Societies*, Honolulu:
University of Hawaii Press,
2000; S. Sassen (ed.) *Global
Networks/Linked Cities*, New
York and London: Routledge,
2002

The combination of the new capabilities for mobility, along with patterns of concentration and operational features of the cutting-edge sectors of advanced economies,
suggests that spatial concentration remains as a key feature of these sectors. But it
is not simply a continuation of older patterns of spatial concentration. Today there is
no longer a simple straightforward relation between centrality and such geographic
entities as the downtown, or the central business district (CBD). In the past, and up to
quite recently in fact, centrality was synonymous with the downtown or the CBD. The
new technologies and organizational forms have altered the spatial correlates of
centrality.[12]

Given the differential impacts of the capabilities of the new information technologies
on specific types of firms and of sectors of the economy, the spatial correlates of the
'center' can assume several geographic forms, likely to be operating simultaneously
at the macrolevel. Thus the center can be the CBD, as it still is largely for some of the
leading sectors (notably finance) or an alternative form of CBD, such as Silicon Valley.
Yet even as the CBD in major international business centers remains a strategic site
for the leading industries, it is one profoundly reconfigured by technological and economic change.[13] Further, there are often sharp differences in the patterns assumed by
this reconfiguring of the central city in different parts of the world.[14]

Second, the center can extend into a metropolitan area in the form of a grid of nodes
of intense business activity. One might ask whether a spatial organization characterized by dense strategic nodes spread over a broader region does in fact constitute a
new form of organizing the territory of the 'center', rather than, as in the more conventional view, an instance of suburbanization or geographic dispersal. Insofar as
these various nodes are articulated through digital networks, they represent a new
geographic correlate of the most advanced type of 'center'. This is a partly deterritorialized space of centrality.[15]

Third, we are seeing the formation of a transterritorial 'center' constituted via intense
economic transactions in the network of global cities. These transactions take place
partly in digital space and partly through conventional transport and travel. The result
is a multiplication of often highly specialized circuits connecting sets of cities.[16]These
networks of major international business centers constitute new geographies of centrality. The most powerful of these new geographies of centrality at the global level
binds the major international financial and business centers: New York, London,
Tokyo, Paris, Frankfurt, Zurich, Amsterdam, Los Angeles, Sydney and Hong Kong,
among others. But this geography now also includes cities such as Bangkok, Seoul,
Taipei, Sao Paulo and Mexico City. In the case of a complex landscape such as
Europe's we see in fact several geographies of centrality, one global, others continental and regional.

Fourth, new forms of centrality are being constituted in electronically generated spaces. For instance, strategic components of the financial industry operate in such spaces. The relation between digital and actual space is complex and varies among different types of economic sectors.

What does contextuality mean in this setting?

These networked subeconomies operating partly in actual space and partly in globe-spanning digital space cannot easily be contextualized in terms of their surroundings. Nor can the individual firms and markets. The orientation of this type of subeconomy is simultaneously towards itself and towards the global. The intensity of internal transactions in such a subeconomy (whether global finance or cutting-edge high-tech sectors) is such that it overrides all considerations of the broader locality or urban area within which it exists.

On another, larger scale, in my research on global cities I found rather clearly that these subeconomies develop a stronger orientation towards the global markets than to their hinterlands. Thereby they override a key proposition in the urban systems literature, to wit, that cities and urban systems integrate and articulate national territory. This may have been the case during the period when mass manufacturing and mass consumption were the dominant growth machines in developed economies and thrived on national scalings of economic processes. Today, the ascendance of digitized, globalized, dematerialized sectors such as finance has diluted that articulation with the larger national economy and the immediate hinterland.

The articulation of these subeconomies with other zones and sectors in their immediate socio-spatial surroundings are of a special sort. There are the various highly priced services that cater to the workforce, from upscale restaurants and hotels to luxury shops and cultural institutions, typically part of the socio-spatial order of these new subeconomies. But there are also various low-priced services that cater to the firms and to the households of the workers and which rarely 'look' like part of the advanced corporate economy. The demand by firms and households for these services actually links two worlds that we think of as radically distinct. It is particularly a third instance that concerns me here, the large portions of the urban surrounding that have little connection to these world-market-oriented subeconomies, even though physically proximate. It is these that engender a question about context and its meaning when it comes to these subeconomies.

What then is the 'context', the local, here? The new networked subeconomy occupies a strategic geography, partly deterritorialized, that cuts across borders and connects a variety of points on the globe. It occupies only a fraction of its 'local' setting, its boundaries are not those of the city where it is partly located, nor those of the 'neighborhood.' This subeconomy interfaces the intensity of the vast concentration of very material resources it needs when it hits the ground and the fact of its global span or cross-border geography. Its interlocutor is not the surrounding, the context, but the fact of the global.

I am not sure what this tearing-away of the context and its replacement with the fact of the global could mean for urban practice and theory. The strategic operation is not the search for a connection with the 'surroundings', the context. It is, rather, installation in a strategic cross-border geography constituted through multiple 'locals.' In the case of the economy I see a rescaling: old hierarchies – local, regional, national, global – do not hold. Going to the next scale in terms of size is no longer how integration is achieved. The local now transacts directly with the global - the global installs itself in locals and the global is itself constituted through a multiplicity of locals.

New frontier zones: the formation of new political actors

The other side of the global city is that it is a sort of new frontier zone where an enormous mix of people converge. Those who lack power, those who are disadvantaged, outsiders, discriminated minorities, can gain presence in global cities, presence vis-à-vis power and presence vis-à-vis each other. This signals, for me, the possibility of a new type of politics centered in new types of political actors. It is not simply a matter of having or not having power. There are new hybrid bases from which to act. By using the term 'presence' I try to capture some of this.

Here the interaction between topographic representations of fragments and the existence of underlying interconnections assumes a very different form: what presents itself as segregated or excluded from the mainstream core of a city is actually in increasingly complex interaction with other similarly segregated sectors in other cities – e.g. a transnational immigrant household, a network of human rights activists, etc. There is here, in my reading, an interesting dynamic where top sectors (the new transnational professional class) and bottom sectors (e.g. immigrant communities or activists in environmental or anti-globalization struggles) both inhabit cross-border spaces that connects multiple cities.

The space of the city is a far more concrete space for politics than the space of the nation. It becomes a place where non-formal political actors can be part of the political scene in a way that is much more difficult at the national level. Nationally, politics needs to run through existing formal systems, whether the electoral political system or the judiciary (taking state agencies to court). Non-formal political actors are rendered invisible in the space of national politics. The space of the city accommodates a broad range of political activities - squatting, demonstrations against police brutality, fighting for the rights of immigrants and the homeless, the politics of culture and identity, gay and lesbian and queer politics. Much of this becomes visible on the street. Much of urban politics is concrete, enacted by people rather than dependent on massive media technologies. Street-level politics makes possible the formation of new types of political subjects that do not have to go through the formal political system.

Through the Internet local initiatives become part of a global network of activism without losing the focus on specific local struggles.[7] The Internet enables a new type of cross-border political activism, one centered in multiple localities yet intensely

[7] H. Cleaver, 'The Zapatista Effect: The Internet and the rise of an alternative political fabric', *Journal of International Affairs*, Vol. 51 1998 (2), pp. 621–640; S. Sassen, "Local Actors in Global Politics," *Current Sociology*, Vol. 52 (4), 2004, pp. 657–674

connected digitally. This is, in my view, one of the key forms of critical politics that the Internet can make possible: A politics of the local with a big difference - these are localities that are connected with each other across a region, a country or the world. Because the network is global does not mean that it all has to happen at the global level.[18]

The large city of today, especially the global city, emerges as a strategic site for these new types of operations.[19] It is a strategic site for global corporate capital. But is also one of the sites where the formation of new claims by informal political actors materializes and assumes concrete forms. The loss of power at the national level produces the possibility for new forms of power and politics at the subnational level.[20] The national as container of social process and power is cracked. This cracking opens up possibilities for a geography of politics that links subnational spaces and allows nonformal political actors to engage strategic components of global capital.[21]

Digital networks are contributing to the production of new kinds of interconnections underlying what appear as fragmented topographies, whether at the global or at the local level. Political activists can use digital networks for global or non-local transactions *and* they can use them for strengthening local communications and transactions inside a city or rural community.[22] Recovering how the new digital technology can serve to support local initiatives and alliances across a city's neighborhoods is extremely important in an age where the notion of the local is often seen as losing ground to global dynamics and actors and the digital networks are typically thought of as global. What may appear as separate, segregated sectors of a city may well have increasingly strong interconnections through particular (and inevitably perhaps particularistic) networks of individuals and organizations with shared interests.[23] Any large city is today traversed by these 'invisible' circuits.

Conclusion

Economic globalization and digitization have contributed to produce a spatiality for the urban which pivots on deterritorialized, cross-border networks and territorial locations with massive concentrations of resources. This is not a completely new feature. Over the centuries cities have been at the intersection of processes with supra-urban and even intercontinental scalings. What is different today is the intensity, complexity and global span of these networks, and the extent to which significant portions of economies are now dematerialized and digitized and hence can travel at great speeds through these networks. Also new is the growing use of digital networks by often poor neighborhood organizations to pursue a variety of both intra- and inter-urban political initiatives. All of this has increased the number of cities that are part of cross-border networks operating at often vast geographic scales. Under these conditions, much of what we experience and represent as the local turns out to be a microenvironment with global span.

As cities and urban regions are increasingly traversed by non-local, including notably global, circuits, much of what we experience as the local (because it is locally sited),

18] I conceptualize th 'alternative' circuits a countergeographies c globalization becaus are deeply imbricatec some of the major dy constitutive of the gl economy yet are not the formal apparatus the objectives of this apparatus. The forma global markets, the ir ing of transnational a translocal business n the development of communication techr which easily escape conventional surveilla practices – all of thes produce infrastructur architectures that car used for other purpos whether money-launc alternative politics

19] F. Engin Isin (ed.) Democracy, Citizenshi the Global City, Londc New York: Routledge, Drainville, op. cit.; A.C (ed.) 1996. Represent: City. Ethnicity, Capital Culture in the 21st Ce New York: New York University Press; J. Co M. Sorkin (eds.) Giving Ground,. London: Vers L. Sandercock, Cosmo, Mongrel Cities in the 2 Century, New York and London: Continuum, 2 R. Hector, Cordero-Gu Robert C. Smith and R. Grosfoguel (eds), Migration, Transnatior tion, and Race in a Chc New York, Philadelphia Temple University Pres

20] There are, of cours severe limitations on t possibilities, many hav do with the way in wh these technologies hav to be deployed. See S. op. cit., 1999; S. Graha Aurigi, 'Virtual cities, s polarization, and the c urban public space', Jo of Urban Technology, Vol. 4 (1), New York: C Taylor and Francis Grou 1997, pp. 19–52; M. "Cyberdemocracy: Inte and the Public Sphere,' D. Porter (ed.) Internet Culture, London: Routle

Reading the City in a Global Digital Age **Saskia Sassen**

is actually a transformed condition, in that it is imbricated with non-local dynamics or is a localization of global processes. One way of thinking about this is in terms of spatializations of various projects - economic, political, cultural. This produces a specific set of interactions in a city's relation to its topography.

The new urban spatiality thus produced is partial in a double sense: it accounts for only part of what happens in cities and what cities are about, and it inhabits only part of what we might think of as the space of the city, whether this be understood in terms as diverse as those of a city's administrative boundaries or in the sense of the multiple public imaginaries that may be present in different sectors of a city's people. If we consider urban space as productive, as enabling new configuration, then these developments signal multiple possibilities.

997, pp. 201-218; Calabrese, J. Burgelman, *Communication, Citizenship and Social Policy: Re-Thinking the Limits of the Welfare State*, Oxford: Rowman and Littlefield; J.W. Anderson, 'The Internet and Islam's New Interpreters.' In: F. Eickelman, N. Anderson, (eds.), *New Media in the Muslim World: The Emerging Public Sphere*, Bloomington and Indianapolis: University of Indiana Press, 2nd edn, 1999, p. 45–60.

1] E.g. C. Mele, 'Cyberspace and disadvantaged communities: the Internet as a tool for collective action', in: M.A. Smith, P. Kollock, (eds), *Communities in Cyberspace*, London: Routledge, 1999, pp. 264–289; M. Jensen, *Internet Connectivity in Africa*, Report, January, 1998, http://demiurge.wn.apc.org/africa/; *The Journal of Urban Technology*, special issue: *Information Technologies and Inner-City Communities*, Vol. 3 (1) (Fall), New York: Carfax, Taylor & Francis Group, 1995; S. Sassen. 2004, op. cit.

2] See, e.g. G. Lovink, and P. Riemens, 'Digital City Amsterdam: local uses of global networks', in S. Sassen (ed.), op. cit., 2002.

3] E.g. V. Espinoza, 'Social networks among the poor: inequality and integration in a Latin American city', in: B. Wellman, (ed.), *Networks in the Global Village*, Boulder, Co: Westview Press, 1999

M. Christine Boyer
Playing with information:
urbanism in the twenty-first century

The generic city

Call them megacities, edge cities, 100-mile cities – finally the city as a topic of intense research has caught the eye of the architectural avant-garde. Conceived as a radical alternative to architecture and urbanism in the twenty-first century, this approach develops visions and scenarios to deal with the instability and unpredictability produced by the ever-shifting territorial growth and unstoppable population expansion of urban territories around the globe. These conditions have produced, in the words of Rem Koolhaas, the 'Generic City'. Yet it must be asked how the architect, the master form-giver, can make sense of this "diffusion with a deficit of meaning", this bigness and ugliness erupting on a tabula rasa, be it Mexico City or Paris, Singapore or London, Shanghai or Tokyo.[1]

It is this very resistance to urban organization that is now being hailed as the vital theory to be addressed by a new urban discourse. Yet there is disagreement: Rem Koolhaas, the leader of this avant-garde, wonders whether this theory expresses "the ultimate oxymoron: chaos as project."[2] Or might the theory arise – as Caroline Bos and Ben van Berkel believe – after architects address the urban field and focus on the many ambivalent forces and complex junctions where public and political dimensions cross paths with structural techniques, mapping strategies, and site specifications?[3]

The return of architects to the urban field after decades of absence implies a major restructuring of architectural thinking: shifting away from philosophical inquiry and towards questions of performance and reception, the design process and experimentation. Such a maneuver entails a pragmatic and operational 'research-based architecture', outlining the necessary steps one must take if the chaos of mega-cities is to be interpreted.[4] In order to describe and especially to historicize the approach of the avant-garde, it is necessary to take a critical distance from their positions. They propose an alternative discourse involving analytical procedures of datascapes and diagrams, the consideration of complexity theory and non-linear urban dynamics, besides computational theories and modeling that influence the way the mega-city is imaged and represented. Their proposals, however, have a long history of development.

Three 'big books' of architecture published in the late 1990s will provide the focus: *S, M, L, XL* by Rem Koolhaas and Bruce Mau, *FARMAX: Excursions on Density* by MVRDV, and *Move: liquid politic*, a presentation in three volumes - *Imagination*, *Techniques* and *Effects* – by the UN Studio.[5] These are not glossy portfolio books of the kind that architects normally produce. Instead they are artist's books that define a

[1] Rem Koolhaas and Bruce Mau, *S, M, L, XL*, New York: The Monachelli Press, 1995, p. 366

[2] Koolhaas and Mau, op. cit., p. 365

[3] Ben van Berkel and Caroline Bos (Kristin Feireiss ed.), *Mobile Force*, Amsterdam: Ernst & Sohn, 1993

[4] Patrik Schumacher, 'Business, Research, Architecture', *Daidalos Architecture. Art. Culture*, 69/70, December 1998/January 1999, pp. 34–35

[5] Rem Koolhaas and Bruce Mau, op. cit.; MVRDV (Winy Maas and Jacob van Rijs), *FARMAX: Excursions on Density*, Rotterdam: 010 Publishers, 1998; UN Studio (Ben van Berkel and Caroline Bos), *Move: liquid politic* (3 vols), Amsterdam: UN Studio & Goose Press, 1999

huge conceptual space, engendering a performance between text and image, and playing on the word 'in-formation'. Such informational images are dependent, more-over, on their surrounding text, remaining opaque without further explanation.

Offering a layered visual presentation of architectural thinking, conceptual formations and organizational maps, these books indicate that architects have become new gatherers of information, diagrammatic analyzers and cartographers, in addition to being most attentive to mathematical models and topological surfaces. Contrary to their stated intentions, however, these supposedly new theorems of visual thinking may not extrapolate into architectural form, for more often than not they make only analogical connections between their diagrams and urban designs. In other words there is always room for a creative leap between the datascape, diagram and map to the resulting architectural design. Yet these books do begin to outline a grammar of graphics and methods of mapping data flows arising from urban complexity and chaos that reflect mega-cities as they stretch out across the globe.

We begin by remembering that Koolhaas is a great scenographer.[6] He chooses to close his discussion about the Generic City by asking the reader to imagine a spectacular Hollywood movie about the Holy Land – although this time without sound and running the film backward. Like the Lumiére Brothers' early silent film of a wall 'falling' back up, the reader is supposedly surprised by the event and forced to see things anew – spaces begin to emerge, the silence is filled with emptiness as the actors disappear one by one until the film is finished. So Koolhaas knowingly pretends: "That is the story of the city. The city is no longer. We can leave the theater now ..."[7] His definition of the Generic City is no less polemical:

> The Generic City is what is left after large sections of urban life crossed over to cyberspace. It is a place of weak and distended sensations, few and far between emotions, discreet and mysterious like a large space lit by a bed lamp. Compared to the classical city, the Generic City is *sedated*, usually perceived from a sedentary position. Instead of concentration – simultaneous presence – in the Generic City individual 'moments' are spaced far apart to create a trance of almost unnoticeable aesthetic experiences: the color variations in the fluorescent lighting of an office building just before sunset, the subtleties of the slightly different whites of an illuminated sign at night. Like Japanese food, the sensations can be reconstituted and intensified in the mind, or not – they may simply be ignored. (There's a choice.) This pervasive lack of urgency and insistence acts like a potent drug: it induces a *hallucination of the normal*.[8]

In spite of Koolhaas' sardonic tone it is this hallucinatory normality that leads him to wonder whether there is any way to theorize the forces that produce this convergence towards a Generic City, a design method – or lack of method – that makes all cities around the world appear to be just like each other? As he maintains, "it *must* mean something."[9] For an example, look at the essay 'Singapore Songlines: Portrait

Koolhaas claims that "the [ar]t of the scriptwriter is to [co]nceive sequences of [ep]isodes which build suspense [an]d a chain of events ... the [la]rgest part of [his] ... work is [m]ontage. Spatial montage." [Q]uoted in Maggie Toy, ['E]ditorial', *Architecture & Film*, [A].D. Profile no. 112, 1994, p. 7

Koolhaas and Mau, op. cit., 1264

Ibid., p. 1250

Ibid., p. 1248

of a Potemkin Metropolis ... or Thirty years of Tabula Rasa".[10] Koolhaas' use of the label "Potemkin Metropolis" sets up an ambiguous spatial antithesis between the real city and an illusory theatrical display of canvas and pasteboard. It was Potemkin, the propaganda minister of Catherine the Great, who quickly erected an artificially constructed image of a modern town to hide the squalid behind-the-scenes space from the eyes of Her Imperial Majesty when she visited the Ukraine. Yet the reader is told that Westerners, when gazing upon non-Western cities, must sever this connection between the authentic city and its imitations, for the dictatorial stage set of modernization is the only thing the spectator must consider as real. In this ecology of the contemporary, Koolhaas asserts, everything is pure form devoid of context, pure intention designed on purpose or willed.[11]

Contemptuous of those who deride its newness (such as cyberfiction author William Gibson, who referred to Singapore as 'Disneyland with the Death Penalty') Koolhaas argues that Singapore stands for something that Westerners can neither imagine nor interpret: it is an effect of the 'operational', of the ability to 'make a city' – something Western architects have long forgotten. For this very reason, the new city and its operations are worthy of study.

In an attempt to get at its roots, the architect sets out to graph this unique city, hoping to understand how information is potentially structuring. He looks at its statistics: location, size, ethnic make-up, its explosive demographics since 1959, and the need to produce an immense amount of urban substance in two short decades, which support his allusion to Potemkin villages. Its weirdness is another subject the architect will graph: the point where the upward curve of tourism meets the downward graph of historical presence, and the point where the lines of no crime and no pleasure safely cross. The architect sets up equations under which lack of freedom is exchanged: no freedom in return for unlimited real estate deals, no freedom in return for no debris and no chaos, and no freedom in return for social stability and collective desires. Finally the architect tries to explore a set of hidden logics or '[w]here these urgencies [to displace, destroy and replace] lie buried.'

With the use of these statistics and equations, in spite of the random and ironical manner in which they are presented, Koolhaas begins to outline an approach for an alternative urbanism of data, graphs and hidden logics. Hoping to understand how information is a form [an in-formation] he therein returns architecture to an intricate play between graphic elements and thinking, symbol manipulation and imagination. The concern is not the reproduction of an exact record of reality, but the logic of the argument, searching for the invisible forces that produce the Generic City. It is a question about the visibility of the argument, how to represent the data according to the rules of graphic specification and how to transform sets of data into planar mappings. Might this analysis eventually be reduced to a mathematical formula, an algorithm that can be expressed numerically – data fed into a computer model and then to a plotter or a screen that reveals something we cannot perceive with our eyes, without the mediation of technical machines and models?

10] Ibid., pp. 1008–1089

11] Ibid., pp. 1013–1017

Playing with information **M. Christine Boyer**

Going in search of deep logics that effect the Generic City requires the application of new graphic techniques and analytical diagrams. Many of these techniques are gaining widespread currency due to the use of computer modeling and graphing. These assumed new techniques, it is argued, will reveal order and meaning that have heretofore been concealed by the use of outdated instruments. This requires the development of a new mode of visual thinking aided by informational images such as diagrams, charts, maps and geometric configurations that borrow heavily from science and mathematics.[12]

Architectural design is a method for giving form to matter and it can do so in two different ways.[13] The architect can offer the spectator pictures, impose forms on urban reality, drawing images – or representations – of what a city or urban project will look like, displaying preconceived geometrical ideals and static forms. Or the designer can offer us models, recipes, and computer algorithms that enable forms to emerge, to be displayed as images on the screen – animated images, three-dimensional images, proliferating, uncontrollable images, maps, and diagrams. No matter how artificial, it is these models, maps and diagrams that become the new tools for thinking about cities and urban projects. The question then is to what extent these forms are realizable as architectural or urban projects? Do they offer us a new image of the city, or only an image of the problems of the Generic City or megacities? In *S, M, L, XL,* for example, an explanation of an architectural project is seldom given. Instead the reader is taught to visually explore the array of images and texts in an open-ended, questioning manner.[14]

Take the project 'Programmatic Lava: Urban Design Forum Yokohama, Japan' (1992), in which a series of mappings are juxtaposed with amusing notations. This is to be an investigation into a 'lite' urbanism – it will infiltrate, or invade like flows of lava into the site, engendering an alternative to the heavy construction of present-day cities. Concept phrases like 'programmatic tapestry', 'montage of events', and 'mosaic of heterogeneous twenty-first-century life' explain that programs and infrastructure are woven together in layers and overlaps, allowing events to emerge from unexpected interactions and juxtapositions. The site already contained two huge market halls and a parking facility, but was busy only between 4 and 10 a.m. Thus, a series of activities had to be invented in order to utilize the infrastructure 24 hours a day, allowing this programmatic lava to flow into every leftover space and gap until it created density without permanence, and facilitated change and flexibility.

12] For more information on information images, see ames Elkins, *The Domain of Images,* Ithaca: Cornell University Press, 1999

3] Vilém Flusser, *The Shape of Things: A Philosophy of Design,* London: Reaktion Books, 1999, pp. 22–29

4] Koolhaas and Mau, op. it., pp. 1210–1237

The project ends with six double-pages of photographs of maps and site plans plotted on top of photographs of a model or tabletop clutter, with inserts of computer-generated site models in the corners. These photos are not intended to specify the project but to underscore the intent of programmatic complexity and the geometry of stacks and arrays. This is not an urbanism that imposes static plans and frozen programs incapable of spontaneously changing form, but a mapping of a non-hierarchicalized field of events and parts that sets up a play between horizontal juxtapositions and vertical splices, generating an indeterminate and improvisational mix. Such a procedure cuts up space in new directions, replacing the plan with the map. These artificial constructions, or mappings, are visually reflexive devices that challenge the normal process of planning by acknowledging that any projected system or mapping is one among many possible systems. It makes the viewer think about the open-ended nature and iterative procedures that describe the complexity of a city. Consider these synthetic mappings to be performative, operational and engendering – anything but representational devices.[15]

Graphing techniques and visual thinking

Following Koolhaas' lead, mapping and graphic notation techniques have attracted other architects – most of whom have worked for Koolhaas' Office of Metropolitan Architecture (OMA) and are thus well versed in the study of hallucinogenic normality produced by the Generic City. These architects are bent on developing new datascapes and diagrams with which to explore the surface effects of deep underlying logics that might explain the urban condition eating away at every city in every country around the globe. In the current flurry of enthusiasm over datascapes and diagrams there is the oft-repeated criticism that our former instruments distort images and play tricks on us. The functional city, produced by representing the city of modernity in two dimensions, produced a static geometry – bifurcating center/periphery, inside/outside. It displaced, destroyed and replaced on a tabula rasa. Instead of this modern aesthetics of transgression, architects now consider field conditions in all their messiness and unpredictability – working in an improvisational way with and not against the urban site, until they produce site-specific, project-based experimentations.[16]

There is nothing really new here, for these architects espousing datascapes and diagrams as a mode of operation are reconsidering field models developed in modern physics at the end of the nineteenth century.[17] At that time the mathematical system of Euclidean geometry, the geometry of straight lines and empty spaces, was based on a number of assumptions that no longer seemed plausible. Among them was the assumption that space was a void that had no intrinsic characteristics and that did not interact with matter. Instead, space-time was considered to be an interactive field of forces operating on objects. A second assumption, the claim that change was continuous, was replaced with the awareness that matter and energy appeared to vary by jumps or by crossing thresholds within interacting systems.[18]

Before turning to explore the operations of these field models and the information images that they produce, we need to explore briefly the history of graphic techniques and visual thinking as they evolved out of two different developments in the nineteenth century.[19] The first utilized analytical geometry, in which a functional relationship between two variables was described as a curve or a line. Statistical graphs could figuratively display this information and by showing smooth curves, the result of averaging data or successive abstractions, they could reveal in a mass of data mathematical regularities that overcame errors of measurement. These regularities embodied arguments about invisible phenomena undergoing change, or interactions

[15] James Corner, 'The Agency of Mapping: Speculation, Critique and Invention', in Denis Cosgrove (ed.), *Mappings*, New York: Reaktion Books, 1999, pp. 213–252

[16] Stan Allen, 'From Object to Field', *Architecture after Geometry*, AD Profile No. 127 1997, pp. 24–31 and UN Studio (Ben van Berkel and Caroline Bos), op. cit.

[17] Pamela Major-Poetzl, *Michel Foucault's Archaeology of Western Culture*, Chapel Hill: The University of North Carolina Press, 1983, pp. 61–104

[18] Michel Foucault's use of archaeologies bears a striking resemblance to field theories. His 'field histories' posit no actors and deal only with webs of relationships in local areas. He avoids causal arguments that link distant elements by big steps and instead explores a multitude of small events viewed in spatial terms. Major-Poetzl, op. cit., p. 64

[19] Thomas L. Hankins and Robert J. Silverman, *Instruments and the Imagination*, Princeton: Princeton University Press, 1995, pp. 113–147

Playing with information **M. Christine Boyer**

between invisible phenomena. Thus graphs were analytical devices, used to help explore an unresolved problem – like that of the Generic City. Perhaps it can even be argued that they enhanced nonverbal reasoning ability.

Developed by William Playfield in 1786, this method was called lineal arithmetic and was based on the concept that lines might represent anything that could be expressed in numbers. Although it was a mathematical method, Playfield recognized it as a universal language, making it possible to record and comprehend a great deal of information in a single diagram.[20] Playfield applied broken line graphs, bar graphs, circle graphs, and pie diagrams – the last three being his own invention – to information about nations. His graphs appeared in a pioneering book entitled *Commercial and Political Atlas; Representing, by Means of Stained Copper-plate Charts, the Exports and General Trade of England at a Single View* (1785). Thus a line on a graph or a section of a circle could be varied in size to show wealth, area, population, or whatever the quantitative variable among geographical units. Playfield considered that the great advantage of the diagrams, graphs and maps of his 'lineal arithmetic' was that they enabled the eye to comprehend instantly what might otherwise require much time or even remain incomprehensible.[21]

The other development leading to an increase in graphic notation systems was the advancement of automatic recording devices. Here, meaning was embodied in the shape of the graphical trace. Étienne-Jules Marey, working at the end of the nineteenth century, wanted to reveal the invisible movement of birds flying, humans walking, horses galloping, blood circulating, or hearts beating. He sought to capture in graphic lines the rhythms and variations of the incessant activity of life - movements that eluded the eye and processes not detectable by human senses.[22] Thus he developed a graphical method for conveying the trace of these movements by telescriptors, machines that generated documentation. These instruments provided access to an unknown world. They 'penetrated' the apparent chaos of objects constantly in motion, and they 'revealed' a pattern where the naked eye perceived only confusion and discord.

The graphic method, Marey wrote, arranges phenomena in 'a striking form that one could call the language of phenomena themselves, as it is superior to all other modes of expression.'[23] His graphic trace diverted attention away from the problem under consideration – how horses gallop, how birds fly – and instead focused on how to decipher the mechanically-inscribed graphs and notations. The question became, how to think about – or with – these informational images?

So once again, this time with the aid of computer-generated experiments, the search is on for a "graphic explanation machine, with tables, lists, diagrams, and statistics intended to help master the profusion of contingencies through quantification," that will instrumentalize the approach to architectural design.[24] All of which has led the editors Peter Davidson and Donald Bates, in *Architecture After Geometry,* to note the 'emergent role of visuality' in the development of new concepts of architectural ordering

[20] Josef W. Konvitz, *Cartography in France 1660–1848*, Chicago: University of Chicago Press, 1987, pp. 129–30

[21] In 1801 Playfield used circle diagrams to represent the proportional size of several European countries, coloring them red if they were a land power and green if a sea power. A red line to the right of each circle gave the population in millions on a vertical scale while a yellow line measured revenue. Konvitz, op. cit., p. 130

[22] François Dagognet, *Étienne-Jules Marey: A Passion for the Trace*, trans. Robert Galeta with Jeanine Herman, New York: Zone Books, 1992, p. 16. See also Joel Synder, 'Visualization and Visibility', in Caroline A. Jones and Peter Galison (eds) *Picturing Science Producing Art*, New York: Routledge, 1998, pp. 379–397

[23] Étienne-Jules Marey, *La méthode graphique dans les sciences expérimentales et principalement en physiologie et en médicine*, 1878, p. 111. Quoted by Hankins and Silverman, op. cit., pp. 139, 113–147. Dagognet, op. cit., p. 63

[24] Gerrit Confurius, 'Editorial', *Daidalos*, 69/70, December 1998/January 1999, 7

and spatial structuring. Visuality and graphic cognition - as noted here - are probably not as new as Davidson and Bates appear to think and there are lessons to learn from exploring the past more closely.[25]

Let us now look more specifically at what are being called 'datascapes'. Manfredo Tafuri pointed out in the 1970s that every building site was a contested field in which building codes, legal restrictions, health regulations, government guidelines and aesthetic preferences, among others, all influence the design process. These external forces are now being visualized as so many quantifiable datascapes that control or impinge on a site. Information is to be manipulated within a series of experimental scenarios that ask 'what if?' What if data were to be extrapolated to its maximum: how would that effect the development of a city? Winy Maas and Jacob Van Rijs of MVRDV exemplify this approach in their book *FARMAX, Excursion on Density*.

'FAR' refers to the New York City zoning ordinance that regulates the total floor area or massing a building can attain by a ratio of allowable height to the site's square footage. Thus a Floor Area Ratio [FAR] of 10 allows the maximum density of 10 times the square footage of the assembled lot. In these 'what if?' scenarios, clearly New York City is one of the mega-cities taken by Maas and Van Rijs for a paradigm of maximum density.

Maas and Van Rijs understand that when architecture becomes synonymous with urbanism, it enters the realms of quantities, infrastructure, time and relativism.[26] They are looking within the chaos of events for the hidden logics that allow gravities to emerge. These are defined as 'scapes' generated from the data that lie behind them: 'scapes' such as the linear towns of villas along the border between Belgium and Holland that have grown up as a result of tax differences between the two countries; or the rise of 'piles' of dwellings just outside the border of Hong Kong before its return to China. Maas and Van Rijs argue that cities can no longer be described as if they are divided into two zones, the center or the periphery. They have become polynucleated, and built containers of density can erupt at any point in their extended field. Processes shape cities, and cities should be seen as indeterminate soft bodies whose form changes, depending on the gravitational field they occupy and the information they receive.[27]

The issue is not one of image creation but of response to economic and social programs. There are market forces, new life-rhythms of the city to be considered, and the time factor becomes important. Maas and Van Rijs argue in favor of an experimental urbanism that draws lines and modifies densities as mathematical formulas generating a virtual urbanism one step ahead of reality.[28] This new city needs space for innumerable combinations and substitutions that will allow density to become its third dimension.

Yet Maas and Van Rijs are not just tweaking the parameters of density. Instead, they argue that events take place in every city yielding surface effects, which appear to

[25] Peter Davidson and Donald L. Bates, 'Editorial', *Architecture After Geometry* A.D. 1992 p. 7

[26] MVRDV, op. cit., pp. 100–101

[27] Ibid., p. 123

[28] Ibid., p. 126

Playing with Information **M. Christine Boyer**

reveal random or chaotic patterns but actually contain deep-structured hidden logics that produce different gravities within dynamic fields. Datascapes are the information-driven descriptions of these spatial organizations. New patterns of data emerge when regulations and rules are expressed under maximized conditions. If regulations such as zoning ordinance impinge on architectural design, then why not take these regulations to the extreme, and see what effects are produced? The behavior of this massiveness when pushed to extremes – data observed, extrapolated, analyzed and criticized – becomes the focus of their research.[29]

As a heuristic technique – the kind these advocates of datascapes support - playing with information is a form of abstract, purely spatial thinking that enables discoveries to be envisioned that might otherwise be overlooked. The pattern and structure of these data distributions are studied as figurative expressions to reveal how they contribute to spatial transformations on the urban scale. What once began as play, experimentation, and inquiry in the hands of these diagrammaticians, however, sometimes appears to be extrapolated into architectural form. Nevertheless Maas and Van Rijs, like their mentor Koolhaas, never seem to explain their design method, and how they translate these datascapes into architectural form.

Look, for example, at 'Statistic Suspense Study for a development of 750 houses in Delft' 1992.[30] This proposal maximizes functions taken from the provided program and applies them to strips or bands of the architectural project. Confrontation across the collateral bands turns into what they call 'a kasbah-like labyrinth' in which the unexpected predominates, enabling architectural form to result in an interlocking sectional jigsaw puzzle. The 1909 Theorem for the production of an unlimited number of sites on a single metropolitan location, an image that Koolhaas repeated in *Delirious New York,* almost becomes a serious method of design in the diagrammatic approach of Maas and Van Rijs.[31] But just how the statistics engender architectural form is an open-ended question.

In addition, Maas and Van Rijs are fascinated with 'chaos theory', albeit metaphorically. Liberated from grappling with the necessary mathematics, they instead make cross-categorical analogies between the absence of order in natural systems and the disorder and disarray of mega-cities. In actuality this involves the application of multivariate analysis, or mathematical procedures which model how changing parameters of some of the inputs generate vastly different and unexpected outcomes over time. In the case provided by Maas and Van Rijs, however, the set of equations is missing, a set representing the state of a system at some given point in time. Instead their statements must be interpreted to be poetical forms of thought, making surprising analogical connections.

Let us now turn to a prototype of maximum density as described in *FARMAX*: the former Kowloon Walled City (KWC) in Hong Kong, to explore how Maas and Van Rijs metaphorically dwell on the theory of chaos.[32] The UN's list of societies ranked by an index of social crime placed Hong Kong in the lowest ranks. Yet Hong Kong is the

[29] Winy Maas, 'Datascape: The Final Extravaganza', *Daidalos*, 69/70, December 1998/January 1999, pp. 48–51

[30] MVRDV, op. cit., pp. 587–613

[31] Jos Bosman, 'Form Follows Function: From Meta-City to Mega-City', *Daidalos*, 74, 2000, p. 30–37

densest city in the world, with a FAR of 10. This paradox inspired Maas and Van Rijs to study Kowloon Walled City further, for in spite of taking place in the world's densest settlement within a very dense city, the public life of KWC proceeds in an orderly fashion. It exemplifies, at least for Maas and Van Rijs, the process by which order is generated out of chaos.

Massing together structures 10–14 stories in height, KWC was eight times as densely populated as the *Unité d'Habitation* and it contained 13,000 persons per hectare compared to that of 91 in New York City. A monolith created out of a series of interlocking, self-supporting blocks, its plan revealed super-deep floor areas where sunlight was eliminated entirely. Mass – flowing into cracks and empty spots, where it crystallized and coagulated – became a fluid concept. The only fluid organizations that remained were circulation, a transient population and services that constantly changed with time. A network of 1 m-wide branching 'streets' encouraged maximum mixing, which blurred inside/outside boundaries, residential and non-residential uses, creating unstable programs of use and function. Only at higher levels, especially the roofscape 45 m above the ground, were there continuous streets. Such hyperdensity forced the infrastructure to operate on a time-share basis: water, gas and electricity were siphoned off through alternately redirected routes.

As early as 1843, KWC was a "massive attractor for illicit activities to run wild."[33] It symbolized chaos and everything negative about overcrowding: opium dens, gambling, triad gangs, cramped living quarters. It subverted reality to its own advantage: changing over time from customs house to spy center, garrison to tourist attraction, administrative center to gambling house. Its superblocks represented 'out-of-control self-organization' generated from many different errors. It had no laws, no taxes, no foundations, no light. Yet it seemed, or at least to Maas and Van Rijs, these romancers of urban density, to thrive. But alas, it was demolished in 1992, because the city authorities thought it was an aberration, the manifestation of a city in perpetual crisis.

If we put aside MVRDV's nostalgia for the underbelly, for the gritty city of unreality, we can explore what the surprising connections with chaos theory reveal. Chaos is more prolific than order, uncertainty privileged over predictability, and open-endedness more realistic than closure.

KWC represented a system that changed abruptly or discontinuously. It was a system that displayed breaks, loops and recursions, and produced all kinds of turbulence and chaos. These are all processes described by a system of nonlinear equations, in which a small change in one of the variables may have disproportionate effects or even catastrophic impact on all the output of all the other variables. Yet what intrigues these students of hyperdensity is not the necessary mathematics, but the appearance of an ordered structure and unexpected stability generated out of seemingly random and chaotic expressions. Chaos seems to be strangely and unpredictably ordered. This is what Maas and Van Rijs seek to understand – the hidden logics whereby order emerges out of the very chaotic nature of megacities.

32] MVRDV, op. cit., pp. 152–173

33] Ibid.

Playing with Information **M. Christine Boyer**

[4] Michael E. Hobart and Zachary S. Schiffman, *Information Ages*, Baltimore: The Johns Hopkins University Press, 1998, pp. 235–269

[5] Ludwig von Bertalanffy, 'The Tree of Knowledge', in Gyorgy Kepes (ed.) *Sign, Image, Symbol*, New York: George Braziller, 1966, p. 27

[6] To consider an example of an algorithm, think of the Arabic notation of units in the first column from right, 10s in the second, 100s in the third. Figures set out in columns makes child's play of arithmetical operations

[7] Norbert Wiener said that the world could be viewed as a multitude of To Whom it May Concern messages – everything sending out an identifying signal. Mankind, in particular, has a wide range of signal recognition, and "learns to recognize and utilized signs as 'feedbacks' for orienting and directing much of his patterned conduct, evoking these signs as guidance." This information processing takes input signals, transforms them into symbols, and interprets them as meaningful messages. People design or articulate patterns of these signals, which are invested with meaning to which they respond with purposeful goal-seeking conduct. Lawrence Frank, 'The World as a Communication Network', in Kepes, op. cit., p. 3

[8] Language was construed as a sequence of symbols assembled according to certain prescribed rules, or syntax. Chomsky called his theory 'Cartesian Linguistics' to emphasis the scientific nature of the study of language, i.e. objective, dispassionate, rational and context-free

[9] *Gyorgy Kepes* Exhibition Catalogue, James R. Killian (ed.), Cambridge: MIT Press, 1978, p. 12

Computational models

One way of exploring the meaning of these graphic analyses focused on chaos theory and field effects is to understand that they reflect a major paradigm shift in our computational theories and in the manner in which we image the city.[34] Logic controls the precise steps of information management that define a computer algorithm or program. An algorithm is a system of symbols connected according to a given set of rules – it is a device for thinking, for performing operations on a string of symbols.[35] As we process these symbols or move them about they emerge into patterns or information. Symbols standing alone mean nothing; they merely constitute a vocabulary without grammar.[36]

The manner in which we create and process digital information is also playful and capricious. By allowing iterative procedures to play out over time we produce new and unpredictable patterns of information. Alan Turing and John von Neumann were the main architects of our information age: they were the two who thought to combine symbolic logic and electronic circuitry. Both conceived of the computer as electronically processing bits of information (in strings of zeroes and units) according to exact and undeviating rules. And both were interested in play: Turing produced the earliest version of computer chess and the poker-playing Von Neumann invented game theory. Thus there are two aspects to the computer: one is based on symbolic logic and the other on the iterative open-endedness of play.

These two conceptualizations of the computer – as a machine for processing symbols or for playing with information – affect the manner in which we envision or image the city. For example, in the 1950s the Massachusetts Institute of Technology (MIT) was a hotbed of investigations into cognitive processes. Norbert Weiner, the father of cybernetics, continued work on his theories of control systems, revealing how bodies in motion achieve equilibrium through feedback loops carrying information from the environment back to the object.[37] During the same period, Noam Chomsky developed Cartesian Linguistics. Fusing symbolic logic with natural language, he studied how thought could be encoded in forms that could be manipulated by purely logical means.[38] Meanwhile, artificial intelligence experts envisioned the mind as an information-processing machine, a manipulator of symbols and signs.

So it is not surprising to find that the visual artist Gyorgy Kepes, also at MIT, and seeking to bridge the gap between artist and scientist, began to consider how information theories, cybernetic controls and symbol-manipulating processors could be applied to the manner in which the landscape was envisioned. Kepes participated in weekly discussions with Norbert Weiner at MIT in the late 1940s. Weiner's ideas of cybernetics and feedback loops or corrective equilibrium greatly influenced his work. From the neurophysicist Warren S. McCulloch, Kepes learned that the capacity to orient oneself in a given environment is based on the ability of the neurological system to discern invariance in continuous transformations. Thus Kepes reasoned, art could aid an individual to achieve a new equilibrium with the surrounding environment, to rediscover the invariant harmony beneath the constant flux and transformations of life.[39]

In the twentieth century, Kepes noted in *The New Landscape* (1956), we have become lost in an alien, menacing world. He called this man-made environment a 'new landscape', in which the appearance of things no longer revealed their true nature. Instead, images fake forms, forms cheat functions, and functions are robbed of their natural sources. Thus humankind maneuvers in a world of incomplete information, in which invisible processes operate. In order to make sense of these invisible things, mankind makes symbols. So Kepes surmised: "It is not with tools only that we domesticate our world. Sensed forms, images and symbols are as essential to us as palpable reality in exploring nature for human ends ... We make a map of our experience patterns, an inner model of the outer world, and we use this to organize our lives."[40]

Yet the distorted environments of everyday reality rob us of the power to make our experience coherent. Thus, Kepes claimed, we need new symbols to bring this new technical landscape into balance with the human environment: "The essence of symbol making lies in the transformation of the ceaseless flow of sense data into clearly defined pictures, words and concepts. Symbol making is based on transformations, on the changing of substances or the changing of forms."[41] Thus the key to creative work lay in symbolic transformation, "the translation of direct experience into symbols which sum up experience in communicable form."[42] This means that the traditional concept of an image as a mirror held in front of nature is obsolete. Instead, the new patterns of information are pictures of processes.[43]

As early as 1944, Kepes had written, "To grasp spatial relationships and orient relations oneself in the metropolis of today, among the intricate dimensions of streets, subways, elevated trains, and skyscrapers, requires a new way of seeing."[44] Working collaboratively at MIT between 1954 and 1958, Kevin Lynch and Kepes conducted a research project on the 'Perceptual Forms of the City'. One of the outcomes would be Lynch's famous book *The Image of the City*.[45] Lynch was interested in finding his way around the city, not getting lost in this man-made environment, and avoiding disorientation. Images of the city offered a sense of identity, well-being, or belonging. They form the basis of our memory systems: they attract attention and make a place memorable, storable in the mind. We associate other ideas with these mental images. Thus the mental image or 'cognitive map' which spectators create as their image of the city can be used to guide subsequent design interventions. If a city was weak in imageability then its urban reformers must address the points where its weaknesses lie.[46]

In the case of either Kepes or Lynch, we are dealing with symbolic logic and computation procedures. Thinking about city form as a logical manipulation of symbols, we focus only on the formal properties of these symbols and the rules by which we can put them together or pull them apart in order to generate good city form — well formed statements following syntactical rules. Thus cognitive mapping establishes an instrumental control over urban space and assumes there are feedback loops from the environment to perceiving man. It implies there is a universal language of normative space allowing comparisons and contrasts to determine how far the image has deviated from good city form. Is it imageable or not? Alienating or supportive?

40] "When unprecedented things confront us, we become disoriented, confuse and shocked. Today, science has made the face of nature alien to us: too much information, too many inventions and an exploded scale of things have made it imperative that we develop a way t map the world's new configurations with our senses ... discover its potentialities for an orderly and secure human life." Gyorgy Kepes, *The New Landscape in Art and Science* Chicago: Paul Theobald & Co 1956, pp. 18–22

41] Kepes, op. cit., p. 229

42] Ibid.

43] Ibid., p. 231

44] Kepes continued: "As the Euclidean geometry was but first approximation in the knowledge of spatial forms, reflecting only a certain limited complex of spatial properties, the traditional forms of visual representation were but the first approximation in sensing the spatial reality. The last hundred years of technological practice has introduced a new, complex visual environment. The contemporary painter's task is to find the way of ordering and measuring this new world. This historical challenge calls him to assimilate the new findings and to develop a new sensibility, a new standard of vision that can release the nervous system to a broader scale of orientation." Gyorgy Kepes, *Language of Vision*, Chicago: Paul Theobald & Co., 1967, p. 67

45] Kevin Lynch, *The Image of the City*, Cambridge: MIT Press, 1960

46] The image must also be flexible (it must be able to change with time, yet respect the past): "Changes, when managed, are meant to lead to more desirable states, or at least to avoid worse ones." Lynch was concerned to maintain some level of per-

Playing with Information **M. Christine Boyer**

The second computational paradigm or information play has different aims. John Huizinga argued in his book, *Homo Ludens* (1950), that play is voluntary activity in which we engage according to rules freely accepted but absolutely binding. Play is freedom, yet it also creates order. It connotes looseness, a lack of closure, and the arbitrariness of symbols.[47] 'In its creative activity, play does not imitate or reflect or correspond or map directly to an outside world, although the resulting order it produces might eventually do so.'[48]

We play with computers as if they are after all mere toys. Computer play generates a profusion of information: the result of human curiosity and exploration, of testing and logic, of imagination and invention, of discovery and application. Furthermore, iterative computer simulations model complexity and chaos. Start with a simple algorithm or a set of rules and repeat them at great speeds, then turn them loose to see what happens as new information is fed back into the algorithm producing startling effects. This form of computer play no longer generates linear predictive ends but new patterns, unpredictable behaviors of complex phenomena, random and chaotic calculation and events.

Hence the iterative capability of computers generates completely novel forms of information.[49] Feedback is essential: as the computer program 'learns' (i.e. takes new information from its environment) it adapts, or changes the situation, altering its properties and structures, sometimes forging completely new orders. At other times, variables in a model are tweaked or toyed with, to see whether transitions into organized complexity might result.[50] Computer modeling, the processing of vast amounts of data, can lead to the discovery of new, emergent properties and structure.[51] The basic assumption behind computer modeling and information play is that it will lead to the discovery of new, emergent properties and structure, those hidden logics invisible to the human eye.

Consequently the metaphor of information processing and complexity theory is gaining explanatory power as it has been applied – without precision – to many emerging and complex adaptive systems, ones that are open-ended, not in a state of equilibrium, and follow the arrow of time.[52] Hence MVRDV used KWC as an emblem of urban complexity, seeing order emerging out of its chaotic behavior. Manuel de Landa states in *A Thousand Years of Nonlinear History* (1997) that the study of urban dynamics requires us to analyze the history of complex physical systems in order to understand the current dynamic state of cities, because we are no longer dealing with energetic equilibrium and linear causality, but with coexisting forms of complexity (static, periodic, and chaotic attractors) and systems that switch from one state to another (a bifurcation), in which minor fluctuations may play immense roles.[53]

In such complex systems, the researcher can no longer focus on planned results but instead must consider the unintended collective consequences of a multitude of human decisions. Since there are emergent properties that take place as the result of interaction between the parts, any hierarchical top-down analysis will fail to

ormance under change and to avoid excessive change: 'Flexible form and action must be coupled with a clear concept of desired performance, and actual performance must be monitored to see how it varies with respect to that standard." Lynch, *What Time is this Place?*, Cambridge: MIT Press, 1972, pp. 190, 200

47] John Huizinga, *Homo Ludens: a study of the play element in culture*, Boston: The Beacon Press, 1950

48] Hobart and Schiffman, op. cit., p. 259

49] Computers model self-organization, or complex adaptive systems that result from the processing of ever-changing information, which returns to them through feedback loops as they adjust and adapt to their surrounding environments. Ibid., p. 237

50] 'Extremely sensitive' to initial conditions means tiny changes in initial conditions can produce divergent results. While 'phase transitions' means sudden transformations of structure or patterns into emergent new order. 'Tweaking or toying' with variables in a model is an investigation to see whether transitions into organized complexity might result

51] Hobart and Schiffman op. cit. *Information Ages*: pp. 248, 259

52] Ibid., p. 2412

capture these emerging properties, which are the result of complex interactions. Taking just one example, De Landa explains how colonization of the New World transformed both Europe and the Americas. By the eighteenth century, towns and cities began to escape the disastrous cycles of famines and epidemics, because not only did they have access to overseas supplies of foods, new 'miracle' crops and better soil management techniques that increased food supplies, but they also had better transportation and communication networks that permitted faster responses to famines. Meanwhile epidemics were controlled by government regulation of sewage and water installations, new compulsory vaccinations and other public health procedures.

Thus by the mid-eighteenth century a threshold was crossed, and Europe moved into a new stable state. Medicine was organized around the hospital, new disciplinary procedures were applied to plague victims and the insane, and to students, workers, prisoners and soldiers. A whole series of sorting devices weeded out the abnormal from the normal. The same disciplinary procedures were applied to animals and plants: new breeding of livestock, new methods of rotating crops, new hybrid plants, and embryonic agribusiness took over the colonies. The result was new levels of population growth, of productivity and consumption, newly affluent societies, new levels of education and leisure activities. Thresholds crossed due to the dynamic interaction of a variety of different variables in the end produced new emergent results.

In order to understand how these ideas have migrated into architectural practice and define an alternative urbanism we have only to look to the project from the Canadian Center for Architecture's 'Design of Cities' competition in New York City in 1999. Here 'emerging' is the operative word: it describes how planning procedures will continuously adapt themselves to their environment or site-specific conditions. The site chosen was the western edge of Manhattan, bounded by 8th Avenue and the Hudson River, between 30th Street and 34th Street. It includes an open railway cut and storage yards for Amtrak, New Jersey Transit and the Long Island Railway. Ben van Berkel and Caroline Bos of UN Studio applied their notion of 'deep planning' to the site: they claim that this procedure 'move[s] away from traditional urban planning processes' and instead 'involves a situation-specific, dynamic, organization structural plan with parameter-based techniques'. Their fascination with 'the emerging global city resides ... in its qualities of mutability and instability':

> Absences, deficiencies and deformations carry a transformational potential ... these emerging architectural and urban organizations reflect qualities that belong to our time, such as vicariousness, transformability and the almost limitless absorption of information. In a sense organization structures emerging in this way can be likened to performance structures as they operate through living forces at physical and public levels ... Structures such as these are no longer seen as the representation of homogeneous, linear systems, but as process fields of materialization. They are scale-less, subject to evolution, expansion, inversion and other contortions and manipulations.[54]

53] Manuel de Landa, *A Thousand Years of Nonlinear History*, New York: Swerve Editions, 1997, pp. 11–22, 149–179

54] UN Studio Van Berkel & Bos Team, *IFCAA PRIZE FOR THE DESIGN OF CITIES 1*, Montreal: CCA, 1999

Note that in one short paragraph, Van Berkel and Bos use 'emerging' three times, searching for unknown properties to employ as the basis of an alternative urbanism or 'critical package' for the global city, including a mixture of scenarios, diagrams, parameters, formulas and themes. The concept 'critical package' is chosen to indicate relational qualities: for any intervention has reverberations on many levels, and therefore in reality always constitutes a package of measures and decisions.[55]

Does this borrowing from the rhetoric of complexity theory present itself as an alternative urbanism?[56] First of all, instead of dividing the city into functional categories based on different land uses such as commercial, residential, and industrial and then imposing a static plan based on Euclidean geometry onto the form of the city, deep planning focuses on modeling information flows through the city of people, uses, objects in shared and leftover territories. There are urban nodes, juncture points, or hybrid spaces where infrastructure and programs come together, where different flows of vehicles, pedestrians, shoppers, tourists, and workers articulate a policy of mobility. Elaborated on the basis of temporal occupation, new types of compartmentalization occur within these nodes or knots, while a new choreography annotates the pattern of these flows.

This dynamic energetic aspect of cities with their vast flows of data inputs can be modeled on the computer as liquefied levels and layered systems in which all kinds of information flow in and out, as parameters constantly change over time. As in the other cases cited above, the set of equations and the appropriateness of their explanatory power remain unknown. Nevertheless, these complex processes are translated into graphic forms; they are successively abstracted, simplified and schematized into informational images. This network architecture, utilizing computer models to combine flows of data with new visualizing techniques, is reminiscent of Marey's instrumental mediation of data flows, which focused on the visible trace of hidden processes, and the notational system employed.

Time-based information becomes potentially structuring when it is visible. Through automated design and animation techniques a deep plan becomes a new abstraction: one that unfolds, proliferates, generates. Extruded to three dimensions it reveals new relations, in which switching between four or five layers becomes possible as combinatorial thinking develops, new concepts emerge, and new forms are imagined. An abstract architectural organization results.

Returning to the subject of how playing with information establishes an alternative urbanism, there is a second change to be considered. Instead of regulatory rules and hierarchical control stemming from zoning ordinances or building codes as city planning normally does, deep planning utilizes 'a network of relations between parameters of program and parameters of site-specific conditions. Control is seen as a relational quality.' Through the search for new forms of ordering principles (not unlike the study of flocking behavior, swarming analysis, and various self-organizing theories), an urban project emerges interactively or recursively. In parameter-based models, variables are

55] UN Studio, op. cit.

56] Ibid.

traced over time: some things are transformed, some things remain constant, and consequently 'the project emerges as if of its own accord.' Data is interactive allowing animation to establish a design path.[57]

Here lies the crux of the matter: since the set of defining equations have yet to be specified, 'deep planning' does not model the underlying forces that determine the disorder and complexity of the city, but allows the animation techniques of computer modeling to generate the design path. We know from film animation, however, that animation fabricates and projects its own illusion, not of life but of visual primacy.[58] The description of an animated figure or diagram is always in the process of being formed or dissolving. It is the line that defines the diagram/cartoon that gives it character, and endlessly changes and transforms its shape.

Hence the third aspect of 'deep planning' as an alternative urbanism is diagrammatic. Think of the slices of a brain scan and how the different parts of the brain in use are colored, then apply this to the performance of materials and how they react to different structural forces. These diagrams make processes visible. New notational schemes develop diagrammatically: like musical notation, choreography, computer flow charts and operating manuals. As Bos and Van Berkel proclaim, "an image is a diagram when it is stronger than its interpretations."[59] These images are not representational but mediated through computer instruments, just as Marey's mechanical instruments mediated what fell outside detection by the human eye.

Conclusion

Does this playing with information, this modeling of processes, produce a radical alternative to urbanism, or merely a new architectural formalism, one that is rather arbitrary and non-methodical? There is, of course, a paradoxical twist in the study of chaos theory applied to mega-cities: how the absence of urban order can be utilized to allow new organizational structures to emerge. And the models remain arbitrary and unspecified in terms of the rules and procedures that might describe how these parameter-based flows of information can be transformed into structural forms. If the analysis stays at the level of diagrams – a notational system for studying flows of data and their effects – we are not talking about re-presentations, pictures or architecture, but about tracings, notations, lines and curves that must be read imaginatively. But when the analysis shifts to display elements of motion that reveal sights undetected by the human eye, patterns emerging from the free play of data, then we have moved into the realm of re-presentations, mediated by new computer modeling, but nevertheless yielding to forms and images.

This cross-categorical translation from graphic notation to the representation of an architectural project is based purely on chance, a 'haphazard leap' or 'arbitrary graft' from notational system to an architectural structure. It is not based on a 1:1 correspondence or methodical translation. Without a set of transformation rules determining what remains constant and what transforms as the designer shifts between

[57] UN Studio (Ben van Berkel and Caroline Bos), op. cit., Vol. 2, *Techniques*, pp. 158–215

[58] Philip Brophy, 'The Animation of Sound', in Alan Cholodenko (ed.), *The Illusion of Life: Essays on Animation*, Sydney: Power Publications, 1991, pp. 67–112

[59] UN Studio (Ben van Berkel and Caroline Bos), op. cit., Vol. 2, *Techniques*, p. 20

media, diagramming as a design language is anecdotal and metaphorical rather than a rational, methodical move.[60]

But let us return to Étienne-Jules Marey for advice and clarification. In 1890, he considered the value of his serial photographs or chronophotographs for illustrators and artists. He knew that his apparatus revealed more than was visible to the naked eye; it brought new pictorial evidence of things in motion, 'positions of visibility' that could only be discerned through the tracings of mediating instruments.[61] His chronophotographs associated movement with a series of static poses as if photographed simultaneously. To understand these chronophotographs the spectator needed to do something with them, for these images appealed to the imagination rather than to the senses. That is, the spectator needed to imagine that he or she could actually see the motion that this series of static poses depicted.[62] Thus it is argued analogically that the mappings, datascapes and diagrams presented here ask the spectator to imagine what aspects of mega-cities in motion the spectator and architect can come to know only through the mediation of computer technology. What invisible aspects do we imagine to emerge, aspects that form the basis of this alternative urbanism?

Epilogue
So let us return to look at the open-ended nature of information play and the emergent properties of the Generic City in *S, M, L, XL*. This book, these projects of OMA, become a data space, a verbal-visual collage of alphabetical dictionary entries running down the margin of pages, juxtaposed with photographs that bleed out to the edge of their pages, and these juxtaposed against written commentary about projects.

Take for example, 'Congestion Without Matter,' OMA's competition project for Parc de la Villette in Paris of 1982. In this *terrain vague* between the greedy needs of the twentieth-century metropolis and the plankton of the suburbs, Koolhaas/OMA designed a program that offered "Density without architecture, a culture of 'invisible' congestion." A series of bird's-eye views in color of Koolhaas' model for Parc de la Villette, lead the viewer into the project. One in particular includes a corner insert of Brandinelli's *Adam and Eve*. Is this a reminder of the Garden of Paradise, from which man and woman have been expelled, never to return? Elia Zenghelis, the co-founder of OMA, wrote: "everything relating to nature, essentially is doomed to disappearance. We are born, we die, we disappear; only ideas, art, the artificial seem to offer some promise of permanence." A few pages later we see dictionary entries along the margin with a double page photographic spread in color of figures standing in an open field in a spiral arrangement. These figures are voters in South Africa photographed by the Associated Press in 1994. On the margins continues the third and fourth entries for 'Lille'. The former explains the various sports fields and walks to be found near the metropolis while the latter describes the site plan of Eurolille as a monster encompassing London, Brussels and Paris. 'Liminal' defines a time and space betwixt and between meaning and action. 'Liquefaction' explains the latest OMA buildings as containers of gel rather than as a series of geological formations or piles. And finally 'Lite City' begins with a drive through Houston.

[ ] Patrik Schumacher, ational in Retrospect: eflections on the logic of tionality in recent design', *A Files* 38, Spring 1999, p. 32–36

[ ] "In representing a movement ... an artist rightly tempts to reproduce a hase, which is visible to the ve. It is usually the preliminary or final phase, which an be best appreciated. hen a machine is in motion, ere are certain parts of it hich are only visible when ey reach their dead points, at is to say, for the brief oment when the direction f movement is changed. And his is also the case with ertain movements in man. ome attitudes are maintained longer than others. ow, chronophotography on xed plates could be used to etermine these positions. ney are recognizable as the nes which have left the ost intense impressions on he sensitized plate – in fact, hose which have had the ongest exposure ... In all possible actions ... there are attitudes which last longer than thers and which may be alled 'positions of visibility.' hronophotography would etermine these with the reatest precision."
.-J. Marey, *Movement*, 1853, . 183. Quoted by Joel ynder, 'Visualization and isibility', in Caroline A. Jones nd Peter Galison (eds), p. cit., pp. 393–394

[2] Ibid., pp. 394–395

These definitions and the photograph appear at least on the surface to be accidental juxtapositions, but even if they are chance encounters, they generate and disseminate meaning of their own. Standing in a line to vote, newly enfranchised South Africans: just an image of people and landscape? Or a reminder of modernism's project, its emancipation from tradition, from the tyranny of history and the Academies, its promise of improvement and reform? Connections and linkages are important but kept open and indeterminate. More bird's-eye views of the model follow, until on page 920 we discover that Houston's urban territory (note that the 'Lite City' dictionary entry was left dangling several pages before in the book) represents an art of erasure or desettlement. It is a less oppressive, less vulnerable kind of urban condition, but one for which 'park' would not be an adequate word, for this 'Lite City' offers catalytic chains and patterns of unpredictable events.

Eventually we arrive at the Initial Hypothesis: Parc de la Villette's program was much too large to create a park, in the recognizable sense of the word. Rather than provide a replica of Nature with some service facilities dotted about it, this park would be an open-ended, constantly changing and adjusting park, reflecting the multiplicity and ambiguity of the dictionary entries that undercut stable and definitive meanings; or like the alphabet when used as an arbitrary encyclopedic order that re-orders the universe as it links words together and arranges them in space.

The park contains an underlying principle of programmatic indeterminacy: how to combine on a given field a series of activities that will interact and set off a chain reaction of new, unpredictable events, like the chain of voters in South Africa? Or how to create a social condenser, an architectural transformer, based on horizontal strips of congestion that constitute the park? The strips that run east-west house the major programmatic elements of the park, while layering creates the maximum length of borders and enables the maximum amount of permeability of each programmatic band. Horizontal strips and vertical entries set up an investigative process: look up a word and consider the information then transfer the data from margins to site. The horizontal and vertical establish the artificial confines of a gridded diagram of space. The grid, the CIAM grille, the graphic notational system, the data space that enabled comparisons to be made on 33 different cities and then facilitated the projection of these comparisons forward onto the homogenized and abstract functional city of Modernity: this is Koolhaas' and OMA's acknowledged patrimony. But Koolhaas' system is less rigid than his modern ancestor's grille – it allows instead for free play.

On top of the grid are layered a network of points and a layer of infrastructure, intended to interact, disorient, blur with and override elements in other layers, just as the page layouts do. The spectator/reader faces two different projects - an alphabetical listing of words and an abstract layering of grids and points - and acknowledges the random play between them. This is not so much a designed landscape as a framework that absorbs a series of potential meanings. And so we return to lists, fragments, associations, and analogies: an ordering of experience performed on a specific frame, determined by the logic of the site, and drawn to experimentation and performance.

But the text, like the strips and layers of Parc de la Villette, shifts meaning about from objective project description to personal anecdote, from random fact to technical detail. It generates a discourse of tension between objects and ground plane, between artifice and nature. It is in the end an encounter, an adventure, a game, and a shifting ground. This data-space begins to 'play with the meaning system' of architecture as art. Seeing architecture as a meaning system that constantly changes sets up a play between past and present forms, establishing ambivalent open-ended conundrums and analogies that make it impossible to assign fixed meanings. This is the basic message behind playing with information – allowing form albeit in an arbitrary and non-methodical manner to emerge from the hidden logics of urban chaos and complexity. This is play at its imaginative best.

Number of inhabitants [p]	3,694,820
Area [km²]	1,215
Density [p/km²]	3,041
Population urbanized (national) [2003]	80%

Los Angeles: Cluster City

Kazys Varnelis

For many, it seems, Los Angeles is the end of the urban line. Condemnations of L.A. are commonpl.a.ce in the contemporary literature on cities, as it has become a synonym for sprawl and the desperate state of the urban itself. The verdict of historian Jon C. Teaford in his *The Twentieth-Century American City* is typical: "By the close of the twentieth century, the 'Los Angelesization' of America was well advanced. The city was lost, and an increasing number of Americans were not even searching for it."[1] But if Los Angeles' influence is pervasive, is it still synonymous with undifferentiated sprawl? Is Los Angeles really the end of the city? Might there still be urban order lurking in the grid?

This essay seeks to address these questions through a more historical reading of the city, marking a distance from the 'L.A. School' of urban geography's spatial approach which currently dominates research on the city and l.a.rgely brackets out the city's historical development.[2] Although the spatial analysis of uneven geographic development allowed an incisive understanding of the plight of the city during the early 1990s it has been less able to expl.a.in the changes in the city during the more recent period of recovery.

That there has been an over-emphasis on geographic analysis at the expense of histori-cal understanding is suggested by the changing nature of the city itself. Until the 1970s, Los Angeles grew through sprawl: constant, diffuse outward expansion into a *tabula rasa* of undeveloped land. By 1990, the city had densified significantly, the amount of land per capita dropping to the point that Los Angeles could arguably already be the densest city in the United States.[3] Ten years later there is virtually no undeveloped land within the Los Angeles Basin. Checked by the lack of suitable development sites and growing commute times, the outward growth of the city has stalled. A recent *USA Today* survey of sprawl in America concluded that between 1990 and 2000, Los Angeles exhibited little new sprawl in comparison to other American cities such as Nashville, Atlanta, or supposedly 'smart growth' Portland, Oregon.[4] Los Angeles is turning in on itself and, in so doing, we have to begin looking at history again, at the conditions already established within the sprawl.[5] It is only by examining the historical development of Los Angeles that we can come to an understanding of its contemporary evolution from field of sprawl to cluster city. Beyond the inherent demands of the subject matter there is also the issue of appropriate ideological viewpoint: in the case of Los Angeles, to ignore history risks colluding in the "history of forgetting" that Norman Klein has identified as a key strategy employed by the ruling ideologists of the city.[6]

To trace a line to the contemporary megalopolis from the beginning of Los Angeles' history seems an unlikely proposition. In response to a perceived threat to its territory in California by the Russians, Spain set up a series of eight missions and three presidios between 1769 and 1777. As the outposts were unable to grow enough food for their needs, the Spanish augmented them with settlements aimed at agricultural production, one of which, founded in 1781, was El Pueblo de la Reina de Los Angeles.

Far from any economic center and lacking any attractive natural resources, the town struggled through first Spanish, then Mexican, and later, American rule. Given the

[1] Jon C. Teaford, *The Twentieth-Century American City* (2nd edn), Baltimore: Johns Hopkins University Press, 1993, p. 152

[2] The seminal text is Edward W. Soja, *Postmodern Geographies: The Reassertion of Space in Critical Social Theory*, London: Verso, 1989

[3] Leon Kolankiewicz and Roy Beck, 'Appendix B. Raw Data for the 100 Largest Urbanized Areas (1970–1990)', in *Weighing Sprawl Factors in Large US Cities*, Arlington, VA: Numbersusa.com, p. 38–41. Online. Available http://www.sprawlcity.org/stu yUSA/index.html. Kolankiewi and Beck point out that although it seems counter-intuitive to argue that Los Angeles is denser than New York City, the reality is that a city's suburbs must be consid ered in judging its degree of density. While Manhattan is far denser than Los Angeles, New York City's suburbs are only 60 percent as dense as those of its west coast coun-terpart. Although the authors caution that Los Angeles is still sprawling, they are using data from the 1990 census whereas the USA Today study mentioned below covers the ten years since then

[4] Haya El Nasser and Paul Overberg, *A Comprehensive Look at Sprawl in America*. Online. Available http://www.usatoday.com/new s/sprawl/main.htm

[5] On the implications of the end of horizontal growth for Los Angeles see William B. Fulton, *Sprawl Hits the Wall. Confronting the Realities of Metropolitan Los Angeles*, Los Angeles: Southern California Studies Center, University of Southern California, 2001

[6] Norman M. Klein, *The History of Forgetting: Los Angeles and the Erasure of Memory*, New York: Verso, 1997

Los Angeles: Cluster City **Kazys Varnelis**

temperate climate, however, Los Angeles grew slowly, eventually becoming the most important agricultural settlement on the Pacific coast. With the discovery of gold in Northern California in 1849, however, the city's fortunes changed. The newly Americanized Los Angeles became a base for suppliers who made a tremendous profit from the prospectors by heavily marking up products brought into Gold Rush territory. The influx of adventurers and the potential for quick wealth generated a dark side to accompany the sunshine: by 1854, L.A. was said to average a homicide a day with a population of less than 3,000. A visiting preacher termed it a 'city of demons.'[7]

Radial city

Real estate investment would soon cancel the city's negative reputation. The completion of the transcontinental railroad to San Francisco in 1868 made the possibilities for Los Angeles apparent. With the 1876 extension of the Southern Pacific line from San Francisco to L.A. establishing an indirect connection from the East Coast followed by the direct line of the Atchison, Topeka and Santa Fe railroad in 1885, rapid access to the city from points east became possible. Uniquely gifted by a climate that stays temperate year round, Los Angeles began to attract migrants fleeing the harsh climates of the Midwestern and the Northeastern United States along with developers eager to sell land to them.

Speculators built up a system of intercity railways following the existing network of footpaths and roadways that linked the city to the other significant southern California settlements: San Diego, Santa Barbara, and San Bernardino. The result was the precondition for Southern California's establishment as one continuous megalopolis. Rather than the traditional pattern of urban growth – with the creation of a dense core that would grow outward – residents inhabited town-like developments, such as Santa Monica, Venice, and Pasadena, located along a pattern of trolley lines radiating from the city center. Thus, the pattern of the city's sprawl and its distinct texture – clusters located along radiating lines – were already established prior to the arrival of the automobile.

Beyond its morphological difference from older cities, Los Angeles swiftly evolved its own ideology of urban growth, combining the promises of progressive urbanism with dollar-driven planning. Together with city government officials, whose elections they bankrolled, developers downplayed the center city, promoting instead the idealized image of Los Angeles as a place in which prairie and city life collapsed into each other and the ideals of the garden city could be realized. A city center catering to commercial and financial needs did of necessity develop, but its existence was taken for granted, the absence of major cultural institutions within it a demonstration of its lack of significance in the collective imagination. Regarding downtown as a necessary evil would later make it poorly suited to a transition to post-industrial cultural and entertainment center in the latter half of the twentieth century.[8]

Demographically, Los Angeles had a composition unique among American cities, a crucial factor in the development of the city. Far from the East Coast immigration terminals

[7] Robert M. Fogelson, *The Fragmented Metropolis: Los Angeles, 1850–1930*, Berkeley: University of California Press, 1993, pp. 5–27.

[8] Ibid., pp. 63–107

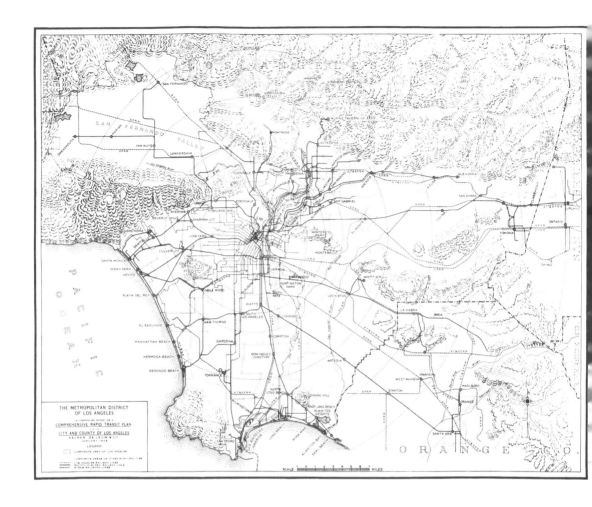

figure 1 The Metropolitan District of Los Angeles, 1925

admitting arrivals from Europe, the city's growth was spurred by relatively affluent families from East coast cities and the Midwestern prairie, where an end-of-the-century increase in food prices gave farmers the ability to buy their way out of agriculture. These new arrivals were either fleeing from, or unused to, the dense urban experience and bustle that typified the early twentieth-century metropolis. Instead of townhouse or tenement living, they wanted detached houses on large plots. The city would be sold to this affluent public through lifestyle marketing. Speculative real-estate developments would often be based on themed life-style ideas: Pasadena became a land of bungalows suggestive of an exotic colonial life of informal luxury; Venice adopted the look of a seaside resort, its streets replaced with canals. Other neighborhoods took on the Spanish Colonial motif and the myth of romantic, leisurely *rancho* life.[9]

The housing typology of the single family house and the desires of the new settlers in Los Angeles came together, encouraging the population of Los Angeles to follow the rails into the countryside and ending the possibility of centralization around a single urban nucleus. The railroads were built by developers not in the first instance as a public transportation system, but rather to serve land speculation. In this, they were successful. With the help of the transcontinental train and the electric streetcar Los

9] Merry Ovnick, *Los Angeles, The End of the Rainbow*, Los Angeles: Balcony Press, 1994, pp. 69–197. On the colonial origins of the bungalow, see Anthony D. King, *The Bungalow: The Production of a Global Culture*, New York: Oxford University Press, 1995

Los Angeles: Cluster City **Kazys Varnelis**

Angeles' population ballooned from under 5,000 to over 320,000 in the forty years after 1870. Once the land tracts were sold off, developers had no interest in maintaining the old streetcar lines. Having served their purpose, these were now a financial drag. Moreover, by limiting development to areas near the lines, the streetcar became an obstruction to continued land development. As automobile ownership rose among the relatively affluent population, they came to see the streetcar lines as a nuisance, and many residents sided with developers to do away with them. Even those who relied on mass transportation put their faith in the bus system's capacity to provide a more flexible and more reliable service. With the streetcar's job done, the car and its more extensive and flexible network supported accelerated expansion. By 1930, the city had grown to 1,240,000 residents.[10]

The city's ban on buildings above 50 meters in height, also greatly encouraged horizontal development. Officially intended to lower the risk from earthquakes, the statute's real purpose was to prohibit Manhattan-like density in the urban core and the drawbacks of a congested city. Following the railway lines and old roads out into the basin, the city developed a radial pattern of boulevards, with main traffic arteries leading from town-like settlements to the central city.

By the 1920s, it became clear that with so many Angelinos commuting to downtown by car, the core was being strangled by congestion. The removal of the trolleys, which frequently broke down and brought gridlock to the streets, was widely seen as a step towards undoing congestion even as it undid future possibilities for mass transportation. The city government turned to freeways as a means of moving people in and out of the city. The result, however, was not so much decongestion as gigantic increase in the territory available for sprawl.[11] Central government of the postwar years supported subsidized mortgages for veterans returning from the war and subsidized the suburb by funding the highway system that made it practical. In Lakewood, for example, as in the more famous East Coast Levittowns, Fordist production techniques were extended to house production. Situated on 3,375 acres of land, Lakewood, the largest single-owner development in the country, would provide 17,200 homes for some 70,000 people, all built by one Louis H. Boyer.[12]

The location of homes further from the city core encouraged various industries – most notably the dominant aerospace and defense sectors – to locate their corporate headquarters and other offices in edge cities on peripheral ring highways. The result was that although the freeways came together at the center, they no longer necessarily led to destinations there. Rather, the center became a hub for the traffic that bypassed it. The congestion that this added to the central area easily undid any benefit the freeways might have brought.

Between 1945 and 2000, downtown's importance steadily decreased as suburban commuters avoided the center, commuting whenever possible from suburb to edge city. After the 1960s, this led to a decrease in Los Angeles' dominant role in Southern California and to massive growth in new postsuburban areas, such as Orange County.

[10] Martin Wachs, 'Autos, Transit and the Sprawl of Los Angeles', Journal of the American Planning Association, 1984, Vol. 50 (3), pp. 297–310.

[11] On the automobile and decongestion, see Scott L. Bottles, Los Angeles and the Automobile: The Making of the Modern City, Berkeley: University of California Press, 1987. Los Angeles' case is far from unique as the seminal study on the American downtown points out, see Robert M. Fogelson, Downtown: Its Rise and Fall, 1880–1950, New Haven: Yale University Press, 2001. On the freeway see David Brodsly, L.A. Freeway, an Appreciative Essay, Berkeley: University of California Press, 1981

[12] Richard W. Longstreth, City Center to Regional Mall: Architecture, the Automobile, and Retailing in Los Angeles, 1920–1950, Cambridge, Mass.: MIT Press, 1997, pp. 335–337

figure 2 Downtown
Los Angeles, the highly-
defensible, preposterously
condensed skyscrapers of
what Mike Davis calls the
City of Quartz.

jure 3 Fortified Housing for
e Elderly in Fairfax, an area
` Los Angeles hit hard by the
992 Riots. More recently, the
anagement has attempted
o lighten the structure's
npression by painting it a
each color

In postsuburbia, daily commutes would be from exurban center to exurban center. The resultant diffuse, horizontal sprawl reconfigured the existing traffic patterns, radically undoing the predictable flow of traffic into and out of the city, in favor of a homogeneous and eventually evenly gridlocked field.[13]

The restructuring of Los Angeles

After a hundred years of positive superlatives, it was perhaps predictable that the backlash against Los Angeles would come in superlatives as well. In the 1960s, the Watts Riots and the Manson Family exposed the hidden fault lines beneath the veneer of suburbia. Only twenty years later, paradise appeared to be lost: the downtown core was becoming depopulated, racial and social tensions were mounting, and with the end of Cold War defense spending in the early 1990s, the seemingly unstoppable Los Angeles economy had run aground.

It was time for theory. The theorists of the L.A. School saw Los Angeles' plight not as a strange exception to urban development but rather as a model of a global restructuring of society and economy. Having begun in the early 1970s, this transition from Fordist mass production to Post-Fordist flexible production reached a crisis point in the 1980s. Its processes, as the L.A. School argued, were visible more clearly in Los Angeles than in any other city.

3] Rob Kling, Spencer Olin,
nd Mark Poster, *Postsuburban
California: The Transformation
f Orange County*, Berkeley:
Jniversity of California Press,
995

4] A summation of the L.A.
school's origins and positions
an be found in Marco
Cenzatti, *Los Angeles and the
.A. School: Postmodernism
ınd Urban Studies*, Los
ıngeles: Los Angeles Forum
or Architecture and Urban
Design, 1993, pp. 5—7

The effects of restructuring on L.A. were perhaps best summed up in Mike Davis's depiction of Los Angeles as the City of Quartz. Davis described a city composed of a heavily fortified city core of 'quartz' skyscrapers, a ring of intense poverty, a series of gated communities on the edge, and a minority population quite literally imprisoned. Davis's main rival, Ed Soja, also saw a massive polarization giving shape to the city but insisted that downtown had been eclipsed by 'Exopolis', or Orange County, and the other communities that had grown up on the periphery of L.A. And whereas Davis had advocated an historical understanding of the city to explain the persistence of darkness beneath the sunshine, Soja urged a more thoroughly spatial understanding that largely avoided history.[14]

figure 4 Development at its
Limits, Pacific Palisades.
Further expansion into the
Santa Monica Mountains is
unlikely because of topo-
graphic conditions, fire danger, and the protection of
unbuilt spaces in wilderness
areas

figure 5 The ocean and the
mountains act as natural
boundaries for Los Angeles as
shown in this computer
reconstruction of the terrain
from satellite imagery.
Vertical relief is exaggerated

If analytically sophisticated, the L.A. School's practical contribution to reshaping the city has been limited. This is partly the result of the L.A. School's approach, which is more analytical and critical than interventionist and partly the result of a new, 'post-political' condition emerging in the city that has made significant planning initiative more difficult. By the 1980s, fractionalization in Los Angeles politics led to a political stalemate that resists any significant new urban interventions. Virtually all the build-able land in the basin was spoken for. With the landscape atomized and under individual control and with the rise of strong neighborhood organizations, expert in the art of endless delays and ceaseless appeals, major urban projects became largely impossible in the basin.[15]

The 1992 riots and 1994 Northridge Earthquake validated the L.A. School's predictions, but they also marked the end of its relevance. Unable to propose any intervention and unable to offer any insight into the recovery of the late 1990s, the L.A. School seems spent, the fatalism of its program having inevitably undermined it.

Cluster city

What then of Los Angeles today and in the near future? Between 2000 and 2015, nearly 2 million people are expected to come to the county, swelling its population from 9.8 million to 11.5 million while the region of Southern California grows from 17 million to 20 million, the equivalent of adding a city the size of Chicago to the area.[16]

Few today put their faith in the construction of more infrastructural solutions. Already by the 1970s, it had become apparent that freeways were adding to the region's traffic problems by encouraging ever-more-distant development. The traditional solution of building more freeways had, in turn, become obsolete in the face of resistance from neighborhood groups and the collapse of big government. New highways are unlikely to be built again in the basin. From now on, the existing freeways will only fill, the coming gridlock accompanied by yet more densification in what is probably already America's densest city.[17]

15] See Mike Davis,
'Homegrown Revolution,' in
City of Quartz, op. cit,
pp.153–219 and William B.
Fulton, The Reluctant
Metropolis: The Politics of
Urban Growth in Los Angeles,
Point Arena, CA: Solano Press
Books, 1997

16] Southern California
Association of Governments,
2001 RTP Social Economic
Forecast Report. Online.
Available at:
http://www.scag.ca.gov/growt
hforecast/gf_report.pdf

Los Angeles: Cluster City **Kazys Varnelis**

Figure 6 Gridlock on the Harbor Freeway, Downtown Los Angeles

Figure 7 The most stringent air pollution laws in the world now allow downtown Los Angeles's skyscrapers to be visible from miles away most days of the year. Note the haze remaining beyond

[17] While growth from 1960 to 1980 was dominantly suburban – adding population beyond the periphery in Riverside, San Bernardino, and Ventura Counties, on the metropolitan periphery, the period from 1980–2000 saw a substantial increase in growth in Los Angeles County, see Fulton and USC, op. cit. p. 11

[18] Mike Davis, Ecology Of Fear: Los Angeles And The Imagination Of Disaster, New York: Vintage Books, 1999

[19] Anthony Downs and Brookings Institution, Stuck in Traffic: Coping with Peak-Hour Traffic Congestion, Washington, D.C.: Brookings Institution; Lincoln Institute of Land Policy, 1992, pp. 27–31

[20] United States Government, Federal Transit Administration, Department of Transportation. Online. Available at: http://www.fta.dot.gov/brt/pr ojects/losangeles.html

While Mike Davis's prediction of Los Angeles' slow death due to ecological disaster coupled with ethnic and class strife is still plausible, the continued advantages of L.A. – temperate weather, the presence of Hollywood, its role on the Pacific Rim – will more than likely counterbalance the negatives.[18] Both air pollution and crime fell dramatically in the 1990s while growing population diversity meant a more interesting, increasingly global city.

That L.A. would flourish or at least continue to function is ultimately a more interesting proposition for urban studies as it points to a possible road out of or beyond sprawl. And, for all the interest in 'solving' sprawl, it seems that new political realities dictate that any solution, however provisional or partial, must come not from the top but from a bottom-up restructuring of communities.

If political stalemate encourages the clusterization of Los Angeles, so too does the gridlocked condition of the freeways. Increasingly, based on empirical observations and technical analyses, transportation planning theorists are coming to understand that once gridlock emerges in infrastructure, individuals respond by traveling earlier or later, using other routes and modes of transportation, or avoiding travel entirely. If more infrastructure is built, they will expand their commutes until gridlock occurs again to once again dissuade them. The result is a new pragmatic acceptance of gridlock as an unavoidable factor, shifting planning concerns away from infrastructural solutions toward solutions in behavior modification and intelligent systems.[19] The new MetroRapid bus system is a successful example of this. Introduced in 2001 on two routes at the cost of a mere $8 million, MetroRapid buses have more limited stops than regular busses and contain transponders that control traffic lights as they approach intersections. The result is a system that can operate some 25 percent faster, often as fast or faster than the subway on trips of under five miles. Over the next twenty-five years, the city transit authority plans to add some twenty-two more MetroRapid lines.[20]

Behind such 'smart' solutions is the acknowledgement that increasing congestion within the Los Angeles Basin will not be overcome. The likely outcome is that the postsuburban periphery will be transformed towards a cluster-based network urbanism.[21] The diffuse field of postsuburbia will give way to a polynucleated field of clusters which will also be linked virtually by an informational infrastructure. Rather than functioning simply as centers to commute to, these clusters will become places with stronger local networks, within which one commutes short distances, often by foot or mass transit. While their geographic morphology will be based on the historical clusters and linear traffic patterns that emerged during the first wave of real estate speculation, they will also be inflected by newer demographic developments.

The most important demographic developments that will affect and reinforce this cluster city are the ethnic reconfiguration of the basin and the splintering of populace. If Los Angeles was once a relatively homogeneous white city, divided only by income, today it has become something quite different. The diffuse and homogeneous sociological texture of Los Angeles has been replaced by a community of virtually unprecedented diversity. Although the grain of such diversity has until now been large scale, with ethnic groups isolated from each other, population pressures appear likely to couple with the reduction of commutable distances to encourage diversity at a smaller scale.

Throughout history, the notion of the urban has been based on the idea of a fixed place and an idea of a unified public or *polis*. Into the 1960s, this was embodied by the idea of the mass market in which consumers would live with others like them, owning a suburban house, a dishwasher and pool, two cars, 2.3 children, and a dog. Splintered by flexible consumption and migration, such a mass market no longer exists.[22]

Nowhere, however, does a mass market exist less than in Los Angeles, a city of ethnic minorities. While non-Hispanic Whites represented 76 percent of the population in 1970, the proportion had dropped to 50 percent in 1990 and is under 30 percent today. Meanwhile, Los Angeles is the sixth largest Hispanic city in the world, the world's second largest city of both Koreans and Armenians, the second largest Chinese city outside of Asia, the second largest Japanese city outside of Japan, and even contains the largest number of British expatriates of any city outside the Commonwealth. Multiple ethnic communities have reshaped the demographics of a city that had formerly depicted itself as lily-white American. Demographically as well as physically, Los Angeles has become a city of peripheries without a center.[23]

The L.A. School was quick to identify the new ethnic communities in Los Angeles, locating future urban tensions in the conflicts between these often-incompatible groups. Over the last ten years, however, the situation has grown yet more complex. Exposed to the post-Fordist market, minorities, both ethnic and white, have fragmented into smaller groups with their own interests, agendas, and ideologies. The rise of flexible consumption and the dwindling of traditional institutions under modernity have made the creation of the self a conscious project; the articulation of difference has replaced the articulation of sameness as the preoccupation of the individual in search of identity.[24]

Although a developing body of writing in sociology has begun to address these issues, a significant geographic analysis of this new condition in the city emerges from the

21] See Fulton and USC, op. cit.

22] This, of course, is a central aspect of post-Fordist society. See Harvey, op. cit.

23] See James Paul Allen, Eugene Turner and California State University, Northridge, Center for Geographical Studies, *The Ethnic Quilt: Population Diversity in Southern California*, Northridge, Calif.: The Center for Geographical Studies California State University, Northridge, 1997

24] On the new, 'reflexive' subject see Scott Lash and John Urry, *Economies of Signs and Space, Theory, Culture & Society*, London; Thousand Oaks, Calif.: Sage, 1994 and Anthony Giddens, *Modernity and Self-Identity: Self and Society in the Late Modern Age*, Cambridge, UK: Polity Press in association with B. Blackwell Oxford, 1991

25] Michael J. Weiss, *The Clustered World: How we Live, What we Buy, and What it all Means About Who we Are*, Boston: Little Brown, 2000, pp. 10–11

Los Angeles: Cluster City **Kazys Varnelis**

market itself. In his book *The Clustered World,* Michael J. Weiss describes the new 'geode-mographic' approach marketers use to understand the contemporary cultural landscape. With the end of mass consumption, top-down marketing strategies aimed at a centered subject have given way to a demographically targeted approach. To this end, over the last thirty years, the Claritas Corporation has developed the PRIZM method to break down the United States into distinct demographic clusters based on age, ethnicity, wealth, urban-ization, housing style, and family structure. Fragmentation of the population is increasing over time: during the 1970s and 1980s, Claritas identified forty clusters in society, by the 1990s, greater diversification from immigration, economic changes, and greater choice in lifestyle led Claritas to identify sixty-two distinct demographic clusters.[25] By 2003, the sixty-two clusters had fractured further, into sixty-eight.

PRIZM serves as a way of identifying, understanding, and targeting consumers down to the individual city blocks, allowing marketers to understand the evolution of differences geographically. The result, Weiss explains, is a revolution in thinking about society: "Forget sex. Forget race, national origin, age, household composition, and wealth. The characteristic that defines and separates Americans more than any other is the clus-ter."[26] No longer is a city composed of solid blocks of ethnic and economic groups. Rising consumerism and demographic fragmentation efface many of those traditional differences as they create new differences. Thus, for example, claims for a unified Hispanic minority disintegrate in the face this demonstration that Hispanics now break down into some eighteen clusters.[27] According to this research, the United States is composed of a landscape of radically small minorities, the largest comprising a mere 3.0 percent of the American population. A politics of group identity and an urbanism of the masses seem to be becoming increasingly untenable options.

PRIZM's demographic clusters are not in the first instance tied to any one large geo-graphic area, but rather exist in a network. Today's new tribes are widely dispersed nationally and globally, connected by telecommunications.[28] On a local scale, people live next to people they like, in neighborhoods they like. Demographic clusters settle into geographic locations based on a variety of factors: historical precedent, housing types, educational possibilities, opportunities for work, retail choices, cost of living, and the presence of like minded people. Moreover, given their status as radically small minorities, clusters rarely dominate an area thoroughly, but rather co-exist with other clusters.[29]

Not only do individuals cluster, businesses cluster also. Face-to-face networking is a constituent part of what Manuel Castells calls "the network economy."[30] Financial institutions tend to be located together, companies serving Hollywood's movie studios group together, and so forth, not only globally but also within a given urban region. The strong inter-relatedness of businesses and infrastructures (be they the port of Los Angeles or fiber-optic cable under Wilshire Boulevard) establishes powerful clustering effects, strongly influenced as well by commuting distances and patterns.[31]

[26] Ibid., p. 178.

[27] Ibid., pp. 30–31. On an example of the resulting hybridity, see David Lott, "The Wizards of Moz; for the Many Latino Fans of the Enigmatic Morrissey, Jose Maldonado and the Sweet and Tender Hooligans are a Lifeline to Their Hero," *The Los Angeles Times,* 19 November, 2000, p. 1

[28] This argument is suppor-ted in Manuel Castells, *The Rise of the Network Society,* Cambridge, Mass.: Blackwell Publishers, 1996

[29] Weiss, op. cit. pp. 24–25

[30] Castells, op. cit. pp. 384–386

[31] S. Graham and S. Marvin, *Telecommunications and the City: Electronic Spaces, Urban Places,* London; New York: Routledge, 1996

Case studies

This essay concludes with three case studies of such clusters developing in Los Angeles. Together, these demonstrate potential models for the densification of the city. The first is Conjunctive Points, a cluster identified by a city design strategy, the second is Wilshire Center, where an abandoned infrastructure led internet startups to cluster together and where cultural hybridity is leading to unexpected results, and the third is downtown Los Angeles, where an existing infrastructural and architectural conditions are leading to very different uses in the center city.

In the first example, Conjunctive Points, developers Frederick and Laurie Smith are pursuing their own strategy of cluster urbanism, attracting creative tenants through careful planning and the architectural design of Eric Owen Moss. In 1987, Frederick Smith inherited a few industrial buildings in the deteriorating 57-acre industrial area of Culver City known as the Hayden Tract. Smith, together with his wife Laurie, decided that the key to successful redevelopment would be the invention of a physical identity capable of drawing in high-tech entertainment industry firms. The Smiths believed that radical architecture would appeal to those firms, given their cutting-edge self-image and the futuristic work that they undertake. Initially, Moss made interventions into these buildings, leaving the vast internal spaces free but adding elements of unique, sculptural design. Over time, Smith augmented these with further renovations and new structures dispersed throughout the area.[32] With Moss's buildings receiving worldwide attention, the area now has an avant-garde prestige and Smith's strategy has proven successful, with area rents increasing some 500 percent. By 2001, it was clear that the center of gravity for creative industries had shifted south and east as a result. Los Angeles' pattern of real estate development that had previously always moved westward from the core.[33]

With the project demonstrating its economic success, Moss and the Smiths found city officials were willing to listen to their ideas, even when it meant radical changes in zoning laws. Thus, the building height limit has been raised from 15 to 70 meters, a move that will allow the construction of two skyscrapers, and changes have been made in parking regulations, open space requirements, and permissions for allowable use.

figure 8 Guthrie + Buresh, Live/Work House, 1996

figure 9 Conjunctive points, Culver City

[32] The strategies employed by the Smiths and Moss fit into the models described in Bert Mulder, 'The Creative City or Redesigning Society,' and Justin O'Connor, 'Popular Culture, Reflexivity and Urban Change' Jan Verwijnen and Panu Lehtovuori (eds), *Creative Cities. Cultural Industries, Urban Development and the Information Society,* Helsinki: UIAH Publications, 1999, pp. 60–75, 76–100

[33] Morris Newman, 'Creative Tenants Making Culver City Fashionable; Ad Agencies, Dot-Coms and Film Companies are Snapping Up Industrial Buildings in Once-Drab Hayden Tract,' *Los Angeles Times,* 21 August, 2001

gure 10 Traffic in Wilshire
enter, an area largely
eserted only five years ago

Moss sees master-planned zoning as inevitably leading to a homogeneity of design and thus to homogeneity of identity. In opposition to this, his vision of Conjunctive Points treats it as an 'Architectural Free Zone' in which design will be unencumbered by such rules. To lend the area broader coherence, he proposes The Palindrome, in which a 1,600 meter-long, 15-meter-wide right of way, originally used by a railroad, will be remade into a park with the potential for having mixed-use office and retail spaces floated above it.

The second example of re-densification and development is taking place along a stretch of Wilshire Boulevard west of downtown. Extending from Alvarado to Wilton boulevards, the area known as Wilshire Center was initially zoned for multi-story residential units and developed large and elegant apartment buildings as a result. By the 1920s, however, motorists had discovered that the width of Wilshire and its lack of a trolley line made it the quickest route to reach downtown from points west. The resulting traffic made the street unattractive for residential purposes while encouraging its commercial development. The speculative apartment buildings lost value and began a slow decline. Continued congestion of downtown in the 1950s led to a revival of Wilshire Center as a business center, with back offices for banks, insurance company offices, law offices, county agencies, and other large bureaucratic organizations moving in. Though located within the central urban texture of Los Angeles, Wilshire Center essentially functioned as a prototype edge city and over twenty office buildings were built in the

4] On edge cities, see Joel
Garreau, *Edge City: Life on the
New Frontier*, New York:
Doubleday, 1991

Kazys Varnelis Los Angeles: Cluster City   **187**

figure 11 Aroma Wilshire
Center. Built for and by
Koreans, this structure
symbolizes the modernity of
Korea and Koreatown,
containing an exclusive
health club and a typical
Korean golf driving range
enclosed by a net

area between 1966 and 1976.[34] By the 1970s, however, decline began again as tenants drifted westward to newer, more attractive office space in west Los Angeles. Mexican and El Salvadoran immigrants moved into the increasingly dilapidated residences and Koreans took over retail functions in the area. As the level of poverty increased, the area became less well-maintained and crime rose culminating in heavy damage during the Rodney King riots in 1992. Remaining businesses took flight. With offices empty and streets deserted, recovery seemed so improbable Mike Davis called it "the modern high-rise ghost town."[35]

Defying that bitter end, however, the area has revived dramatically in the last few years due to the presence of an invisible factor: the existing telecommunications infrastructure.[36] In the late 1980s, expecting that the offices in the area would continue to be viable, Pacific Bell laid down a fiber optic trunk line, creating a three-mile loop from Norton Avenue to Coronado Street and equipping some thirty buildings with fiber optic links. Following the mass exodus of businesses, however, the fiber lay virtually unused. In addition to inexpensive office rents, the low cost, high bandwidth pipes lured in telecommunications and new media companies. The latter found the location of the area, not far from Hollywood an added bonus.[37] Office vacancy rates plummeted from 35 percent in 1994 to 14 percent in 2000.[38] The apartment buildings have also benefited from this trend, their retro elegance appealing to young professionals who work in the new services companies, as well as to aspiring movie stars.[39]

35] Davis, op. cit., pp. 375–37?

36] On the adaptation and
reuse of existing infrastructures for new purposes and
on the role of city centers in
development of telematics-
rich areas, see Graham and
Marvin, op. cit., pp. 290,
323–324

37] Nola L. Sarkisian,
'Mid-Wilshire Making a
Comeback; Fiber-Optic Cable
Line Lures Internet
Companies to Area,' Los
Angeles Business Journal.
Vol. 21 (39), September 1999
p. 1

38] Laura B. Benko, 'Low
Rents, Cable Lines are Luring
Many Tenants,' Los Angeles
Business Journal. Vol. 21 (43),
October 1999, p. 53. Margot
Carmichael Lester, 'Market
Emerging as Popular
Alternative for Telco Deals,'
Los Angeles Business Journal,
Vol. 23 (5), January 29,
2001, p. 41.

39] John Grimmett 'Jewels in
the Rough: Apartments from
Hollywood's Golden Age are
Restored in Wilshire Center,'
Los Angeles Downtown News,
21 October, 2000, p. 1

Los Angeles: Cluster City **Kazys Varnelis**

Figure 12 The SBC/Pacbell Central Office at 400 S. Grand, the central office for Los Angeles's telephone system

Figure 13 One Wilshire, Telecommunications Hub for the Pacific Rim

Figure 14 Fiber Opticlines running into One Wilshire

Overlaying and reinforcing this recovery is Wilshire's central role in Los Angeles' Koreatown. New investors with Korean ties have purchased property in the area, with Dr. David Lee, a Korean American internist from the San Fernando Valley, controlling some fifteen buildings or 45 percent of the market's total floor space.[40] Negotiating coexistence between the high-tech service firms and the Korean community has been delicately handled: in efforts to discourage the idea that the area excludes non-Koreans, the community decided to limit the amount of Korean characters in signage and to refer to it as Wilshire Center. The most important symbol of the resurgence of the area is a $35 million spa, mall, fitness and exercise complex called Aroma Wilshire Center. Developed by Hanil Cement Company, a major Korean construction firm, Aroma Wilshire Center implants Korean 'member culture' into Los Angeles, creating an exclusive environment for the Korean American elite. Lifetime memberships cost some $22,000.[41] Although built by the rich for the rich, Aroma Wilshire Center serves not only as an icon for the area – topped by a gigantic video screen for advertising – it symbolizes the resurgence of the neighborhood as both a Korean American cultural community and as a high tech center, celebrating Korean economic success in America.

The third case study is the clusterization of downtown Los Angeles. As has already been mentioned, the city's core has been in a state of decline for at least half a century. As with Koreatown, the recession of the early 90s following the Rodney King riots pushed the downtown core into a condition of outright collapse, leading to nearly 30 percent vacancy rates in the area.

As with Wilshire Center, existing infrastructural advantages led to the emergence of a high-tech cluster in the area. Seeking to bring long distance telephone communications

[40] Sarkisian, op. cit.

[41] Roger Vincent, 'Luxury Spa to Open its Doors to Wealthy in Koreatown,' Los Angeles Times, 18 June, 2001

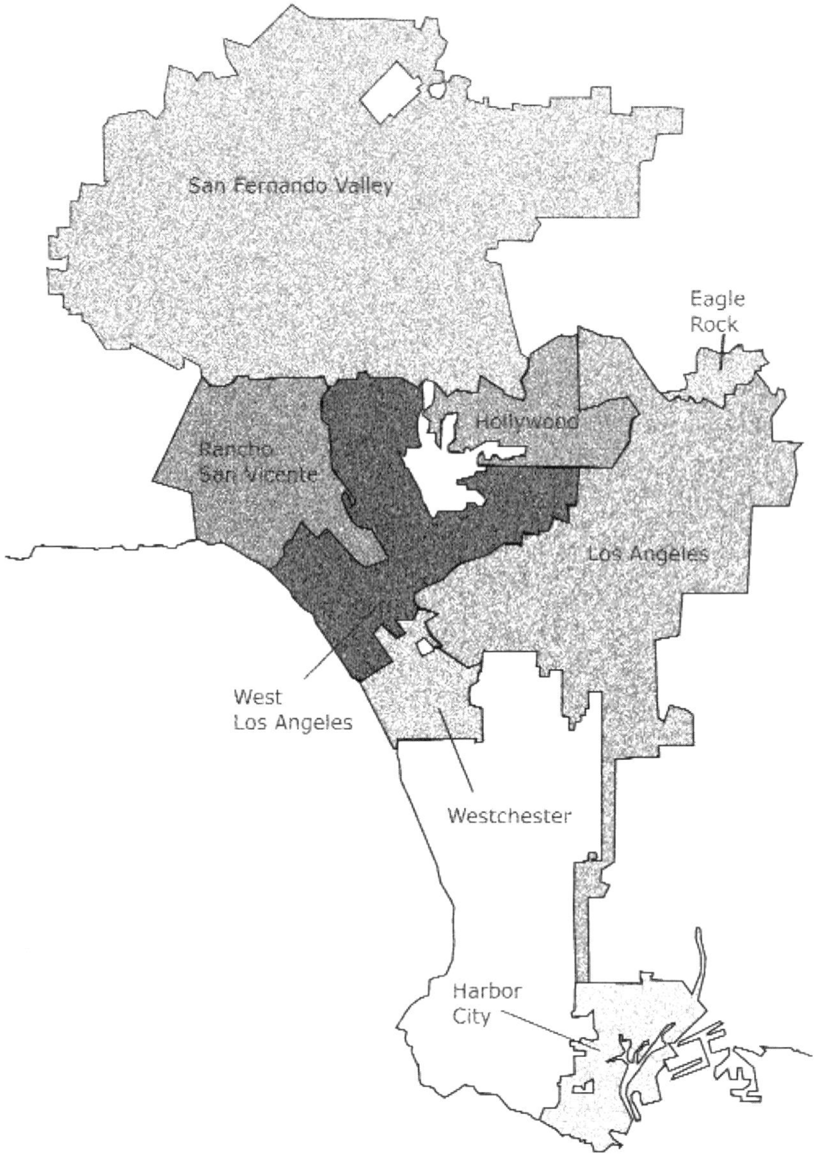

figure 15 Map showing proposed secession areas from Los Angeles

San Fernando Valley

Eagle Rock

Hollywood

Rancho San Vicente

Los Angeles

West Los Angeles

Westchester

Harbor City

into the city core where the city's central telephone station was, telecom firm MCI mounted a rooftop microwave station on the modernist tower at One Wilshire, at the time one of the tallest buildings in downtown.[42] Fiber optic networks were connected into the tower to connect with the microwave lines and as fiber's networks grew, the confluence of lines at one point became more and more influential. The building's management devoted the fourth floor of the structure to a "Meet-Me Room" in which telecoms could freely interconnect. Following congressional deregulation of local telephone services in 1996 and the internet explosion of the mid and late 1990s, telephone, data, and networking companies found this ability to make private peer-to-peer connections crucial. The proximity to such a fiber network has led telecoms and networking companies to locate in One Wilshire or in existing office buildings in the area. Some thirteen buildings, vacant since corporations departed for the skyscrapers built in down-

42] Peter F. Hartz, 'L.A.'s Telecom Hotel. Downtown High-Rise is information Superhighway's Grand Junction', L.A. Weekly, 10–16 September, 1999

Los Angeles: Cluster City **Kazys Varnelis**

town's Bunker Hill in the 1980s or to West Los Angeles, now began to fill as telecom hotels. In the space of two years, one such building's occupancy rose from 30 percent to 91 percent.

A highly publicized downside of these telecom hotels is that circuitry and equipment does not demand a substantial employee presence. There may nevertheless be a benefit to this occupation of the city by stealth. While adding to property values and tax rolls in the area, allowing necessary maintenance of the hard infrastructure, the data hotels do not increase congestion on the streets. Jack Kyser, the chief economist for the Los Angeles Economic Development Corporation suggests that the promise of access to this massive concentration of infrastructure will lead companies, especially multimedia entertainment companies reliant on high-capacity digital networks, to move in.[43]

In the old structures of downtown's former Banking District, too far east of the central switching station to be viable as data hotels, developers are creating loft spaces for residents interested in a more typically urban living experience. Just as Moss's cutting edge architecture in the Hayden Tract underscores the cutting edge nature of the work being done there, downtown's historic architecture and gritty character appeals to creative professionals seeking a dose of urban chic. Perhaps nostalgically repeating the experience of the urban pioneers in New York's SOHO and other revived city core areas of the last forty years, these new inhabitants have to brave a city core that lacks many typical amenities such as supermarkets, shopping possibilities and night time activities. The high ceilings and unobstructed spaces within downtown's loft buildings makes them appealing to creative professionals, who frequently live and work in the same space. Avoiding rush hour, downtown's residents are able to take advantage of the ring of freeways to commute to other areas in Los Angeles and the San Fernando Valley relatively swiftly. If the predictions of the Los Angeles Downtown Center Business Improvement District come true, the area will experience even more rapid growth in the near future, its 12,600 residential units growing to over 18,000 by 2004.[44]

[43] Stephen Gregory, 'Telecom Boom Revives Declining Neighborhood; Growing Industry Concentrates Local Network Operations in Downtown L.A. Hub. But Few Workers Accompany the Facilities,' *The Los Angeles Times*, 17 November, 1998

[44] Karen Lindell, 'As More of L.A.'s Historical Buildings are Converted to Residential Units, People are Leaving the Sprawl of Suburbia for the Diverse and Vibrant Heart of Downtown,' *The Los Angeles Times*, 4 March, 2001

As these case studies demonstrate, faced by an end condition of sprawl and postsuburbia, Los Angeles has begun to transform into cluster city, congealing into centers and nodes within a formerly diffuse field. As we investigate the future growth of this city, we need to take account of the inherent demands of this condition, keeping one eye on the conscious shaping of identity in an era when not only the mass market but also traditional minorities are being atomized by processes of continuous diversification, and the other toward history and spatial structures left over from the past, for it is often on the deformations in the spatial field, often invisible and infrastructural to our conventional statistical and sociological viewpoints, that the clusters seem to congeal.

Postscript: November 2003

In 2002, the city was almost torn in half by a measure that would have allowed the San Fernando Valley with a resident population of 1.3 million to secede. Advocates of secession believed it would lead to lower taxes, better representation, improved governmental efficiency and services, and a more equitable distribution of funds. Critics argued that the Valley would most likely be followed in secession by Hollywood and the Harbor area, dramatically shrinking the city and stripping it of vital industries. Moreover, residents of wealthy West L.A. and Venice proposed seceding as did groups in the Echo Park, Silver Lake, and Eagle Rock neighborhoods. The remaining city would have been reduced in the main to ghettoized communities of poor Latinos and African Americans and surrounded by a ring of affluent and independent suburbs.

In fairness, however, the Valley itself is increasingly Latino, it would hardly have been a return to a version of the Los Angeles of old. Minority communities both there and in the city at large often supported secession, arguing that smaller cities would be more responsive to their needs. The failure of the measure, however, proved that clusterization could coexist with a broader collective metropolitan identity. Los Angeles as a single urban entity still remained attractive to the voter.

In the last weeks of October 2003, however, the darker side of clusterization re-emerged. The long-awaited Disney Concert Hall designed by local architect Frank Gehry was depicted in the press as the jewel in the crown of downtown L.A. as a revived center of culture. Day after day, Angelinos were treated to live radio and television coverage of the opening festivities in the city core. As this was taking place, however, downtown's boosterists joined the rest of the city to watch in horror as the largest wildfires in the history of the state swept the periphery of the city, burning thousands of homes and hundreds of thousands of acres of woodland. The city core was choked in smoke and in the early afternoon the stainless steel façade of the concert hall was bathed in the red light of the obscured sun. Angelinos were warned to avoid exercising outdoors and to stay indoors with windows closed whenever possible.

It is a mistake to think that the banal, prefabricated suburban homes built in ecologically sensitive areas were somehow part of a different reality to what was happening downtown. In fact the two events were intimately linked. The construction of Disney Concert Hall was made possible through the intervention of billionaire Eli Broad. Known as the 'King of Sprawl', a founder of Kaufman Broad (now KB) Homes, Broad made his riches by building more cut-rate homes in suburban America between the late 1950s and 1980s than anyone else. Over the last twenty years, Broad increasingly withdrew from home-building, managing instead a large insurance firm and promoting real estate investment in downtown. But this was no moral retraction. On the contrary, for Broad the home-building market had become too risky for investment. Although it would be easy to see his public beneficence downtown as penance, akin to the building of cathedrals by barons to justify the pillaging of the surrounding countryside, Broad insists that this is not the case. For him both suburban sprawl and the culture core downtown are appropriate reactions to the local condition.[45]

45] Mark Arax, 'Convention is Just an Introduction to Eli Broad's vision of Downtown; Once the King of Sprawl, Billionaire Turns his Sights to Reviving the City's Heart', *The Los Angeles Times*, 6 August, 2000

Disconnected from the field of sprawl they punctuate, the monuments of L.A.'s new downtown serve as an *alibi*, promoting the idea of am urban environment even as they draw attention away from the realities of everyday life in the city and its increasing banality, unaffordability and unsustainability. Only by confronting the realities of the broader condition of post-sprawl Los Angeles while understanding the consequences of clusterization, will the city be able to address its own reform.

Number of inhabitants [p]	736,045
Area [km²]	219
Density [p/km²]	3,361
Population urbanized (national) [2003]	66%

Amsterdam: Beyond Inside and Out
Stephen Read

A connected city

Amsterdam grew as a trading city, connected to the world, infected with the accents and attitudes of faraway places and stimulated by the friction between the parochial and the exotic. At a time we sometimes imagine to have been firmly fixed in place; contained within walls, and between town hall and church spire – it already occupied a position at the intersection of networks of commerce extending way out into Europe and the rest of the world. Amsterdam in the sixteenth and seventeenth centuries was a bustling center of dealing and bargaining: prosperous, expanding rapidly, regularly bursting through and remaking its outer walls. Its streets and quays were alive with an abrasive mix of merchants and shippers, shipbuilders and fishers, bankers and middlemen, rubbing shoulders with a motley collection of economic migrants, itinerants and refugees from less hard-headedly broad-minded attitudes and mores. This was no sleepy village; the foreigner and stranger were commonplace in its streets and coffee shops. But at the same time Amsterdam was a city of citizens and of neighborhoods, inhabited by people linked by a sense of common identity and with a sense of belonging in its streets and squares.

In the eighteenth century Amsterdam experienced an extraordinary reversal. Like Rip Van Winkle, it fell asleep (at least as a significant continental and global player), and arrived at the end of the nineteenth century only just beginning to spill again out of its seventeenth-century walls. Dutch cities missed a great many of the changes experienced by other European centers as a result of the Industrial Revolution. In Amsterdam today there is no typical central business district; the concentration of power to the center experienced by Paris and London, for example, with their radial spreads of workers' and middle-class districts, happened in a much more limited way. Instead, the twentieth century arrived in a city just waking from a long winter of economic stagnation, with its seventeenth-century plan, its residential character, and even its architecture, rather shabby and threadbare but substantially intact. First the welfare state with its state-sponsored housing, and then infrastructure and the explosion of mobility with the drift to the periphery, were the shapers of the further expansion of the city. In between, in the second half of the twentieth century, Amsterdam, despite its small size and population, and despite (or perhaps because of) a paradoxical urban decline linked to global economics, played a central part in the emergence of a global urban culture. It was a center of the popular urban radicalism that emerged in the 1960s and it contributed the Provos, the Kabouters and the New Babylon to the story of the emergence of 'the urban' as a 'question'. It also generated a huge folklore around its involvement in the 'permissive', the hippie and pop cultures,[1] from which it still lives as a youth tourist destination today.

Amsterdam itself remains very substantially a residential city; its politics to a very significant extent, even today, focused on the struggle to maintain the center as a liveable and (barely) affordable living environment.

[1] See G. Mak, *Amsterdam: A brief Life of the City*, London: Harvill Press, 1999

Amsterdam: Beyond Inside and Out **Stephen Read**

Located in the networks

The city occupies a strange position between the world 'out there' and the world in our heads.[2] Its materiality is incontestable, as is the way it presents itself as a visual scenery of types and styles of buildings, standing apart from and looking over the lived flux of the city and its processes. At the same time, however, this physical thing indexes and orders the world of our everyday actions and social interactions so pervasively that it is difficult to separate it from the lives we live and the structures we recognize as 'community' or 'society' or whatever. Beyond its material surfaces, beyond the object we stand apart from and observe, lies a city we understand rather more sensuously and immediately as an underpinning for something else. Here is a city we experience and recognize, like the background awareness we have of the positions of our limbs, through the shapes, sequences and rhythms of our actions and interactions, and the things we encounter in the course of those actions - through the way we *live* it and encounter others living it, and use it to make real and to order our everyday lived social experience.[3]

Amsterdam today is a city 'known' by many millions of people. Images of its streetscapes and even its plan are instantly recognizable across the world. It is the subject of countless travel books and documentaries, brochures and advertising features, a product for consumption in a world made accessible by airline travel and commercial tourism. But being there is something else, being there is about being *immersed* in a setting whose shape and atmosphere is itself an integral part of the structure and order (the 'habitus'[4] in Bourdieu's terms) of people's lives. The difference between the city of the traveler and that of the inhabitant goes way beyond simple issues of local knowledge and familiarity; it has to do with the different worlds and viewpoints they bring with them. It has to do with *perspective*. But these worlds are also not separate from each other, and they don't simply meet in the arrivals hall of the airport, or on the harbor-front of seventeenth-century Amsterdam. Rather, they intersect in dynamic patternings of space in the city, in the networks of streets and squares; conditioning, shading and coloring habitus and place, articulating relationships between differing worlds, differing perspectives on and commitments to the place. The space of the city itself is articulated into different levels and qualities of public-ness; identifying and structuring different orders and levels of significance, and of community and belonging.[5]

Other worlds

Negotiating a passage through the rabble of backpackers and other loiterers installed on the steps of the Albert Heijn food hall and supermarket, under the lumpy architecture of Het Paleis (the official royal domicile in Amsterdam). Dreadlocked and pierced, a young couple, speaking Italian, share the lunch they have just bought with the border collie at their feet.

Exit the mass by turning right down a side-street. Half a minute away and one enters another world; also 'Het Paleis', a neat but unprepossessing café, one of a small network, distributed through the center and nineteenth-century belt, of trendy meeting places for the city's bright and beautiful. Quiet and orderly after the throng in the next street, it is

[2] The whole idea of there being a world 'out there' opposed to the world in our heads is perhaps questionable - a product of Cartesian thinking. Nevertheless, this Cartesian split highlights how the city is more than its status as an object could account for, and how it can change fundamentally without there being a lot of change in the physical fabric we observe in the center itself

[3] See for example T. Ingold, *The Perception of the Environment*, London: Routledge, 2000, especially Ch. 10 'Building, dwelling, living' and Ch. 11 'The temporality of the landscape'

[4] The habitus is society written into the body according to Bourdieu (P. Bourdieu, *Outline of a Theory of Practice*, London: CUP, 1977). One of the ways this writing is performed, I suggest, is through the body's being embedded in the scaled networks of the city. The 'habitus' is not simply related to place through static occupation; it is also a product of the dynamic intersection of these different worlds with all that implies for the copresence and encounter with other worlds

[5] If the space of the city is an astronomically dense web of relations continuously being constructed in our everyday actions and interactions, then place is this web seen from one point. The properties of place (or at least the interesting properties) are seldom found in that place itself. Rather, they are found in the way place is a product of this space

figure 1 Nieuwezijds
Voorburgwal, Amsterdam

less than half full in the early afternoon of a sunny Saturday. A late-twenty-something with dyed jet-black hair sits over the newspapers and her address-book in the middle of the café making calls on her mobile phone. A long-haired man in well-cut jeans comes in from outside to meet his wife and two school-age children, who are drinking cappuccino and cola. He shows off the quality of the marijuana he has just bought in a coffee shop around the corner (this is Amsterdam!). These are also travelers, many of them almost as familiar with the languages and the hangouts of London, Paris and Berlin as they are with those of Amsterdam. Here they are at home, their worlds shrunk again to the comfortable familiarity of the routes around their inner-city neighborhoods and their favorite haunts. Their space is woven into the tree-lined canals and straight narrow streets, behind and between those over-priced shopping and tourist spaces one step removed from the network of freeways, stations and airports that delivers the throng just 100 m away.

Cities today still deal in the basic business of structure and articulation – shaping the worlds of stranger and inhabitant, local and larger scale interests – and the inhabitant and the stranger still embody two opposite polarities of dwelling in the city. While a great deal, from Bachelard[6] to de Cauter[7] has been written about the impossibility of any longer *dwelling* in the city, it is not my intention here to dwell on the 'crisis' highlighted by cultural philosophers. Designers deal with the issue at a different compass and with a different intent. They seek opportunities where commentators seek trends and make of them universals. Designers are happy to find niches where their craft can be exercised, and by close observation, we find countless ways the city still articulates

[6] G. Bachelard, *The Poetics of Space*, Boston, Mass.: Beacon, 1969

[7] L. de Cauter, 'The capsule and the network: Preliminary notes for a general theory', *OASE 54*, Nijmegen: Uitgeverij SUN, 2001

gure 2 Café 'Het Paleis'
aleisstraat, Amsterdam

the social and existential worlds of different urban populations, and the way it still, to a very large extent, supports the everyday real-life sociality of the urbanite. More of these niches may be uncovered, re-invigorated, perhaps re-invented once we understand better how this process works. We need to explore the poetics of today's space, to point a way to re-engaging with a contemporary mechanics of urban dwelling. By finding out how dynamic urban populations are structured in space, and more importantly how their relationships and interfaces with each other are structured, we may discover that we still have it in our power to integrate and connect multiple layerings of social existence.

Absorbing change

The number of 'worlds' we deal with in any city are more than multiple, they are multitudinous – split along all the well-known lines of division: ethnic, lifestyle, age-group, class, and so on. They are split also along ever-new lines that seem to multiply endlessly as the world changes around us. And yet the urban center seems somehow to absorb all of this: not without conflict and friction, but certainly in a way which is reflected and becomes legible on the face of the city itself – in the characters and conditions of its spaces and places, in their decayings and changings and in their surprising recoveries.

A real issue today, in relation to cities, is how so much of the stuff we associate with an urban community: the corner grocers and bakers, the traditional brown cafés, the amenities for a way of urban life familiar perhaps from the times we stayed over with our grandparents (and cast in the cozy, rosy hues of those memories), are changing or are disappearing seemingly from under our noses. In their places have emerged and are emerging other characters and amenities, generated by and targeted at a different, a more dispersed and mobile, a more worldly, less committed population. It is clear that something is changing – but it is not always so clear exactly what that is, and what we should do about it. It is nevertheless also apparent that the center in a very direct way accommodates these changes – it doesn't simply provide space, but also seems to find a place for them.

Changing worlds

The workers' district of the first half of the twentieth century, with its straight streets lined with almost identical white-trimmed and cheaply-built housing, its daily market, its brown cafés, small shops and smelly industries, had, by the time my neighbor moved there, become the volksbuurt *(people's neighborhood) with its culture of local engagement and annual rituals of rent-increase resistance and street beautification. There had been fewer chain stores along the Ferdinand Bolstraat, the local high street when, as a student, she had moved into a small squat in the side street she still lived in. Her window, which had then looked out on the back of the old brewery, gave out now on a new supermarket and new shops and restaurants which catered over weekends to crowds of younger people with money to spend.*

The anonymous throng of shoppers on the high street gave way to a scattering of passers-by on her side street, each, by their presence and in a way she could read effortlessly, embodying the multiple stories of the buurt. *Each of the half-decades she had been there had seen a new story begin. And each story had been layered over previous ones, so that none of them ever seemed really to end. The rather earnest left-bankish cafés of her time on the other side of the Ferdinand Bolstraat were still there, catering to many of the same people – older now and with jobs in design and the theatre or in the voluntary sector, and to a new generation of the people they had been – artistic types, readers and movie-viewers. The neighborhood had attracted ethnic minorities in the more recent past who brought with them cheap eateries and exotic shops and smells. It was now becoming the yuppie neighborhood, with its overpriced apartments, its sushi bar and its designer cafés.*

The daily market is still there, along with a decent number of long-standing residents, who had resisted (or who could not afford) the drift to the suburbs. Their regular complaint, besides the way rents were going up, is of the transformation of the market from a place where one could buy daily provisions more cheaply than in the supermarket, to a place where teenagers buy € 10 tank-tops, and tourists, whose space extends just this far out of the historic center, come to buy their Amsterdam souvenir T-shirts.

These changes are very largely a matter that runs ahead of a well-meaning planning bureaucracy. They are a matter of appropriation, the taking over of a place by new tendencies and new times. The idea of appropriation runs counter to many of our preconceptions about place. It appears to be a matter of openness rather than of fit, and insofar as multiple and overlapping appropriation seems possible, it seems to make a nonsense of

Amsterdam: Beyond Inside and Out **Stephen Read**

the idea of social territories. Insofar as it happens opportunistically and repeatedly, by populations who often see in the place nothing but a temporary refuge, but end up making of it a home, it forces us to question the idea of collective memory, or where exactly this 'memory' may be located – in the (collective) head or in the space of the city itself.

For the planner or designer today, this is not in the first instance an issue of authenticity, as if place was a matter of scenery, of architecture made in an appropriate (or not) style or of serving any particular history. The processes taking place in the city today are delivering changes to urban centers, and the problem, rather than being one of making *fit* localities, seems to be becoming much more one of resisting contemporary tendencies for localities to disconnect from one another socially, to break up into separate territories and to disengage from a continuous urban experience. Design begins to be about giving back to the urban subject the opportunity to themselves construct complex meaningful realities out of their embeddedness in continuous connected urban fields.

Process of place today: from civic enclosure to urbanized landscape
The space of seventeenth-century Amsterdam was clearly contained in relation to its immediate surroundings. It was a world apart, defined against a hostile outside prone to devastating flooding, and by its walls. Contact with the outside proceeded above all through the harbor front. The inside had its dangers, but they were dangers domesticated by the fact of their being contained within a delimited social space. To venture

outside the walls meant crossing a threshold – from a socially ordered inside into an unpredictable dangerous windswept outside. The predominant relations across this landscape were with other enclosed entities, other cities that were partners and rivals in commerce and in struggles for political and economic influence.

The space of modern Amsterdam could hardly be more different. Amsterdam today, after the economic and urban decline of the eighteenth and nineteenth centuries, is once again animated by traceries of activity and movement at regional, continental and global scales. The harbor as point of contact with the wider world has been replaced, at the exact location of the center of the old harbor, by Central Station, which is connected not only to the region and to other national centers beyond the local network, but also to the high-speed train network connecting Brussels, Berlin, Paris, London and Milan. Other continental and global travelers stream into the city through Schiphol Airport. Amsterdam sits in the second rank of global cities, as part of the network of business and finance linking London, New York, Tokyo, Frankfurt and Paris.[8] Flows of information, people, and especially ideas and finance, leapfrog the region and even the nation to funnel wealth and power into and through the city along highly controlled conduits.

Without doubt, though, the factor that has the most significant larger-scale effect on the space of Amsterdam today, and the way it effects the character and experience of the city as a place or matrix of places, is the general increase in mobility of the modern urbanite. Where just half a century ago, the lives of the overwhelming majority of the city's population were bound up within the city, today the rush-hour traffic on the trains and the freeways, is as much between cities as within them. It is commonplace for people to live in one urban center and to work in another, and people's social circles and their places of everyday business and entertainment spread themselves out in a network whose reach extends well beyond the old urban boundaries.

New social condensers

Spotting a colleague ahead of me, I pick up speed, overtaking him just as we reach the door of the train that will take us both to our work. The rest of the journey is spent swapping notes and catching up on the progress of a joint project.

Reflecting later in the day on the state of contemporary urbanity (as one does), it occurred to me that we had experienced another of those unremarked inversions of conventional wisdom that seem so to characterize the state of our urban lives. As a relatively new inhabitant of the inner-city neighborhood I call home, I cannot say I know a great many of my neighbors – nor does this seem to be a particularly unusual situation. It is only rarely that I bump into someone I know in those traditional urban condensers, the local high street or the neighborhood street. What's more, I don't experience this as a loss, nor feel that it diminishes the value of my neighborhood as the local support for the processes of my life. I inhabit simultaneously many spaces, many complexes of relations, and it is no longer obvious that the space of my most social and personal life will be the most local. Many – no, all – of these spaces I inhabit adhere to and merge with coherent

[8] S. Sassen, *The Global City*, Princeton, NJ: Princeton University Press, 1991

Amsterdam: Beyond Inside and Out **Stephen Read**

ure 5 Central Station,
nsterdam

movement or communications networks, and clearly this is where many new social condensers will be emerging – at urban, regional and even international nodes, as well of
course as in telephonic and electronic space.

My local area with its buzz and variety, and with all the amenity that buzz and variety supports and attracts, becomes setting (more than that overloaded notion 'neighborhood'); a
public extension to my private realm, an aspect of the identity I choose to project; not only,
but also a decor to my life. Personal social neighborhood, in so far as it is possible to specify, exists in a far more complex and multiplex configuration of geographic, network and
virtual space. The local setting is still rich and deep with complexes of relations, but set
up on the basis of an urban mechanics that is formed less around spaces and scales
which relate immediately to my personal space and experience, and more to generic
processes of scale and movement related to systems of urban networks. These processes
are still able to establish the conditions of overlap and social multiplicity and diversity
that characterize those places we point to when we refer to the seductive pleasures of
the urban experience. The urban place (even in the urban center) is constructed in
metropolitan and not in medieval space. Simmel's blasé individual still treads the
pavements. Old-fashioned community is possible amongst children playing in the
side-streets but is a silly fantasy for people who live their lives in metropolitan space.

There is a new scale in the present-day urban spatial field led by the mobility of people – by the new dimensions of everyday human activity as these eclipse the physical
limits of the old center. 'Outside' has disappeared from the old 'inside–outside' of urban

Stephen Read Amsterdam: Beyond Inside and Out   203

figure 6 Gerard Dou Plein, Amsterdam

center and periphery, and it is the scale and intensity of the flows within the new extended urban field that is redefining for us what urban space is, and forcing us to reconsider its nature, as well as reconsider our thought-habits of 'inside-outside' and 'edge-center'. But the new urban social-spatial scales and their effects don't limit themselves to the peripheries of old centers; centrality and peripherality seem increasingly to invade every sector of the urban landscape, weaving through each other, flipping old orders on their heads, establishing an often discordant space whose collisions and inversions have become an ever more familiar part of our lives.

A new centrality has emerged from the dynamic, a diffuse, amorphous, centrifugal new center which infuses the infrastructural networks of the periphery. At the same time, however, other centralities have not disappeared. The centripetal forces generated by the focus of the infrastructure towards the historical core – by the knots in the web, the increasing fineness of the mesh and density of connectivity as one approaches the center – are if anything stronger by being opposed to a powerful alternative polarity. The whole system, seen at the regional or metropolitan scale, will in any event generate unevennesses, nodes within the network, 'edge cities' tied to strategic positions in the regional web. The traditional centers will tend to be strategic positions in this web anyway, but then supercharged by their intense mesh of connectivity at the finer scale, and by the density of embedded lives and interactivity.

So the traditional center, at first sight an opposite polarity of the centrality of the regional network, is also fed by this network. European centers have become stronger,

more intensely used than ever they used to be. But at the same time their programmatic logic has changed. The whole city is no longer the traditional center; rather, the
center is a component of an extended node-and-network urbanization which includes
those encapsulated, controlled, monofunctional spaces on the regional network, and
which has to be considered as a whole if one wants to understand the way other orders,
including those of class and power and that of community, are spatialized.

It is also clear that the respective centralities of the center and the periphery – each
with their own characteristic speeds and scales – don't each remain tidily in their own
places. There is increasingly, also within the fabric of the traditional center, a weaving
of the orders and scales of activity of each through the other. And this weaving clearly
doesn't, as one might perhaps at first expect, lead to an increasing uniformity of the
scales and intensities of activity within the urban field. Rather, it seems to generate
increasing contrasts within an increasingly complex configuration of urban places as
the new centrality of the periphery penetrates deep into the old urban 'inside'.
Infrastructural connection at the metropolitan and regional scales mean that at these
scales connective efficiencies increase, but in terms of a matrix of adjacent central
urban places, spatial and functional fragmentation is more the character of the new
order. The old urban grid, the integrating spatial matrix of the traditional city, is in
danger of giving way (even within the limits of the traditional center) to a matrix of
high-value places, often highly designed and highly connected to the new scales, which
come or are designed into being, interspersed within a low-value, relatively unconsidered,
relatively unconnected space whose nature is becoming increasingly problematic. The

Stephen Read Amsterdam: Beyond Inside and Out

figure 8 Wibautstraat, Amsterdam

ambitious and boosterist plan for the area along Amsterdam's waterfront in the vicinity of Central Station is a case in point.

The contained, circumscribed space–time and experience of the medieval city with its shared significant localities and shared significant moments has given way to an extended, vectorized space–time, where the limits between the city and the world dissolve, and where shared experience and shared place are the result of being absorbed within a concentration of people brought together and divided in a whirl of movement. The bulk of this movement is generated through the larger-scale networks, opening up new swathes of territory on the periphery, but squeezing itself also into the space of the traditional center, where delicate networks of places are transformed forever.

Schisms in social space

The Wibaut Axis, seen in plan, is an inner-city boulevard stretched through the urban fabric from Amstel Station in the south to the waterfront in the north. On the ground however, it is marked by the noise of its traffic, by the general dilapidation of the surrounding fabric at its southern end and by the rather alien, disconnected, edge-city-like business-node urban renewal to the north. The Wibaut Axis has stood high in the priorities of Amsterdam's spatial planning department for many years and continues to resist all efforts to make of it a district with some kind of relationship with the urban fabric in which it is physically embedded.

A knot of slower-moving cars held up the stream of traffic and the lights turned red in front of us. I wished now I'd taken the ring road. She had been considering crossing in

Amsterdam: Beyond Inside and Out **Stephen Read**

front of the slower cars but had thought better of it. As the lights turned green she wheeled her bicycle loaded with shopping bags over the pedestrian crossing towards the baker on the corner of the 1st Oosterparkstraat.

In this city with more than its fair share of pedestrian and bicycle traffic, most people experience the Wibaut Axis from their cars. Many of them experience it only in passing, on their way by the route of least resistance from Amsterdam South-East to Amsterdam North, because the Wibaut Axis is directly connected to, is in fact an integral part of, the regional motorway network. Some motorists use it as a distribution route into the center itself – into Amsterdam South and Amsterdam East – but only at one or two points of crossing with the Wibaut Axis itself.

An urban boulevard is more than a mobility axis. It is a piece of urban fabric knitted into the plan by its crossings, completed as functional space by the interdependence of axis and crossings (and the social material they carry) which feed each other and in their exchange establish the life and identity of the area. But the Wibaut Axis knows few of its crossings, and its crossings know it only as a noisy obstruction. This is a spatial relationship between lives operating at radically different speeds, speeds whose differences thwart contact and prohibit interaction. Axis and area are at best indifferent to one another. One cannot really even speak of copresence, nor is there any significant intersection of economic lives at the street edge. Here we have a shearing of the social space that has everything to do with the insertion of the alien speed and scale and the dis-located one-dimensional vector space of the periphery into the complex two-dimensional social-spatial fabric of the center.

figure 9 Damrak, Amsterdam

The changing shape of the traditional center

The urban place of the underside of the rail viaduct with its dispirited homeless and heroin-whores is a product of these processes and transformations, as is the Kalverstraat with its chain stores and boutiques and its hordes of Sunday regional shoppers. This is about the way urban space is lived in the first place. The mechanics of the city are an emergent mechanics, and the social-spatial structure an emergent structure, a product of the aggregations and condensations of clouds of micro-effects, producing structure which reveals itself not just in activity patterns but also in urban condition and character. The attractors, the shape-givers in this restless fluid field, are the infrastructures, tissues and webs, the physical armatures that gather, concentrate and condense the flux at different levels of scale. The clouds of micro-effects even seem to *seek* these armatures in a complex gridded fabric and may flip relatively suddenly from one to another, as fluxes and their scales and intensities alter.

Conflicts and contradictions between different scales and different speeds and mobilities, underlie many current quarrels and controversies about development in Amsterdam. The historic core, highly connected to the region via Central Station, has found a new vitality as a regional shopping and entertainment center. At the same time, people who manage still to live relatively cheaply in the center (and remember this was a key achievement of the popular activism of the late 1960s and 70s) find this possibility under threat as rents and the demand for retail space and expensive city-center apartments rise. In fact, the space of the historic core has in the meantime performed one of those 'phase changes' from being one thing to being quite another. Popular

gure 10 P.C. Hooftstraat,
msterdam

conceptions (and this one can read in any number of local election manifestos) still hold onto a notion of the center belonging to the city itself and to its municipal inhabitants. Meanwhile, its space and centrality has increasingly been absorbed into that of the metropolitan region. The key element in the displacement of the center at the scale of the traditional city itself is Central Station, and processes of change were already under way soon after it was built.[9] These processes have only gained force and accelerated as the mobilities of the general population have increased.

Displaced centers

Walking down the Damrak towards Central Station on a Saturday morning, one can hard-ly help noticing that one is moving against the tide. The station spews them out: groups of youngsters from Alkmaar and Purmerend out on the town, mothers and daughters, arm-in-arm on shopping sprees, couples, singles, old and young; all making a day of it. Dodging to the other side of the road to avoid the worst of the crowd, one has to sidestep the cars of lost visitors and tourists, circling in limbo, in vain hope of finding parking. The Kalverstraat, the center's quality shopping street of the first half of the last century, concentrates now on jeans and jackets fashion and fast turnover, while Emporio Armani, DKNY, Mexx and Joop have found a home for themselves between the cafés and restaurants on the PC Hooftstraat far to the south.

M. Wagenaar, 'Amsterdam
860–1940: een bedrijvige
tad', in E. Taverne and I.
isser (eds), *Stedebouw: de
eschiedenis van de stad in de
ederlanden van 1500 tot
eden*, Nijmegen: Uitgeverij
UN, 1993, p. 220

This is where you are most likely to bump into faces familiar from the TV, or the establish-ment figures of Dutch literature, film and theatre and Amsterdam's assorted minor glitterati in their Porsches and Mercedes. Here and on the adjacent sections of the van

Baerlestraat and the Willemsparkweg is the gathering spot for the well-to-do of Amsterdam South. It is also home to the Concertgebouw, the Stedelijk and Rijks Musea, and a few more of that dispersed network of trendy hangouts.

The Vondelpark is a central social mixer, attracting the local rich as well as the poor from further away – as is the Leidseplein entertainment area, but a short step away, which comprises a few hundred cafés, bars and restaurants.

The mobility flux at traditional city scale has found itself a new center, or rather a string of centers (including both the PC Hooftstraat area and the former *volksbuurt* already mentioned) around a spatial armature which defined the edge of the city as it was in the early twentieth century. We are not experiencing the first 'flight to the periphery' in the city's history. Indeed, it may be that the movement of centers to edges is a generic spatial effect related to scale increases – to increases in city size combined with accompanying increases in mobility.

A new metro line is proposed that will connect the South Axis, a new commercial development on the ring road, with Central Station and the historical core. The North-South line will form part of a network of improved inner-city mobility – but it is also directly connected at both ends to the regional network and will draw the influence of the new regional centrality still further into the fabric, beyond the historic center and well into the old *volksbuurten*. Accelerating already established processes of gentrification, it will change places of *buren* (neighbors) and *buurthuizen* (community centers) still more rapidly into places of high-priced pieds-à-terre and wine and sushi-bars, while at the same time relatively peripheralizing – consigning to the 'new outside' – adjacent stretches of fabric.

The popular opposition to the metro comes from local interest groups who have read the writing on the wall all too well. Proponents of the metro point out that the urban community no longer accords with its popular image; the *buren* have long been dissipating to Almere and Purmerend, regional satellites of Amsterdam, to be replaced by successive waves of the young, the footloose and economic migrants, and more recently by the yuppies and soupies (slightly older urban professionals) attracted by the density of amenity and entertainment and the anonymous, uncommitted conviviality that the center offers.

The new urban machine

We live in a time when we all seem to have become travelers. What distinguishes our lives from lives lived in the past is that we feel, or imagine we feel, the loss of a sure foot in a rooted and permanent 'somewhere', located by spire and clock tower and embodying a centered place and an ordered time. We can imagine therefore that we have lost the possibility for a centered place in our present-day urbanism, that the conditions that produced that kind of place have gone and that we are doomed forever to rehash a more substantial past in mannered interiors, protected from the rush of contemporary existence. We can forget that movement has always been the motor of our urban experience and that time has always been differentiated by rhythms and continuities in space, speeds of movement, and location relative to the dominant networks of the system as a whole. The experience of the traveler and that of the inhabitant are both mediated by movement; the difference between them is one of degree, of a different proportional relationship in the intersection of space and time and the inhabiting of differently scaled and speeded networks. The space of the contemporary city may be characterized by a dizzying increase in speed, but this increase is by no means constant over the urban field. It is still highly differentiated and still offers multiple opportunities within its variable surface for the dense, solid experience of place.

There was a clear logic to the pre-metropolitan city; and it was one which related to movement rather than to program. It was a logic that was read over and over again through people's everyday movements, through perceptual encounters with a richly-structured, immersive urban world, and it was a logic through which people experienced their relationship with others and with society as a whole. These movements related the part to the whole by way of elements we all knew and understood. The spaces of the neighborhood centered themselves on high streets, and it was through the high street that contact was made with a wider, more diverse and anonymous public. These centers had the ability to adapt to social trends and influences, and to reflect the times we lived in. In fact it was often on the streets of these sorts of places that change first made itself known. These were (and are still, in the best cases) the centers that made 'provision for the fact of history, for the unintended, for the contradictory, for the unknown'.[10]

Amsterdam demonstrates the remarkable spatial and urban logic that still exists within the urban field. Many of the changes we experience in our cities today, far from being chaotic or unpredictable, are a more or less systematic consequence of changes in the scales of our lives (of the addition of larger scales to already existing layerings of scales). We are not going to alter the fact that the city has become something else. What we need is the knowledge, political insight and will, and the planning instruments to establish socially and culturally open and diverse 'footholds in the flux'; centers that are immersive environments not just in the surface furniture of public space, but in the way as environments, they structure the relations between dynamic populations, opening viable interfaces between circuits of local and higher movement scales. Our task in planning and maintaining the city is not so much to provide access and space, as it is to make place. And that seems to be a matter of animation, of close attention to the real world and the details of lives and how they add together in urban space. The world we make can be one that originates in the mean abstractions of access and program, or in the richness of a finely observed choreography of urban social space as it really is. The case of Amsterdam points us in the second direction.

[10] R. Sennett, The Uses of Disorder, New York: Norton, 1970, p. 99

Number of inhabitants [p]   1,500,000
Area [km²]   100
Density   ---
Population urbanized (national) [2003]   51%

Local Navigation in Douala

AbdouMaliq Simone

figure 1 A street scene in Douala

Reviewing Douala

Douala is the largest city in sub-Saharan Africa without a substantial history of being a political and administrative center. While national capitals have been relocated in Nigeria, Tanzania and Cote D'Ivoire, the largest urban centers in these countries have largely been developed by virtue of their former administrative functions. Douala is unique in that its development trajectory is almost exclusively accounted for by commercial activities. This accords a character to the city that imposes a sense of economic dynamism upon what can often seem a markedly disarticulated social field.

The basic infrastructure of Douala is notorious for its state of disrepair, with extensive flooding during the long rainy season, quarters cut off from main arteries, the vast port barely linked to transport corridors, and so forth. This state of disrepair is frequently cited as a metaphor for the city's lack of social and political integration, and the way in which its freewheeling entrepreneurial culture fragments the city into disparate domains. These domains are then viewed as unwilling and unable to assume some kind of collective responsibility for improving life beyond an entrenched insularity. Indeed, Douala is a patchwork of settlements. During Douala's early history, different social groups converged upon it, forging varying links to different colonial powers and specializing in markedly different economic and cultural orientations to a broader external world. A multiplicity of social and economic infrastructures was the result, reflecting various investments in international trade, political competition, emigration and the consolidation of ethnic neighborhoods. Lacking a substantial history of political administrative institutions, urban politics today (dominated by the youth) is played out, not so much in competition over control of specific sites or institutions, but in configuring intersections within a social fabric largely disarticulated in the past. In other words, they attempt to connect various territories, actors, activities and capacities – to get

ure 2 Food stalls in
nanjo, the administrative
arter of Douala

them to acknowledge each other, while not necessarily integrating them. In the latter
sections of this chapter, I look at the hesitant emergence of some of these efforts.

As the commercial center of Cameroon, Douala certainly has a broad range of political
institutions located within it. But as the city has not been primarily built on administrative activities with the concomitant salaries upon which large numbers of extended
families throughout urban Africa have come to depend, surviving in Douala entails a
larger measure of individual entrepreneurial initiative than is characteristic of many
other African cities.[1] Even with large numbers of unemployed, the overall sense in the
city is one of residents making ends meet.

[1] J.F. Bayart, *L'Etat au
Cameroun*, Paris: Presses de la
Fondation Nationale des
Sciences Politiques, 1985

At the same time, the relative absence of political institutions and dependency on public employment means that important instruments of urban socialization are absent, i.e.

figure 3 Small commercial
activity near Bessengue Akw

domains around which social collaboration and solidarity can be fostered. Historically, cadres of civil servants, public sector unions, and local authority networks, played a critical role in fostering a sense of social cohesion in many African cities. As the burden of survival in Douala is much more incumbent upon individuals and households, greater value is placed on the autonomy of operations than on fostering social interdependency.[2]

This tendency also produces a greater divergence in the characteristics of individual quarters. Without strong gravitational fields generated by critical political and civil institutions, quarters are more inclined to 'go their own way.' Some are characterized by a strong sense of social cohesion forged through particular histories of settlement, ethnic composition, location, access to resources and the nature of local leadership. Other quarters have little to distinguish them as coherent places except for an administrative designation or a particular reputation.

Without either strong institutional supports or impediments, some quarters have been able to proficiently mobilize local initiative and resources to provide essential urban services in a judicious and cost-effective manner. On the other hand, for some quarters, the absence of a strong political focus means that there is little basis for residents to come together for any significant form of cooperation. In these instances, quarters can easily become overwhelmed by the absence of regulation and planning, as there are few mechanisms for land use control and waste disposal – particularly thorny problems given Douala's tropical climate and riverine setting.

While urban households may be adept at securing livelihood and opportunity, the largely *ad hoc* manner in which this is pursued means, as indicated earlier, that there are

[2] J.P. Warnier, *L'espirit d'en-terprise au Cameroun*, Paris: Karthala, 1993

massive problems with critical urban functions, such as circulation across the city, drainage, refuse collection and security. At the same time, it is difficult to see how applicable the array of local solutions often effective as stopgap measures in many other African cities with more substantive histories of social cooperation would be in Douala. So the city combines heightened ingenuity, a high degree of urbanization of behavior and social outlook, a largely inadequate institutional framework for regulating urban processes, and a highly contentious relationship to the political regime in power – all dynamics which make innovative urban development planning both necessary and difficult.

While Douala may experience substantial deficits as a 'social city', thanks to its limited experiences of solidarity and social cooperation, it is embedded within a national context that has a strong sense of national identity. The bulk of Douala's residents live within ethnically homogenous domains – most usually clusters of households or blocks within ethnically cosmopolitan quarters. In other words, the majority of the city's residents have immediate neighbors who share a common ethnic identity, even though no ethnic group predominates in any one quarter. In part, this represents the highly varied trajectories of settlement inflows to the city and a strong measure of national identification.[3]

As a commercial city, Douala's residents have a long history of engagement with the wider world, and travel and migration are not uncommon. But – and in this Douala is unlike many other African cities – there is no 'overvaluation' of things coming from beyond the nation's borders, nor any generalized urgent impulse to leave Cameroon, and most residents seem to want to remain in the city.

[3] J. Forje, 'The Politics of Democratization, Ethnicity and Management in Africa, with Experience from Cameroon', in *Anthropology of Africa and the Challenge of the Third Millennium*, Paris: UNESCO; Ethno-Net Publications, 1999

AbdouMaliq Simone Local Navigation in Douala

While both municipal and national political life may be strongly ethnicized, Douala has not experienced the debilitating ethnic conflicts that frequently divide many other African cities. There is a long history of different ethnic groups living together, and whereas specific ethnic groups may be stereotyped as having proclivities and/or privileges in specific domains or activities, in the end, these are largely perceived as at least potentially complementary rather than conflicting.[4] Such a social framework means that in a city with high degrees of urbanized behavior, social differences, and entrepreneurial attitudes, there remains some foundation for the cultivation of a viable public sphere. But again, the shape of such a public sphere and the kinds of public and civil institutions that will elaborate it – particularly given the critical infrastructure developments urgently required – are not clearly evident.[5]

A process of ethnic *métissage* has been an important aspect of substantiating the dynamism of economically fragile urban quarters. The tendency of distinct ethnic identities to mix and to create specific new identities has generated a certain circulation and extension of households across the city. For if the offspring of inter-ethnic marriages are still under pressure to be something specific in terms of ethnic identity, how will they choose? To avoid the implications of a 'wrong' or contentious choice, as well as to prevent too much investment in trying to recruit such offspring to specific ethnic associations within a quarter, these offspring will often move to another quarter, where the implication of whatever choice they make will usually turn out to be less severe.

As levels of hardship and concomitant social tensions grow within quarters, families must find ways to turn to each other under conditions that undermine the strength of family solidarity. Under such conditions, the dispersal of family ties also has its implications. After all, households are, in part, seeking to send their offspring to new quarters. Without territorial proximity and its strong socializing effects, family networks are often subject to more coercive and damaging means of enforcing different kinds of cooperation. Critical family affairs and life events, such as funerals, baptisms, and weddings are increasingly subject to various tensions.

These affairs are often settings for attempts at extortion. For example, one side of the family must come up with a specific commodity of a precise weight or volume in order to avoid exerting some kind of ominous influence over the affair. Mutual demands and threats, and their resultant economies of compensation, establish the need for a precise accounting of equivalence, which, in turn, reinforces an obsession with the need for balance. Opportunities to circumvent these calculations must be exploited with increasing secrecy. At the same time, that secrecy reinforces the very fears and anxieties that largely motivate such economies of compensation in the first place.

As in other African cities, Douala has formally pursued a policy of decentralization, and the metropolitan region is divided into five municipalities. These municipalities have limited power and capacity, as the bulk of administrative, development and budgetary functions remains in the hands of the national government. All five municipalities are controlled by the political opposition, and this continues to be a major factor in their

[4] R. Clignet and F. Jordan, 'Urbanization and Social Differentiation in Africa: A comparative analysis of the ecological structures of Douala and Yaoundé', *Cahiers d'Etudes Africaines*, 1971, Vol. 11, 261–296

[5] J. Takougang and M. Krieger (eds), *An African State and Society in the 1990s: Cameroon at the Crossroads*, Boulder, Co: Westview Press, 1998

Local Navigation in Douala **AbdouMaliq Simone**

ongoing underdevelopment as local authorities. Nevertheless, there is the emergence of a critical attitude on the part of politicians and technicians and an awareness that new modalities of social collaboration and governance are urgently required.

Douala has benefited greatly from the political turbulence in Abidjan, with many commercial enterprises relocating their regional headquarters to the city. In part this is attributed to the city's longstanding commercial infrastructure, but also to the perception that Douala is a city for business, not politics. Consequently, a strong desire persists on the part of most political actors to keep political conflict within manageable bounds.

Again, the types of social conflict evident in many other African cities are far removed from the proclivities of the Camerounais national character: most Camerounais regard peace as the most important dimension of everyday life. Important steps have been taken to regularize the activities of the port and commercial activities. The city's infamous reputation as a place of massive theft and confidence trickery has been attenuated in recent years, in part due to an escalating national embarrassment over being known as one of the world's most corrupt nations. The general perception of a discernible reduction in corrupt activities comes not only from some highly publicized prosecutions but also from a growing determination on the part of Douala's residents not to allow themselves to be duped.

These tendencies toward rationalization remain limited, however, due to the deficiencies of social organization in the city. The persistence of local fiefdoms as the predominant form of local authority reflects the continuation of largely ethnicized residential patterns, although many quarters have instituted development commissions representative of key local interests and associations. But representation in most quarters of Douala is a complex issue. The persistence of parochial settlement patterns and traditional local authorities, combined with otherwise highly urban behaviors, means that both the identification of critical local interests and issues often remain clouded.[6] When dealing with what is perceived as a inherently hostile political or public domain, residents may invoke parochial identities and support traditional institutions. In all other aspects of daily life, residents may largely ignore such identities and institutions, as they may have little relevance for how they go about their everyday lives.

When practices of livelihood formation are largely concentrated outside the scope of political and civil institutional life, no clear modalities of representing residents' interests come to the fore. In some quarters, local power interests are clearly invested in deferring substantial improvements in urban services and the quality of life. This is either because power and wealth accrues to them in terms of compensating for the misfortune derived from poor living conditions or because they control the space of mediation between the quarter and important political actors outside the quarter. In quarters where substantial efforts have been made to secure a decent living environment, there is often a reluctance to expend much local political capital in engaging at larger metropolitan levels, even when there is recognition that continued growth and protection of local gains may require such engagement. In some 'virtual quarters', zones

6] A.J. Njoh, 'The Political Economy of Urban Land Reform in a Postcolonial State', *International Journal of Urban and Regional Research*, 1998, vol. 22 (3), 409–423

figure 5 The first well in Bessengue Akwa. The well is an example of citizen participation as it is part of a regeneration programme of Bessengue Akwa. The well serves as a source of drinking water, a place for small-scal commercial activities and a meeting place for the local youth

on the outskirts of the city where current inhabitants are few, but where hundreds of housing plots have already been sold, struggles for local predominance are already under way.

These dynamics raise the issue of who becomes a legitimate and effective interlocutor for the kinds of social collaboration perceived as necessary by key municipal officials. When the characteristics of different quarters – even of contiguous quarters – are highly divergent, it is difficult to institutionalize local representation and planning processes in any formulaic way. One of the difficulties faced, for example, by a new city-wide organization known as Network for Inhabitants is that the diversity of local power centers and interests makes the transfer of local problem-solving across quarters and the consolidation of a metropolitan advocacy force very difficult.

Additionally, given the large swathes of unregulated settlement that run across the city, the provision of urban services and efficient infrastructure will require the uprooting of many people. Given the contentiousness and profiteering that ensued from the displacement of residents in Zone Nylon, the city's largest suburb, during the restructuring activities of the 1980s, municipal actors have been slow to pursue similar projects that might provide some impetus to the social reorganization of many quarters.

As in many African cities, such impetus for urban change is likely to come from the young. But the trajectories of youth are also contentious, as young people explore different pathways to address what they perceive to be increasing exclusion and declining opportunities.

On the one hand, young people are more likely to criticize the persistence of the old mores and values as impediments to change and effective social mobilization. For example, traditional associations are viewed as reinforcing assumptions about gender roles and household authority that no longer hold good in the urban realities of present-day Douala. Attitudes about men's roles produce situations where fathers are either unable to face their households or face them with exaggerated displays of constraining authority – to compensate for the inability to really exercise a sense of economic, social and psychological support. In this way, traditional associations constrain households from actualizing new ways of working together to improve their situations.

On the other hand, young people are more likely to interpret contemporary urban crises as crises of moral values. Thus, they are more likely to either support the resuscitation of traditional values and institutions or devote their time to a host of religious sects aiming to constitute a 'holistic' universe for their devotees while discouraging participation in other activities. Intergenerational conflict is escalating, particularly as young people have borne the brunt of the security operations carried out with extraordinary force by the military – including detention, nighttime raids, constant identity checks, and even assassinations.

Militancy among young people is increasing. This derives partly from the escalating boredom they experience under curfews, which restrict them to what are perceived to be claustrophobic quarters and household situations. It also derives from an increasing tendency for youth to live in household arrangements independent of the family. Along both trajectories, young people are demanding both institutions they can call their own and a greater part in the deliberation of local affairs.

Although their attempts are confused and diffuse, many young people are trying to put together an urban identity that attempts to go beyond both ad hoc entrepreneurial sensibilities and the lingering power of ethnic affiliation. At the same time, this identity forges itself through reinvented memories of the practices that emerged during the formative periods of the city's original quarters. This is not so much a revisionist history as an attempt to identify elements of dormant capacity for diverse residents to create a powerful urban life. Thus Douala is best understood, not in some overarching view, but in the hundreds of stories that proliferate across the city – stories that produce shifting social spaces through which to navigate new possibilities in an urban environment where so many things do not work.

Reassembling Urban Life
Story I
Bessengue Akwa represents one of Douala's quarters where the struggle to remake urban life has often been most marked and confusing. It is a very dense quarter built between two of North Central Douala's main north-south thoroughfares and south of a lateral road that connects them. On the southern boundary runs a large swampy creek. Most households are quite literally living on top of each other, with bad sanitation and barely navigable narrow thoroughfares. There are major problems with security, waste collection, and clean water.

Because the area beside the lateral road used to be an area of dense bush, the initial settlers, relatively well-off households able to construct two- or three-story compounds, encouraged informal settlements behind the compounds in order to provide security. But within two decades, the area has become a sea of contiguous makeshift tin roofs organized in highly ethnically parochial domains. Largely out of general view, the quarter is well known as a cheap refuge close to the city's center.

The quarter's chief is a dynamic and towering young man with a quiet demeanor and the political skills and persistence to corral a motley assortment of the quarter's residents into an effective development committee. This committee has wangled commitments from the municipality to substantially restructure the quarter, i.e. plans to install electricity, build usable roads, clean up the creek and provide clean bulk water supplies. That the provision of these services means that many of the present residents will have to be moved – and is thus a contentious issue – has not so far proved a major obstacle to mobilizing community support as such a prospect often is for many such communities. In part, this is attributable to the chief's and several other activists' efforts to make the development committee as inclusive as possible, even though the chief has no direct role in coordinating its functions.

An important part of the development effort in terms of service provision has been these activists' conviction that the effort provides an opportunity to inculcate a sense of 'moral partnership' among residents who are already overstretched with having to manage delicate territorial relationships. In other words, it is perceived as an exercise in getting residents to take responsibility for each other in ways that exceed their immediate household and local ethnic ties. It thus takes a chance on a variety of local personalities, without clear institutional status, to try out various ways to, for example, mobilize young people locally or organize women's support groups. This reframing has, in turn, encouraged patience with the slow pace of negotiations with the municipality. Despite these efforts, even the more militant residents seem to remain largely passive observers waiting for the change that must come and hoping that the deteriorating environmental and social conditions will not overwhelm them. It is understandable that any external assistance would be eagerly taken up, and great efforts are made to be hospitable to an array of potential 'external partners'. But this accommodation also signals the extent to which members of the development committee cannot see what operates within Bessengue as potential resources. There is a sustained affirmation that residents must behave differently with each other, not so much in order to activate greater local potentials or skills, but to deactivate something insidious that has been released in the prolonged neglect of the quarter.

Near the northwest entrance to the quarter stands the tallest and best-built structure in the area. It is a structure that is not being used, and to all appearances stands empty. This emptiness is somewhat ironic, given the effort the development committee is now making to raise money to build a youth center from the shell of an overgrown abandoned house. The building was intended as a kind of *auberge* – a guest house for stays of various length, with some facilities for meetings and even performance.

A former Bessengue resident, Bernard, who had made a little money after emigrating to Europe, initiated this construction as an investment in the quarter, a signal of the viability of its urban future. But as soon as the building was finished, the owner disappeared. Apparently it was not a matter of the lack of proper permits, land deeds or continued funding. Rather, the common assumption was that powerful forces in the quarter did not want the business to succeed. The possibility of success – which was good, given the quality of the construction and its discrete yet highly central location – would bring in a flow of outsiders, and perhaps open up this section of the quarter to more scrutiny from the outside. Whatever the reason, everyone talked about how the owner had been scared off.

In trying to find out a little more about this story, I was told to find a dancer, Frances, who worked at a strip club in the center of the city and who had reputedly gone out with the owner for several months during the time the *auberge* was being built. She also happened to rent a room in the second tallest building in the quarter – a five-story shell of an apartment building some 100 m from the *auberge*. Frances had come to Douala two years before from the outskirts of Yaounde in order to pursue a singing career. Earning less than a $100 a month, she pursued what is called the 'usual supplementation', i.e. occasional sex for money. Although she wouldn't or couldn't say where Bernard was, she did indicate that he frequently called her late at night on her cellphone, usually with cryptic instructions to pay close attention to certain spots behind the shuttered windows of the *auberge*. She could report back whatever she saw the next time he called, but more importantly, she was to phone a variety of 'associates' and tell them what she witnessed.

What she did see, however, was almost always impossible for her to put into words – which Frances, someone to whom conversation came so easily, experienced as a pleasant surprise. So she took to simply inviting those to whom she was instructed to report over to her room at least twice a week before sunrise, and together they made their attempts to peer behind the building's opaque visage.

Sometimes, some of her guests took notes and passed them around, although Frances says that she couldn't make any sense of them. They would then make coffee and talk about their days. The guests would inquire whether or not the others had completed certain tasks, whether they had made sure to send certain express packages, fetch people from the airport, or wait in the lobbies of certain big hotels. Frances kept saying that it was never clear to her what they were really up to; rather, they seemed to relish each other's assignments and recommendations, and that somehow by simply assuming different positions in different sites that things were made to happen, and that events precipitated others. Though she was reluctant to have me simply drop by at these appointed times, I was told I might be interested on certain mornings to stand quietly down by the *auberge*, to watch the determined, even joyful way her guests fanned out from Bessengue at sunrise.

What is insidious in the neglect of Bessengue largely concerns an acceptance of marginality and a blindness as to how the quarter fits or could fit into the larger city. But as the chairperson of the local youth committee told me, what was really troubling to most residents was that the place was being used by unseen others in ways that they could not control, and so inactivity became, by default, a means of such control. This brief story of the watchtower is axiomatic, is about this blindness and the way it is constructed. But it also concerns how others, whose identities and purposes we really don't know, come to operate in such a field, in invisible ways we cannot know or anticipate. Perhaps in the near future, local development will require ways of imagining how better to 'go with such flows'.

Story II
President Paul Biya established Operation Command on 20 February 2000 as a means of rectifying the alarming increase in violent crime taking place in Douala. At first residents across the city widely applauded this military operation, as they had become increasingly terrified of venturing anywhere in public, even during daylight hours. It was common for people from all walks of life and in all quarters to tell stories of being held up at work, on the street, or in their homes. Equipped with vast powers of search and seizure, as well as arbitrary detention, Operation Command quickly zeroed in on a vast network of warehouses harboring stolen goods, as well as illicitly-acquired cars, houses, and consumer goods.

As the net widened, almost everyone came under greater suspicion. During raids on homes, if the residents were unable to immediately provide receipts for items like televisions or refrigerators, these items would be immediately confiscated. Increasingly, the Doualaise came to see Operation Command as organized military theft. There were also reports about large-scale extrajudicial killings, of detainees disappearing from prisons. Bodies of suspected criminals were often found in the streets with signs of torture and bullet wounds.

On 23 January, nine youths from the Bapenda quarter were picked up after a neighbor had reported them as having stolen a gas canister. They were taken to a police station in Bonanjo, on the other side of the city, where they were allowed to receive visits from their families and correspond with them, although they reported being physically tortured. On 28 January they were transferred to an Operation Command post, whereupon all communication from them stopped. The parents were unable to find any information as to the location of their children. Following the disappearance of the 'Bapenda Nine', Douala witnessed the first in a series of marches and demonstrations which were brutally suppressed by the police.

During this time there were many reputed sightings of the disappeared, usually at night and usually in quarters considered highly dangerous. The sightings would describe the boys as beaten and emaciated, but desperate to hide from the expected onslaught of Operation Command, from whom they had inexplicably escaped. There was widespread concern that if there were any validity to these sightings, everything possible should be done to keep the boys alive as witnesses to the assumed killing of thousands.

It is common practice in Douala to take in young girls from the rural areas as unpaid domestic servants. Many rural households can no longer provide for their children and so either throw them out of the home or sell them to intermediaries. These girls remain the 'property' of the households they work for and are usually badly mistreated and have little freedom of mobility. As Marc Etaha, Frederic Ngouffo, Chatry Kuete, Eric Chia, Jean Roger Tchiwan, Charles Kouatou, Chia Effician, Elysee Kouatou and Fabrice Kuate – the Bapenda Nine[7] – served as a kind of 'last straw' for the public patience with Operation Command, there was a uneasy mixture of guilt, anger, impotence, and mysticism wrapped up in the larger public response to their disappearance.

Whether people actually believed in the reputed sightings of the disappeared or not, in some quarters of the city a ritual developed consisting of efforts to feed the disappeared. Because the sightings were most frequently in very dangerous parts of the city, households would send their girl domestics, often great distances, to deliver food. From one sighting to the next, from one part of the city to the other, these girls ran the risk of their own disappearance on these feeding expeditions. In the process, however, they crossed Douala at night in ways that were at the time were without precedent. Sometimes they would meet up with other girls they had met on previous journeys and share what they had seen, as well as embellish stories and invent new ones. The danger entailed became secondary to the excitement of this sudden and usual daily freedom, for soon they would meet up in particular spots and go where they wanted, whether or not it corresponded with the destination they had been instructed to seek out.

Amnesty International, Cameroon: The Government must throw more light on the disappearence of 9 children in Douala, 2 March 2001. Online. Available, http://www.amnestyinternational.org

They would leave ciphers and other marks on cars and household walls, on store windows and security grates, or pile up empty pots and pans at key intersections. They would then tell their respective employers that the disappeared were attempting to leave messages, to communicate with the residents of the city about what was really taking place. Word spread that these girls had become not merely deliverers of food, but interlocutors between the disappeared and the city. Their capacities were greatly inflated in a city where the reputations of those able to navigate the world of the night were already inflated. And so several of the girls started being sought out by various officials, businesspeople, and even top personnel of Operation Command itself. They came not so much for direct information about the disappeared themselves nor to interpret their supposed messages. Rather, they wanted interpretations for their dreams, advice on new ventures, insights on the wheeling and dealing of colleagues and competitors.

Girls of 13 who not long before had gone hungry in rural areas experiencing thorough economic and social deprivation, who had been sold to fetch water in perpetuity, now suddenly found 10,000-CFA notes pressed into their hands, and started demanding more. Although I never saw her, stories spread how one of the girls, Sally, would hold court by the pool at the Meridien Hotel, cellphone in hand and surrounded by an entourage of bodyguards.

This story points to the marked rearrangement of moral economies underway in many African cities. A significant aspect of this rearrangement concerns an intensified ambiguity in the positionalities of subaltern populations, as well as inversions in hierarchies of generation. Those apparently entrapped in positions of actual or near servitude find turbulent spaces of some autonomy in navigating an array of spectral worlds and multiple temporalities that are as real as anything else in the city. In this way, children are credited with significant capacities, acquire significant financial resources, and give shape to new social groupings, at the same time as being viewed as possessing dangerous powers.

Throughout urban Africa, possibilities of a viable future are foreclosed for increasing numbers of youth. Without clearly structured responsibilities and certainties, the places they inhabit and the movements they undertake become instances of disjointed histories, in which places are subsumed into mystical or subterranean orders, prophetic universes, or highly localized myths that 'capture' their allegiance, and movements are daily reinvented routines that have little link to anything.

At the extreme, as the material underpinnings of the confidence in once reliable local institutions fades, larger numbers of Africans 'disappear' into a receding interior space – a kind of collective hallucination moving 'away' from the world. This can be a highly volatile space, for even if comprising intricate geographies of spirit worlds, it can upend ordinary civil life in an inchoate mix of cruelty and tenderness, indifference and generosity. At the same time, new relational webs are pieced together with different cultural strands and references. These webs sanction a capacity for residents to be conversant with sites, institutions and transactions at different scales; in other words, a capacity to know what to do in order to gain access to various kinds of instrumental resources.

Conclusion

The people of Douala know that they cannot go it alone, but who exactly to go with is another matter. For Douala has experienced a substantial disintegration of conventional social ties. There are no clear maps; no grand visions for a viable future, as in turn, there is little intact from the institutional 'archive' to be returned to life or to be reinvented. As one of the cities most renowned young artists, Malam, puts it:

> We in Douala always seem to imagine ourselves as somewhere else. While we don't necessarily want to leave this place, we act as if we have already left and this attitude works in several ways. On the one hand, those who are neighbors, who share, this street, for example, sometimes act as if they don't see what is going on. The life around them doesn't bother them because they are not really here, they are living their dream, and so people are more free to do what they want to do. On the other hand, because so many people are in so many other places in their minds, this can be their only common point of view, and so they can't really ask each other for anything, can't rely on each other because no one has a sense of what they are really experiencing. Also it means that things are speeded up; the children have already left the house and gone somewhere else; the father is already old, the mother is already old; the normal rhythm of growing up, of dying, of leaving and coming is all collapsed into a single note that everyone sings, and as such, can't hear each other, can't hear each other being criticized, being scrutinized, being liked or disliked, being told to stop what they are doing or do something different. It is a way of living everywhere and nowhere at the same time.

Number of inhabitants [p]	1,635,254
Area [km²]	360
Density [p/km²]	4,542
Population urbanized (national) [2003]	52%

Belgrade: Evolution in an Urban Jungle

STEALTH Group

Ana Dzokic | Milica Topalovic | Marc Neelen | Ivan Kucina

It did not come about overnight. At first, you would not have noticed the difference, perhaps here or there a glimpse of change. But then, in a sudden shockwave following the silence after the implosion, it was everywhere: all parts of this city suddenly started to move, to grow, to mutate. A new urban substance started to overtake its boulevards, its modernist structures and even the old districts. The city we were familiar with had ceased to exist and started to come intensely to life.

Triggered in an instant, the process, with its time ruptures and accelerations fed by the multitude gushing through it lasted for more than a decade. The city turned into a host of rapidly-growing colonies of urban mutants, which took over its land, its body, the water and the air. It felt as though the process was inevitable, as though the only course available was to watch it materializing.[1]

The virus

Approaching the city through its western gate, one first encounters its modernist suburbs, erected from the 1950s to the 1970s on the no man's land just outside its previous perimeter. Across the brutal open spaces of 'Block 45' or 'Block 70', a softening is apparent; countless small objects for trade and living infiltrate the large-scale ensembles. The sturdy, prefabricated apartment buildings are susceptible to the infection too, their ground-floor flats becoming shops, balconies being made to enclose new rooms, roofs being extended or turned into supports for new buildings. The most rigid structures mutate most quickly and most obviously. New Belgrade, once a showcase of internationalist planning, has invented and promoted its own pervasive logics of transformation, as follows:

Every form can be altered
Any building changes by extension and any typology changes by hybridization; rural houses emerge on top of skyscrapers.

[1] In the 1990s, against the background of the disintegration of the former Yugoslavia, the city of Belgrade faced a collapse of its economy, its governmental structures and its planning systems. The UN Embargo in 1992 brought matters to a head; the city imploded in all domains – economically, demographically, socially, etc.

Emergent processes started to replace the city's failing primary systems in the domains of trade, housing production and public services. What the 'institutions' no longer provided was now supplied by innumerable private initiatives with improvisation, *ad hoc* interventions and opportunistic solutions. The examples taken from the case of Belgrade describe the situation that existed from about 1991 until 2000. The decade of turbulence largely ended with the revolutionary events in October 2000, when a change of government took place. Some of the processes are still highly active, while others lost their intensity in the process of post-crisis normalization

Belgrade: Evolution in an Urban Jungle STEALTH Group

Architecture of camouflage
When the size of an extension is to be boosted over the permission limit, 'ghost' floors feature a mushroom-shaped roof envelope as a formal disguise. Construction goes on, while the architectural envelope becomes a cover-up.

Crossroads shall be centers
No man's land in New Belgrade, located on a major traffic junction, becomes the location targeted for street trade. In the space of only five years, it becomes the largest trading center in the country, and continues to grow through successive waves of legislation and informal invasion.

An entry for exotic agencies
In an unanticipated scenario, the first Chinese immigrants arrive in Belgrade in the mid 1990s. Their swift and silent infiltration targets a large vacant shopping center in Block 70 and turns it into an economic anchor point of the expanding Chinese community.

Edges are attractors
Along kilometers of riverbank, uncontrolled or deliberately overlooked developments in the leisure sector reach a peak. The 'boats' are moored not only in straight lines, but spread from the edges outwards into a floating fabric.

Function follows commercial potential
With a minimum of intervention, buildings explore the borderlines of their functionality: as long as it is economically attractive for it to do so, a public swimming pool functions as a private tennis court.

Leaving New Belgrade behind and crossing the river, the more densely built-up nineteenth century city is approached. The strong city axes, such as the monumental Boulevard of the Revolution, are being filled up with fragmentary objects which align

along the lines of flow, group around crossings and take over open spaces. Coagulating out of recurring waves of sedimentation, these objects change over time from mobile, light, additive structures to solid constructions. Their organization is highly sensitive to local conditions; all of them are continuously adapting to microshifts in context, both in the functions they perform and in the material forms they take.

Solidify in steps

A plastic 'temporary' kiosk placed on a sidewalk of the Boulevard over two years extends into a wood-framed café space, grows a concrete basement and adds a roof awning, while a concealed living space is created inside it. Linear repetition of this type of adaptive structure, along the sidewalks of principal streets, produces commercial strips.

A ground floor is a commercial asset

The entire 'ground floor' of the old city becomes part of the spread of commercial activity through fragmentary, individual conversions. Community centers, flats, houses and storage units give way to shops.

It is not only the physical urban ground that changes; the city's infrastructural services alter in parallel through a multitude of on-site solutions that are taking over from faltering formal institutional schemes.

No organization is stable

A critical shortage of gasoline and spare parts is an incentive for the transformation of the city's public transport system. The alternative model is not fixed, but distributes itself between the core of the old public company and numerous new 'one man, one vehicle' enterprises.

Efficient locations are tested on the ground
A network of mobile petrol traders quickly consolidates and leads to the building of new private petrol stations; constructed on sites that have been tested out by mobile predecessors at times when the regular gas stations are left without supply.

Leaving the city behind, the road continues outwards into territory of a less distinct character. In just a few years, entire districts of individual houses have covered the agricultural land, their ubiquitous brick glaring red on the skyline. Piles of construction materials are lying next to the roads. In a rush of opportunism, self-appointed developers have started constructing parts of the future city here.

Plan equals infrastructure
One of the new 'wild' housing areas in Belgrade's outskirts consists of over 1,000 houses. It is built on city land that even before passing the process of 'denationalization' (i.e., being given back to private owners) is already sold to developers. Fearing that their constructions could be demolished because they do not adhere to the regulations, the 'wild' builders obtain an existing official plan for the area, and reproduce the same street pattern themselves.

Fixed typologies hybridize
On a wide belt of public land surrounding the city, 'wild' houses range from the modest to 'dreamland' villas. In an habitual playing with an individual house type, the owner of a private transport company merges his house with his bus garage.

An alien presence has surfaced in the city, inserting itself into, and bending its structures. Instigated by a decaying institutional body, it has become an ubiquitous, corrupting, but vital force.

The city has become a generative, expanding organism that quickly adjusts and adapts to every possibility, while driven by an instinct to keep its primary systems functioning. As Kevin Kelly has said:

> We find many systems ordered as a patchwork of parallel operations, very much as in the neural network of a brain or in a colony of ants. Action in these systems proceeds in a messy cascade of interdependent events. Instead of the discrete ticks of cause and effect that run a clock, a thousand clock springs try to simultaneously run a parallel system. Since there is no chain of command, the particular action of any single spring diffuses into the whole, making it easier for the sum of the whole to overwhelm the parts of the whole. What emerges from the collective is not a series of critical individual actions but a multitude of simultaneous actions whose collective pattern is far more important. [2]

The nature of cities and the way we look at them has begun to change sharply in recent years. A full range of concepts and practices, from transnational mobility, the global economy and communication technology to cloning and terrorism have only recently begun to be considered. As the social structures and urban models of the 'first modernity' fade, changing economic forces, different power structures and individual dynamics alter the workings of urban systems, and speed up their total dynamics.

The example of Belgrade connects to these large-scale processes, not as a conventional example but as a compressed and extreme case; an instance of the fallout from collateral events of this changing reality. The first striking manifestation of it is the

[2] Kevin Kelly, *Out of Control*, London: Fourth Estate, 1994

[3] Kelly lists the advantages and disadvantages of distributed or dispersed systems. Ibid., pp. 28—30

dazzling chaos – or, more accurately, the apparent chaos. What is perceived as a cacophony of events is rather a city in movement, a large, dynamic system.

With growing entropy in the urban environment and an ever increasing degree of freedom, the viability of the practices of architecture and planning in these conditions remains an open question. But if approached from another angle and with a different set of rules, the behavior of urban dynamics may become accessible.

Firstly, to capture the character and effects of dynamic systems, studies in various fields (from parallel computing to biology) point to certain characteristics: such systems are adaptable, resilient and capable of evolving, they cannot be contained within prescribed boundaries, and they encourage novelty. However, these systems also have drawbacks: they are non-optimal, non-controllable, non-predictable, non-intuitive and non-immediate. In a different framework, these drawbacks will read as positive qualities, too.[3]

Maximize the margin

Satisfy multiple goals

Assuming these characteristics have also been at play in the case of Belgrade, an attempt has been made here to interpret and describe the city as such a large dispersed system. Its principal 'laws' are listed here: [4]

Maximize the margin
Margin [<-> center]. In ecology, the greatest diversity of species occurs on the boundaries between ecosystems. Similarly, emergent processes favor the margin in urban territory, in search of (physical and regulatory) no-man's land in which to test new possibilities. A lively fringe is the source of innovation.

Organize through heterarchy
Heterarchy [<-> hierarchy]. The actors in the urban system are connected through a large distributed network. Control rests at the bottom; the total escapes central governance. Each individual actor acts within his local conditions and negotiates his position against others who are doing the same. Heterarchal systems foster adaptation.

Disperse control
Dispersion [<-> centralization]. The behavior of an urban system is distributed over a multitude of smaller units, creating a complex that is more resilient and powerful than the sum of its parts. Distributed systems promote survival and evolution.

Use positive feedback
Positive feedback [<-> negative feedback]. The system promotes its own reproduction by increasing returns (the 'snowball' effect). Rapid intensification of newly-evolving processes is possible. Successful moves act as catalysts for subsequent developments, mapping out further potential.

[4] The 'laws' of Belgrade are inspired by the 'Nine Laws of God' Kelly compiled for evolving systems. Ibid., pp. 602–606

Belgrade: Evolution in an Urban Jungle STEALTH Group

Organize through heterarchy   Disperse control   Use positive feedback

Grow through continuous transformation   Seek interaction

Satisfy multiple goals
Omnidirectional [<–> efficient]. A large and heterogeneous system will seek to satisfy a multitude of goals by continuously exploring and testing new paths. Efficiency is traded for multiple effectiveness. Acting omnidirectionally keeps open numerous routes to success.

Grow through continuous transformation
Development through transformation [<–> stagnation]. The transition from a simple to a more complex form takes place over time. Large, complex urban systems emerging need time to grow and establish themselves. Complexity develops through successive waves of trial and error, from simple organizations to more sophisticated ones.

Seek interaction
Interaction [<–> sum of parts]. Distributed urban systems have a tendency to find modes of interaction and influence within the system as well as towards centralized institutional systems. Each part starts to influence the other and ultimately to change the organization of the total. A complex system keeps adapting its relations while it develops. With these 'laws' for its behavior laid out, one starts to imagine 'managing' the city in a different way – approaching it from within the motives of the system. This will make it possible to understand its emergent behavior and to intervene within the spirit of its own logic.

This city is not a designed masterpiece. It is alive, non-optimal and capable of evolving, and it shows a surprising agility in exploring opportunities and possibilities. Its innovations are present at all scales and on all levels: spatial, physical, typological, programmatic and organizational. It has become a mutating body, influenced by the virulent power of micro-entities, and it should be understood as such. Its innovative character is the result of infection by an urban virus.

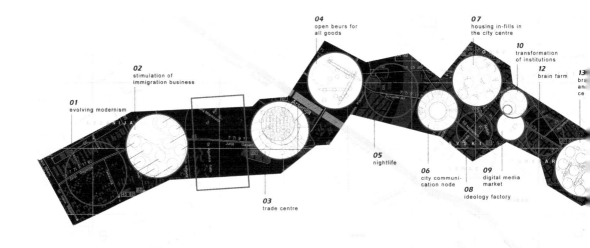

01 evolving modernism
02 stimulation of immigration business
03 trade centre
04 open beurs for all goods
05 nightlife
06 city communication node
07 housing in-fills in the city centre
08 ideology factory
09 digital media market
10 transformation of institutions
12 brain farm
13 bra an ce

Hunting and engineering

Some software designers at the experimental forefront of their field speculate that the software of the future, rather than being designed, will be pretty much grown, in a suitable digital environment.[5] The subjects of these experiments are advanced computer viruses, which work as pieces of self-transforming code. These viruses are regarded as among the most sophisticated examples of software in existence, and recent developments in this field of research have been astounding.

What places viruses above most other software is that they display traces of intelligence. Even very small virus strings can be self-replicating and self-evolving in response to given 'environmental conditions'. In an experimentally created 'digital-primordial soup', viruses unleashed at a massive scale will quickly deliver more and more sophisticated generations – a true 'digital evolution' through rapid mutations. It required a change in thinking to understand that the relentless power of these 'creatures' should not be seen as malicious, but that it can be used to address complex questions. Given enough time and curiosity, 'beneficial viruses'[6] would potentially be able to surpass even the most mature creations of a software engineer.

The designer in this situation is no longer the maker of an actual, finished software but the one who selects it, cultivates it and, primarily, creates the right environment for the process to unfold. This change in roles recasts the experimenter in a more exploratory role: the unidirectional software-designer becomes a 'digital ecologist'.

If this approach helps to determine solutions for such complex environments, can it be of influence in designing a city? Belgrade provides the ideal conditions for such an experiment. During its decade of rapid transformation, the city has acted as an incubator for permanent urban innovation; one that permits and encourages the formation

[5] An inspiring example of research into digital evoluti can be found in Tom Ray's computer world, called 'Tierra'. Ray set out and observed an incredible evolu tion of self-replicating pro gram strings (basically virus like structures) into complex software, which already sur passes the programming abi ities of today's software eng neers. He found that a degre of imperfection has to exist in the system in order to pro duce newness. His ambition to release these viruses (strings of programming code) into the space of the World Wide Web. Due to its vast size, the Web would act as an enormous jungle, an environment in which the viruses could develop. Ray sees the software engineer c the future as a hunter in the jungle, seeking out desired program strings that could b adapted for use

[6] Julian Dibbell 'Viruses are good for you', *Wired*, February 1995

and development of new urban species across different scales. As in the digital evolution model, these 'species' will often surpass in their originality the products of a designer's imagination and sharply conflict with routine solutions.

The forms of 'urban evolution' that feature interesting physical and organizational performance cannot be understood without studying the processes that create or breed these outcomes. The possible role of architects and planners is not only in recognizing and extracting 'spontaneous' urban production, but in influencing, designing, shifting the processes themselves – which means a shift of focus from designing objects to designing processes. In this approach, practical interest in physical form, shape or growth patterns is secondary to interest in the character and behavior of the urban process itself. The question is therefore not so much 'what can I use it for?' but 'how does it work?'

The processes observed in Belgrade cannot simply be called chaotic. They are largely going through similar patterns of changes; there is a specific set of behaviors connected to them. They are based on a series of actions: negotiations and transitions between the inherited 'top-down' and the emerging distributed systems. When these actions are anlysed chronologically, it becomes possible to determine the patterns of interaction between the different actors. In this way, their physical and organizational change can be further mapped, in order to highlight qualities such as speed, attraction, strength, success, failure, etc. An analysis that follows this approach might be called 'urban genetics'.

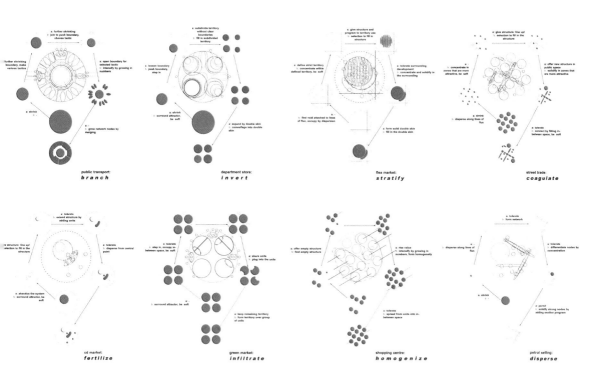

Among the initial conclusions, such an analysis shows that in nearly all of the studied processes, ranging from street trade to the city's transport, emergent organizations have been achieved through conflict and negotiation between institutions and individuals. Symbiotic systems are formed, in which the small elements are in charge of producing newness and flexibility, while the large elements (mainly 'institutional' actors) maintain the minimum of stability required to keep the system running. Analysing these urban genes (expressed as strings of action) gives an insight into the logic of their seemingly chaotic behavior: within the framework of a very complex range of possibilities, the set of rules that is applied remains fairly simple.

Now that the logic of these emergent processes has been opened up, is it possible to develop strategies to steer these processes? Starting from urban genetics, it has been possible to develop a basic simulation tool that makes it possible to enter the still largely unexplored territory of forecasting and then navigating the possible outcomes within what might be called 'evolutionary' design.

Perhaps a profitable field for further experimentation will be in the realm of computing. One can imagine developing urban genes as algorithms by translating them into software. This is possibly a field where knowledge from different disciplines can intersect and cross-fertilize.

Understanding cities as complex adaptive systems, which do not behave along traditional lines, poses numerous questions: can architecture and urbanism be open towards 'spontaneous' innovations; can they be flexible in interaction with the environment, and better equipped to take part in the animate urban network? Can the process of working within the real spectrum of urban production be opened up and move beyond the present scope of the discipline? The apparent suggestion is that designers and planners might want to formulate more operative attitudes. It would be a move from top-down, unilateral and project-based architecture toward an open-ended approach, with emphasis not on individual projects, but on the process of creating environments and on means of steering their course.

One of the perspectives here could be framed as sense-and-respond architecture[7] or, more precisely, a sense-and-respond urban environment (and urban planning), capable of dealing with the complex interactions and the hyperdynamics of urban worlds. The first step for designers is to capture and play with the mechanisms of such urban behavior, and assess, through this, the possibilities for their own world.

[7] John Thackara, 'World' is a verb, *Hunch* (4) 2001

The article in this book is based on the research Wild City: Genetics of Uncontrolled Urban Processes (www.archined.nl/wildcity) whose findings have been translated into an open-source simulation software (www.processmatter.net) with the aim of building a tool that deals with the spatial impact of urban evolution.

Number of inhabitants [p]	6,803,100
Area [km²]	1,102
Density [p/km²]	6173
Population urbanized (national) [2003]	39%

Hong Kong: The Experienced City
Gary Chang

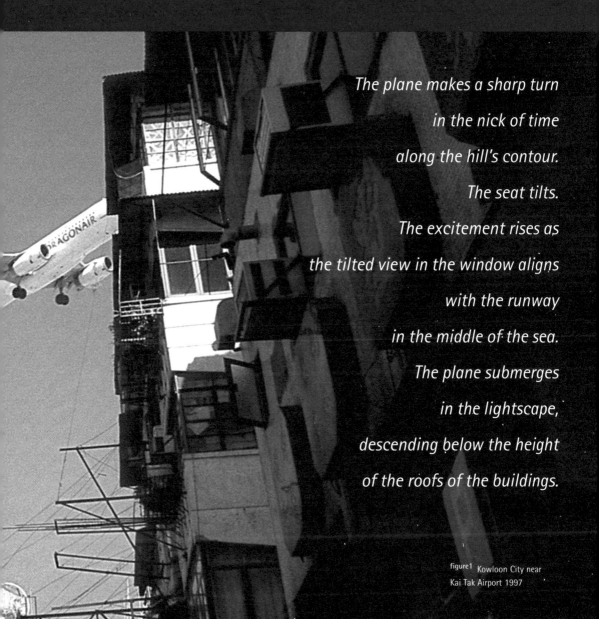

The plane makes a sharp turn
in the nick of time
along the hill's contour.
The seat tilts.
The excitement rises as
the tilted view in the window aligns
with the runway
in the middle of the sea.
The plane submerges
in the lightscape,
descending below the height
of the roofs of the buildings.

figure1 Kowloon City near
Kai Tak Airport 1997

Plane cabin, 6 p.m.

Water condenses into droplets on the window. I find an image compacted into each of them: a small autonomous world contained in each transparent hemisphere. Each miniature 'world' is placed against a bigger version of itself: glittery lights, densely packed into this small city.

Plane cabin, 7 p.m.

Plane descending. My lips move, but no words come.

The 140 decibels create a momentary silence. The aircraft lands safely, thanks to the light guidance system on top of a seafood restaurant. The crowd resumes its bustle.

The city mass is infected with radiant voids and glowing objects. Brilliant windows mark out the contours of buildings. Monstrous neon signs attach themselves everywhere. Can the host buildings support these invasions?

Runway, 7 p.m.

Dark wheels descend from the body of the plane and begin a frenzied spinning upon touching the runway.

Hong Kong: The Experienced City Gary Chang

figure 2 Kowloon City, 1997

figure 3 Terminal Building at
Kai Tak Airport, 2002

Terminal Building, 5 p.m.

The bowling ball drops heavily from his grip and starts a smooth rolling upon touching the alley. It disappears into the gutter.

Section G is filled with bowling alleys; sections A–C of the departure lounge are taken up by the mini-kart race; a second-hand car showroom has been opened in Sections J–O. The transportation terminal transformed into a space of consumption.[1]

Plane cabin, 5.25 p.m.

He tries to move: the fastened seat belt imposes a rigid constraint on his movement.

Gary Chang Hong Kong: The Experienced City

Home, 2 a.m.

He can hardly move: the rusty mesh hems him in.

Cage house. An adapted space of three-dimensional modules.

Chessboard. A simulated battlefield on a grid. Every movement is subject to strict rules.

A chessboard and the pieces occupy the center of the common space, surrounded by iron mesh cages. Each cage measures 180 cm by 90 cm by 90 cm, intersected by 90 cm passageways. Stacked up three high, the cages are packed with people.

Minimum privacy, maximum intimacy.

Looking through the iron mesh I find the slow chess game always going on, with lights occasionally flickering between the silhouettes of the old men, fragmented TV images projecting on the chessboard.

The same scene plays out every day, from dawn till dusk. It will go on for another 30 years. In the heyday of this cage house, there have been more than 60 residents in as many cages in this apartment of 70 sq m. People come and go, but it is always the same fellowship of the aged, the sickly, the addicts.

The pantry and the bathroom are shared; so are the inhabitants' lives.

Hong Kong: The Experienced City Gary Chang

figure 4 Quarry Bay, 1996

figure 5 Tenement Building in Tai Kok Tsui, 2001

figure 6 Tenement Building in Tai Kok Tsui, 2001

figure 7 Hill Road, 2001

Home, 2.30 p.m.

In this situation of extreme verticality, the sense of verticality is diminished.

My apartment is next to the motorway; my apartment is on the nineth floor. Between my window and the floating concrete strip is a 3 m gap.

Static rooms and mobile spaces.
Cars speed by at 50 km per hour, on this winding road in mid-air snaking down towards the seafront. The window shakes. Double-deckers roller coaster. Signboards shake and swing. At 25 metres above ground, the car disappears into a jungle of habitation.

Directly underneath, pedestrians move at ground level. The disconnection and reconnection of space. Propinquity redefined.

The escalator starts at 7 a.m.,

going downhill.

At 2 p.m. it starts going

in the other direction.

It stops at 11 p.m.

Length: 800 m.

Estimated number of riders:

20,000 per day

(actual figures on weekends

may be twice that).

Total number of footbridges

in Hong Kong: 550.

Travelator: hybridized horizontality and verticality. A huge but simple external transportation machine. I am traveling on the longest outdoor escalator in the city. Commonly called the 'pedestrian escalator' by locals, it is officially the 'Central Hillside Escalator'. Distinguished by its length as well as the brutality of its implementation, it cuts abruptly through the central part of the city built on the hillside. More and more of these cuts are envisaged in the old fabric in the near future.

As I move along, the adjacent buildings are at arm's length. I can almost peel off the aged mosaic tiles. A family's television tells me the morning news.

The escalator changes direction daily, washing the human tide up and down this metal canal between dense concretes.

Mall, 2.30 p.m.

The escalators climb into the 30,000 sq m mall. On the other side of the glass, the greyish tenement building looks like a shabby doll's house. The vehicles give the impression of colourful matchboxes scattered around.

Inside the mall, layers and layers of shops are stacked one upon another. Brightly-lit temporary stalls fit into every corner of the atrium. Signboards flash past – a shower of capitalistic commercialism.

Hong Kong: The Experienced City Gary Chang

The mall is the shrine, a citadel within the city. Public space uninterrupted from 15 stories above to five stories below.

I lounge around, join the crowd and stroll to the next floor, till I move to another mall by a hodge-podge network of bridges.

Or I follow the ubiquitous signs for the Mass Transit Railway. Both ends of the train are out of sight. From station to station, one can transect the city from south to north in 30 minutes, enjoying the luxury of the air-conditioning all the way. You are not alone; more than 2,200,000 people pass the same way every day, doing the same thing, heading in the same direction. Getting off at any stop, one is greet-ed by the same view: each station opens into a mall.

figure 8 Central, 2000

figure 9 Office Building in Quarry Bay, 1997

figure 10 Shopping Mall in Mong Kok, 1998

figure 11 Shopping mall in West Kowloon City, 1999

Gary Chang Hong Kong: The Experienced City

Street, 1 a.m.

"I want what I want to say to go without saying." [2]

The hardware stores retreat into the buildings. Another order of male consumption emerges out of the dark. Streets with neon signs aglow stimulate the sensation of temptation. Multicoloured arrows point out where the brothels are, speaking of furtive stories behind shanty façades. I only watch, having no expectations. The laughter and the ecstasy are cheap – cheap as the fluorescent lights that are continually broken by the police, but put back by the pimps the next day. Yet this free-floating architecture lures me: it is flexible and direct, telling nothing and everything in a wink. No words. The lights in the night seem to say that they should not be saying anything.

figure 12 Sheung Wan, 2000

figure 13 Reclamation Street in Mong Kok, 2001

Hong Kong: The Experienced City Gary Chang

Labyrinth, 11.15 p.m.

The lights gradually fuse in a labyrinth of brightly-lit alleys crowded with food stands. Crude stoves out front. Scrap metal and assorted other junk packing every corner. One 'restaurant', from the tables to the kitchen, efficiently wedged into an alley that is literally a few feet wide.

No public seats, but hundreds for the customers. Hundreds of tents and kiosks packing the ground. Hundreds of signboards and awnings sprawling overhead, fashioning a cover above the low, rusty corrugated steel roofs. The hustling ferments and will last through the night, a smorgasbord of experience.

A cure for my insomnia.

Boxes, 6.30 a.m.

The dawn empties the bustling labyrinth. The street becomes five times wider. Puddles dot the ground and reflect the morning sky. A row of green boxes is left on both sides. As the stores retract behind metal sheets, so does the life of the street. This is the transience of a 24-hour city.

figure 14 Night Market in Yau Ma Tei, 1996

figure 15 Night Market in Yau Ma Tei, 1996

Façade, 8 p.m.

Excavations in the air. Visible shells attached to the dense city blocks, floating over the labyrinth of speed, stopping your gaze, hiding my life – the sight is unbalancing. Nomadic structures for urban nomads.

Layers of apartments stretching all around. The sky is filled with hundreds of balconies, one above another, each one fronting an apartment. The soot-blackened buildings seem even murkier at night. Rusting assemblies of air conditioners rumbling. The gust sweeps across the room a meter above my head.

I peep at the concrete of the newer residential buildings through the unblocked half of my window. The apartments there have windowsills instead of a balcony. I hang my clothes and potted plants on the balcony. They pile their windowsills with books, toys and knick-knacks.

Hong Kong: The Experienced City Gary Chang

Construction site, 9 a.m.

An ingenious structure created with a thick mat of bamboo and plastic netting. Wrapping becomes the vernacular public art.

Plans and changes, construction and demolition: a renaissance under way.

Green-mirrored towers of office space are the rule. I cannot keep my eyes off the walls of glass – so tall that they seem to blend into the sky. Among them lattices of simple bamboo twine more than 100 m into the air. Shortened lifecycles in exchange for vitality.

figure 16 Causeway Bay, 1998

figure 17 Mong Kok, 1998

figure 18 Quarry Bay, 1999

Hong Kong: The Experienced City Gary Chang

figure 19 Central, 2000

figure 20 Bus, 2001

Bus, 6 p.m.

Double-decker cruising at 45 km per hour.
A humid day with the thermometer reading 34°C.
The artificial airstreams give me goosebumps.

"There's things going on outdoors," so the LCD screens
say. The four of them and the numerous speakers turn
the compartment into a miniature theatre – music
videos and programs and advertisements providing a
diversion for lonely bus travellers. It is as if I am at
home watching TV: a compact version of the same
program on the regular channels.

I turn to the fleeting views outside this air-conditioned bus compartment. The tinted glass adds an
odd hue to the scenery, which is blurred as vapour
condenses on the window. The view is clearer on the
screen. 'Outdoors' is interiorised.

[1] On 8 July 1998 Kai Tak
Airport was closed after the
opening of the Chek Lap Kok
Airport. Its terminal building
has been converted into an
entertainment mall

[2] Martin Creed, interviewed
by Chris Coombes. Online.
Excerpt available: www.chan-
nel4.com/turner/MartinCreed
Main.htm

Number of inhabitants [p]	1,256,211
Area [km²]	182
Density [p/km²]	6,902
Population urbanized (national) [2003]	67%

Milan: Urban Footnotes
Stefano Boeri

Monuments

Peter Fischli and David Weiss frame the stereotypes of the Milanese touristic imaginary - the Duomo, the Velasca Tower, the fog - from 70 m above the ground. And from above they reveal the buildings jockeying for position in the mass of urban volumes.

Milan is a five-story city; an artificial slab 15–20 m high and 6 km in diameter, frayed at its edges, carved by regular fissures, as flat as the ground it lies upon. The few buildings that rise above this homogeneous fissured slab have access to a rarefied world of isolated individualities, paradoxically more democratic than the one at their feet where the marble or the brick, the stairways or the lobbies mark the distinction between elite and ordinary buildings. Above 20 m, the vertical volumes, though different in form and age, seem instead to be unified: structures of steel, glass, reinforced concrete, skyscrapers, tympani, bell towers, campanili, look at one another across a distance, conscious of their privileged condition. Lacking the wide monumental boulevards and baroque rhetorics of Rome, Naples, Turin, Milan preserves the sky as a space of celebrative redemption, the square for its vertical monuments. The rarefied panorama that is offered at their higher levels enfolds them all.

From the opposite direction, Guido Guidi stops to look upwards at the vertical surfaces of Milan, capturing parts of the post-World War II period — ordinary parts, which we usually observe without attention, out of the corner of the eye: plasters with faint colors, yellowish, pink, light green, that are the visual background hum of contemporary Milan.

However, framed by Guidi's lens, the plaster displays much more than a surface; it is a sensible and porous skin, which reflects and shows its age, its imperfections, its misfortunes and lack of upkeep. The poorer the building's skin, the more plaster is required to make up for its physiognomic defects: it substitutes its swerves and its profiles for the stone friezes, the embossments at street level, the stone ornament around the entrances. The more lavishly this substitution is extended, the more it is exposed to interferences, to crudeness, to degradation. The fragile skin of this 'city within a city' is a delicate and precious sensor of the present time; the public surface which seems to be the extension of the everyday story of life and its tensions.

Figure 2 Milano, 1998,
Guido Guidi

One could try to apprehend in a few frames an entire urban dimension. Thomas Struth does not capture places; he rather takes samples of spatiality, or better, *amplitudes*. His is, literally, a work on urban interiors exposed to the public gaze: covered interiors of the huge cathedral and others without their roofs, a medieval street, a nineteenth-century square, a wide, tree-planted avenue. Struth compiles a catalogue of empty spaces, probably struck by their capacity to generate proportions and rules in the compact texture of Milan: between blocks, between façades, between the corners of the buildings that look onto street crossings. His is a reduced and compelling catalogue, also because it recalls by counterpoint another set of Milanese interiors. Behind the palaces, the façades, we can indeed imagine the invisible and diffused presence of other more intimate and inaccessible interiors, typical of a city used not to show off its treasures: courts, lobbies, kiosks, places of interactivity and exploration.

The places par excellence of intellectual production in Milan – private art galleries, professional offices, research institutes, ateliers – are often invisible from the public space; isolated environments, yet frequently connected with the whole world. In an urban society which no longer has the personalities or institutions capable of linking knowledges and cultures, this archipelago of excellent and invisible monads, isolated and immersed in a vast homogeneous texture which does not connect and that in a certain sense struggles to establish relations elsewhere, represents the other face of the regular and constant Milan of the historical center and of the nineteenth-century expansions, but it also gives a clue to its polemical, forward-looking modernity.

figure 3 Via Morone,
Milano, 1998,
Thomas Struth

By scrutinizing the bases of the columns of San Lorenzo and the profiles of the Roman bas-reliefs of the Archaeological Museum, Mimmo Jodice does not abandon the contemporaneity of Milan. He seems rather to seek here the 'deep structures' of the city. The anatomy of the ancient stones, a study on the variation of figures that are similar yet always different, suddenly reveals what usually remains unknown, or poorly visible, absorbed by the ordinary texture of the city. It is a covert world of stratifications and accidents, which in Milan shows itself in discreet points.

Jodice reveals to us the frightening familiarity of some of these archetypes that the city shelters and then forgets, such as the remains of the Roman Circus, or the frescos which ornament the apses of many churches; spaces extraneous to the touristic flows and often caressed by a distracted, frenzied daily life, which we know without having ever really observed them.

Precisely because it is almost never coincidental, rhetorical, the ancient in Milan is redeemed in the particular, in the detail. It forms the image itself, provided that a sophisticated and rigorous gesture is able to isolate it, restoring its aura.

figure 4 and 5 Anamnesi, 1998, Mimmo Jodice

Moving through the spaces of the Milanese periphery today, as Gabriele Basilico and John Davies do, means encountering – among other things – the urban facts produced in the Milan of the 1980s. Among these Davies isolates a few episodes, locating them on a background of a landscape of void spaces and samplings of the ground.

Basilico instead brings with him the proportions that rise from a long dialogue with twentieth-century Milan: the Milan of the blocks and of the avenues, of the extensions of the ancient urban fabric, of the sober and clear façades that cover dense volumes and inaccessible courtyards. With eyes filled with the Milan that forms a fabric, that value the connective tissue rather than the exceptions, that absorb the variations on a theme as long as they respect the rules, Basilico meets the awkward silhouettes of the city of *Tangentopoli*.

The glossy and disjointed shapes of the towers of the Giambellino district are not dissimilar to the skyscrapers of the State Railway Company in the Garibaldi-Repubblica area, to the towers at Ortica or to those in Via dei Missaglia, to the office slabs in Via Gratosoglio, to the subway stations of Line 3 of the metro, cases that have become symbols of an extended social and urban condition.

Tangentopoli has become suddenly the story of an entire construction phase of the city: the multi-story building with penthouse, the office tower with the service slab, the interstitial glass-clad low-rise. It is a story of recurring motifs – the modular reflecting panels, the absence in the cladding of any identification of the internal spaces, the strident juxtaposition of materials (aluminum and stone, wood and plastics) – and of anomalous procedures – the rotation of the winners of the competitions, the percentage on the professional fees, the 'black' payments to the political party, and the 'envelope' to the city official.

Basilico's gaze measures this exuberant and awkward city, attracted by its surprising and dull plasticity. And he shows us how most of the constructions that comprise the Milan of the 80s embody a certain spectacular complacency: the 'out of scale', the ostentation of richness, a formal arbitrariness so clumsy that it never becomes transgressive. Its monuments – today almost all are abandoned – are a caricature of the great buildings that were simultaneously changing the face of other European cities, enriching them with services, museums, stations, libraries or airports. They are like fragments of a colonized Third World stuck like a crown on the compact city, just before the vast metropolitan extent of the one family houses and of the industrial sheds. Yet for good or ill, they form an integrated, absorbed part of this city of ours. Basilico's gaze sadistically lays these buildings bare, exploring them without preconceptions and inducing a sensation of distaste, as if we are looking at our dirty laundry.

Figure 6 Milano, 1998, Gabriele Basilico

figure 7 and 8 Milan: Real Estate, 1998, John Davies

Solitary waiting constitutes, in Milan, the symbolic form of public space. The figures of the passers-by photographed by Paul Graham are alone; if the movement in the city is collective – a flux of compressed monads – waiting is almost always individual. One stops in public space only to wait for something that triggers movement once more: a tram, a friend, a lift. Many are waiting, but waiting alone.

Graham's still presences, poised to be on the move again, carry with them objects that identify them and that protect them from the opportunity of any communication. These are typical objects of a solitary and mobile use of urban space, labels of an otherwise anonymous sample of figures: satchels, backpacks, handbags, dogs, books, newspapers. During the wait one does not know exactly where to put them, yet exactly for this reason they occupy the waiting time. There are many specialized places for solitary waiting – probably the only really designed elements in public spaces – yet potentially it happens everywhere: in the interstices, in niches, at the borders of the areas of great flow, in front of a monument, in a peripheral road, under a portico.

If we could rotate Graham's camera, we would probably discover next to these solitary figures a presence that is complementary to them. We would see another symbolic form of contemporary Milan, the huge billboards that cover entire façades of the Milanese buildings. On the illuminated vertical panels, fashion photography, even portraits, have ousted text. The walls of Milan today play host to huge, dressed, made-up, entwined bodies that try to monopolize the entire scene of avenues and crossroads. Like the passers-by photographed by Graham, they too are static supernumeraries, yet temporary amidst the cars and pedestrian flows – which, flowing, barely glance at them.

Waiting

figure 13 Milano, 1998, Vincenzo Castella

The asphalt is a broken puzzle. On the right-hand side, a vast, weed-covered space is occupied here and there by stone slabs extracted from the road. Three contiguous and non-coinciding series of black-and-white lines direct the quick footsteps of 26 passers-by. Seven waiting cars are scattered randomly on the edge of the road and the foot-path. Six (probably disused) tram tracks cut the cobbles. Lamplights, tram posts, road signs, billboards, 'men at work' barriers, bus shelters – and off to one side, 25 white 'panettoni' traffic bollards lined up for no discernible purpose.

With two successive moves, the gaze of Vincenzo Castella catches unprepared and at the same time holds, a portion of Milan's ground-plane; it surrounds it, suddenly cap-turing samples of objects, figures and surfaces that otherwise, if there were more time, would probably manage to recompose themselves.

The first move takes place at the moment of the photographic shot. The oblique angle of the telescopic lens produces a sort of photographic axonometry that redeems from indifference and anonymity the city's surface. The city's ground is no longer only some-thing that exists alongside us, as a big neutral support, but it becomes the protagonist of the urban scene. It acquires thicknesses, unevenesses, diverse transgressions –

Milan: Urban Footnotes Stefano Boeri

wrinkled, slippery, dusty – as broken terrain, marked out by the bodies and the volumes of the city. An articulated surface where there are no shadows, in a city where light is often feeble and diffused, with no source. A city almost without squares, where there are no places of rest, that offers an often dirty and therefore paradoxically rich ground. Because it absorbs the small traces of daily life – cigarette butts, public transport tickets, syringes, dog shit – this is a terrain that is often too little or too heavily illuminated.

Milan is also a very particular surface. It is a disregarded yet paradoxically continuously overwritten public space, always being re-elaborated by the copious maintenance works of municipal districts, by gas and telephone companies, by traffic control. A sterile and perennial building yard.

The second move, made possible by digital re-elaboration, gives depth and precision to the photographic image. The translation into a digital code of the negative increases in fact the capacity of the instantaneous image to capture information and controls its output during the printing process. On one hand the high resolution of the negative frees the image from its ephemeral status and simultaneously opens it to a slow, accurate, precise inspection of what it is in a piece of urban ground surface that becomes the scene of a simultaneity of events; infinite things happen in this frozen portion of space, and each figure seems to leave a clear track. Dynamics to be studied, explored, predicted in their next moves. The time of fruition is prolonged thus in the many possible zooms, in the scale leaps, in observing and isolating details.

On the other hand, digital color selection filters the chromatic excesses and brings back to a common ground the materials of the city, without irreversibly canceling differences, as happens with black and white. It is enough, in fact, to let one tonality emerge. Urban space re-acquires discrete, vital points: the overalls of the building-site workers, the lines for public transport, the rainbow colors of a fruit and vegetable hawker. Digital color manipulation is an explicit and controlled way to articulate the field of urban materials and to let the whole dimension of daily life emerge: that of the temporary, unstable, mobile lives of a city, of the public spaces that burst into life and fade out again in the vicinity of transport nodes and spontaneous public events, of the places of encounter of erratic and often dislocated communities. It takes a little time and effort to see this uneasy Milan; one has to slow down, stop, sharpen the eye.

This photography is a research program. An atlas of other sectors of the urban surface, frames of asphalt and cobbles upon which gestures and costumes show themselves become a precious instrument, which can be used for the purpose of in-depth study to facilitate a better understanding of Milan and along with it many other cities.

A

Mumbai

Tokyo

Tokyo

Beijing

Mumbai

E

Tokyo

Buenos Aires

Singapore

São Paulo

Hong Kong

F

Cairo

Tokyo

Shanghai

Bangkok

Los Angeles

C

D

Mumbai

Beijing

New York

Bangkok

HongKong

Buenos Aires

B

Johannesburg

Las Vegas

New York

Cairo

Beijing

Los Angeles

Johannesburg

Mumbai

Moscow

Singapore

Singapore

Kuala Lumpur

The Image of Metropolis
NEXT Architects

ALIEN [tourist industry] In 2000, there were nearly 700 million tourists exploring the globe and in 2020 there will be around 1.6 billion. By some measures tourism is the world's largest industry, accounting for 11% of global GDP and a similar proportion of world employment.[1] [hotels] From 1980 to 2000 the world's hotel capacity doubled to 29,34 million beds.[2] [tourism destinations] France 75.5 million, United States 50.9 million, Spain 48.2 million, Italy 41.2 million and China 31.2 million.[3]

BUSINESS By their sheer size the world's transnational corporations have become major [world players] sales of Japan's Itochu Corporation exceed the gross domestic product of Austria, while those of Mitsui and General Motors exceed the GDP of all sub-Saharan Africa combined. TNC's now control two thirds of all world trade and 80 per cent of foreign investment.[4] [business tips] Arrive 30 minutes late when meeting Indonesian counterparts. Get emotional when doing business with Russians. And if you're a man, shave of your beard before a business trip to Taiwan since hairy faces are considered unclean. Saudi law prohibits the wearing of neck jewellery by men, and Westerners have been arrested for neglecting to observe this rule. The standard Chinese greeting is "Have you eaten?" Even if you haven't eaten, give a simple "Yes" answer, since this is similar to "How are you?" in the English-speaking world.[5] [China] With over 300 million families owning a television, and over 900 active television stations, China is the biggest market for international advertisement. [India] Call centres are booming business in India. With the ability of Indians to speak English, India is taking over many of the back office tasks of the world. In India they do it better, cheaper and quicker. A London consumer, calling a local helpdesk with the question whether the salmon is fresh, may have his phone call transferred to India where an Indian with perfect accent may answer his question. The Londoner notices nothing.[6]

COCA COLA [trademark] Coca-Cola is the world's most recognizable trademark, known by 94% of the world's population.[7] [Coke] Coca-Cola Company policy is that everyone in the world should be confronted by the word 'Coke' at least once every five minutes.[8] [beverage] The world downs 11,574 of the Coca-Cola Company's drinks every second. [refrigerators] In 1997 the Coca-Cola Company gave 50,000 free refrigerators and ice chests to Africans who were prepared to become vendors. [beach] In Central America, there is a beach, a large market and a bus stop named after Coca-Cola.

DISNEYFICATION [it started with a mouse] In 1937 Disney made film history by releasing 'Snow White and the Seven Dwarfs' and shortly after came up with the world's first theme park. Nowadays the Disney Company is involved in books, magazine and newspaper publishing, producing and distributing feature-films, cable TV, music recording, live stage shows, real estate development, North American major league baseball and ice hockey, video production and sales, shops, product licensing, computer software and on-line services. In 1995 Disney took over the USA's ABC broadcasting network and became the second largest media group in the world. [The World] In Shenzhen China, 118 world tourist spots can be visited on a 480.000 m² site. The Grand Canyon, Mt. Rushmore National Memorial, the Niagara Falls, the Pyramids, the sphinx of Egypt, the Acropolis of Athens, the Leaning Tower of Pisa, the Kremlin, the Eiffel Tower and the Taj Mahal are all built to scales of 1:5 1:10 and 1:15.[9] In [Tokyo] A 500m indoor ski track with real snow peeks over the houses. The nearest metro station is packed with Japanese youngsters carrying snowboards under their arms and wearing snow glasses in the middle of summer. In [Cairo] a floating ice-skating rink has been built on the Nile, where the outside temperature is 30 degrees. [Chinatown] After a long history as self-orientated introvert societies a remarkable shift has now taken place, turning many Chinatowns into tourist attractions and transforming Chinese tradition and cultural significance into a flat iconography. [Singapore's] cultural heart is its Chinatown. Years ago it provided a setting for the Chinese immigrants that shaped and built modern Singapore. Chinatown has been rede-signed. Colonial shop fronts have been torn down and replaced by plastic substitutes.

ELECTRONICS [mobile users] Worldwide there are 1.3 billion mobile phone users; more than all existing landlines. [short message service] More than 50 billion SMS text messages were sent over the world's GSM networks in the first three months of 2001.[10] [possibilities] Cell phones can get you dinner reservations, movie tickets and dates. Dial *88 on your cell phone in Hong Kong and feed your personal details into a computer. When another client with matching details is nearby, their phone rings to let them know.[11] [Dolphins] Teenagers have been quick to realise the benefits of the SMS. Without making appointments they 'float' in cities, meeting up opportunistically and spontaneously, liberated from fixed locations by their cell phones.[12]

FABRIC [urban size] Rank Urban Area Population Square KM /1 **New York** 17,800,000 8,684 / 2 **Chicago** 8,307,000 5,499 / 3 **Atlanta** 3,500,000 5,084 / 4 **Philadelphia** 5,149,000 4,659 / 5 **Boston** 4,032,000 4,496 / 6 **Tokyo–Yokohama** 29,950,000 4,429 / 7 **Los Angeles** 11,789,000 4,320 / 8 **London** 12,232,000 4,144 / 9 **Dallas–Fort Worth** 4,146,000 3,644 / 10 **Houston** 3,823,000 3,354 / 11 **Detroit** 3,903,000 3,266 / 12 **Washington** 3,934,000 2,997 / 13 **Miami** 4,919,000 2,890 / 14 **Buenos Aires**

11,200,000 2,771/ **15 Minneapolis** 2,389,000 2,753 / **16 Nagoya** 8,030,000 2,745 / **17 Paris** 9,645,000 2,722 / **18 Seattle** 2,712,000 2,471 / **19 São Paulo** 16,800,000 2,460 / **20 Rio de Janeiro** 10,300,000 2,331[13]

GATED [privatization] Over the last 30 years, massive privatisation of the local government functions of over 230,000 housing developments containing almost one-sixth of the population of the United States, has changed the appearance and organizational structure of American urban areas. CID (Common Interest Development) housing has become the predominant form of new housing construction in the USA. About one-third of the housing constructed in the USA since 1970 has been in CIDs, and in many metropolitan areas more than half the housing is in CIDS. [São Paulo] One of the most notorious and oldest examples of a gated community is Alphaville, a private development started in 1974 in São Paulo. Alphaville consists of 14 residential areas and is home for some 20,000 people. Each residential area is surrounded by high fences and has only one entrance. Residents enjoy the services of a private hospital, a cinema, a newspaper of their own and a complete education system. Residents use entrance passes and it is possible to retrieve a list giving the dates and times at which your wife went out through the gate.[14]

HOUSING [urban density] Urban Area Population Pop/Sq KM / Hong Kong 5,522,000 28,427 / Cairo 9,900,000 23,166 / Tianjin 3,737,000 21,535 / Seoul 14,600,000 20,277 / Manila 7,948,000 19,798 / Mumbai 17,500,000 18,262 / Surabaya 2,473,000 17,682 / Delhi 10,300,000 17,675 / Jakarta 8,223,000 17,069 / Shanghai 9,000,000 16,391 / Bangkok 6,357,000 14,966 / Beijing 7,500,000 14,479 / Lagos 4,400,000 13,591 / Mexico City 17,250,000 11,685 / Calcutta 12,100,000 11,680 / Karachi 10,100,000 10,832 / Guangzhou 2,916,000 10,425 / Montevideo 1,350,000 9,477 / Rosario (Argentina) 1,100,000 9,438 / Singapore 2,705,000 8,703.[15]

INVENTION On every street corner in [Tokyo] you can find vending machines that provide people with their daily needs; hot coffee, meals, milk or underwear. There are five and a half million vending machines in Japan, that's one for every 22 people. Coca Cola owns half of the machines.[16] In [Kuala Lumpur] (as well as in Tokyo and Bangkok) trains have dispensed with the services of the driver. Sitting in the front makes you feel as if you are driving the train yourself. In [Singapore] every taxi is equipped with a computer and connected to the Internet. An e-mail message can reach all of the 20,000 taxis in the city simultaneously.[17]

JUNKFOOD At high altitudes, the sense of [taste] decreases by about 30%. Airplane food is therefore spiced up by 30%.[18] [research] The human palate can distinguish 275 flavours. But companies have an interest in a world with a uniform palate. Standardizing taste is just more efficient; it's also profitable. To persuade people to adapt to a Western diet, multinationals produce foods that have no local flavours. It's called fusion. Strong flavours are becoming milder in different countries so they please more people.[19]

KEEPSAKE [Bilbao] An estimated 80% of all visitors to Bilbao are either drawn there by the museum or add an extra day onto business trips in order to see it. In its first year, the museum was responsible for adding an estimated $160 million to the economy. Already 16 cruise ships have put Bilbao on their itineraries and a new dock is being built to accommodate more.[20] When the I.M. Pei glass pyramid entrance to the [Louvre] opened in 1989, visits nearly doubled to five million visitors annually.[21] The souvenir market for replicas of these icons is booming.

LANGUAGE [diversity] There are many ways of measuring the world's cultural diversity, but the best indicator may still be the state of its languages. As cultural diversity decreases, the number of languages decreases. Linguists project that most endangered languages, particularly those no longer spoken by children, will be extinct by the year 2100.[22] [projection] Today there are about 6,000 different languages spoken in the world. By 2100 there will be only 3,000 different languages.[23] [Penan-people] Threats to cultures are threats to unique perspectives of life. The Penan-people in Borneo, have one word for 'he', 'she' and 'it' and six words for 'we'. What lessons could the Penan teach about social cooperation?[24] [English] In 1989 the European Union proposed to require EU children to be taught at school in at least two different languages. The proposal was rejected by the United Kingdom. English has evolved into a lingua franca, the international language of science, commerce, diplomacy and pop culture.

McDONALD'S [history] Since the 1950s, McDonald's family-oriented restaurants have revolutionised the fast-food business, making the company one of the best known in the world. [restaurants] McDonald's has 23,000 restaurants worldwide and is represented in 118 countries, worldwide it employs over 1,800,000 people. Each day around 33 million people visit a McDonald's somewhere in the world. [progress] It takes only 24 hours to construct a new outlet and to make it fully operational. A new outlet opened every five hours, which is about the length of time it takes to digest a hamburger.[25] [lessons] TV commercials were used to teach Russians to dunk McDonald's Chicken Mc Nuggets in those plastic cups of sweetened sauce. Russia's first McDonald's, which opened in Moscow in 1990, served more than 30,000 customers on its first day of operation, setting a record for the most people served by one restaurant in a single day. [health] the World Health Organisation says that the spread of America's sugary diet round the world is producing a diabetes epidemic. [think global, act local] Despite the idiom of 'M', uniforms and interior design there is a remarkable degree of adjustment to the local culture. In [India] where Hindus shun beef and

P

Singapore

Sergey | 22 years | Moscow

S

Kuala Lumpur

O

Hong Kong

Puhaa | 19 years | Mumbai

Beijir

Bangkok

Jason | 20 years | New York

Chicag

STOP

Tokyo

FOR
YOUR HEALTH
PLEASE AVOID
USING
SILOM ROAD
DURING
1.00 - 3.00 PM.
THANK YOU FOR
YOUR CO-OPERATION

Johannesburg

Alex | 23 years | São Paulo

Los Angele

N

Bangkok

Las Vegas

Ziehong | 22 years | Shanghai

PILOTO

Santiag

Beijing

R

T

Cairo

Beijing

São Paulo

Tokyo

Bangkok

Hong Kong

Q

Kuala Lumpur

Bangko

oxyvital
FRESH CLEAN AIR
OXYGEN BAR'S
NOW AVAILABLE

Kuala Lumpur

Hong Kong

Watinee | 20 years | Bangkok

São Paulo

Mumbai

Mexico City

Gaston | 21 years | Buenos Aires

Tokyo

Tokyo

274

Muslims refuse pork, burgers are made of mutton and called Maharaja Macs. In [Tokyo] they sell a Teriyaki Burger, a sausage patty on a bun, served with teriyaki sauce. In [Singapore] McDonald's has evolved into somewhere where schoolchildren can escape from their cramped apartments to meet friends and do their homework. In [Hong Kong] business people eat their breakfast of Egg McMuffin behind their office desks. In [Shanghai] toddlers are not given French fries to eat because they are good for them, but rather because they are sold in a clean environment. In the [United States] McDonald's is anything but hip while in [Moscow] getting married at a McDonald's is a sign of status.

NEW TOWN [China] plans in the next ten years the construction of four new metropolises each to be inhabited by 30 to 45 million inhabitants. Furthermore, in the next 20 years 40 new metropolises each with five million inhabitants will be built.[26] [Shenzhen] Since China drew up the regulations for Special Economic Zones in 1980, the population of Shenzhen has increased 120 times. [Hong Kong] In the New Territories apartment towers are built at a density of 300 dwellings per 10,000 sq m., producing the most staggering vision of uniformity imaginable. [New Mumbai] To relieve Mumbai of it's urban explosion (3,000,000 to 17.500.000 inhabitants in the last half century) from 1970 onward construction on the virgin land of New Bombay started. Today New Mumbai has a population of 200,000, includes 95 villages, an industrial zone and large tracts of agricultural as well as barren and marshy lands. A huge fraction of the residents commute to Mumbai daily.[27] It is a ghost town.

OXYGEN [health] Throughout the world, atmospheric pollution affects more than 1.1 billion people, mostly in cities. An additional 2.5 billion are at risk from high levels of indoor air pollution. Indoor and outdoor pollution together kill nearly 3 million people every year – about 6% of all deaths annually - and 90% of them occur in developing countries.[28] [most polluted cities] 1. Mexico City; 2 Cairo; 3 Beijing; 4 Jakarta; 5 Los Angeles; 6 São Paulo.[29] [Mexico City] has the world's highest levels of dangerous air pollutants. Most days, unless it rains or there is sufficient wind, airborne particles create heavy smog. Just breathing the air in [Mumbai] is equivalent to smoking 20 cigarettes a day, hence the popularity of recently opened 'oxygen bars'.[30] In [Guangzhou] traffic police die at an average age of 38; 52% die of lung cancer, 47% of lead poisoning.[31]

PUBLIC SPACE [substitute] Malls scattered across the metropolis are providing new types of or substitutes for public space. In these malls climate, safety and time are all controlled and a safe and clean environment is provided for leisure. Public space in malls intrudes deep into buildings and provides a place for children to meet, play and to experience their first kiss. In an attempt to revive the traditional excitement and variety of real-life city centres, roller coasters, skating rinks and amusement arcades attract customers. The appearance of the scenery in traditional public spaces is reproduced, with awnings, artificial trees, recorded birdsong and synthetic scents. Malls are the ultimate entertainment destinations: controlled kingdoms outside a traditional messy urban space and time where the weary can give free rein to the pleasure principle and consume in a holiday spirit. Canada's West Edmonton mall, the [biggest mall in the world], covers a space equal to 100 football fields. The Age of Access, contains the largest indoor amusement park in the world, the largest indoor waterpark, a golf course, 800 shops, 11 department stores, 110 restaurants, an ice-skating rink, 13 nightclubs and 20 cinemas.[32]

QUOTE [Sergey (student in Moscow)]: "My most valuable possession are my parents. I live with them in the centre of Moscow. Moscow is beautiful but not clean. Smog is its major problem. If I had the choice, I would like to live near the Black Sea, in a 2-storey house." [Watinee (student in Bangkok)]: "The traffic is a very big problem in Bangkok. Everyday it takes me 4 hours to go from home to school and back. I like the city though, it's colourful. When I'm older I would prefer to live somewhere in the country, nearby a forest." [Gaston (student in Buenos Aires)]: "I like my city, it's beautiful, but my neighbourhood is very, very bourgeois and I'm still stuck with my parents. Later I would like to live in the country, in a big house with a toilet designed by Rem Koolhaas." [Puhaa (student in Mumbai)]: "I wouldn't mind to live in another city, like Barcelona. Still I like it here. The multiraciality, the diverse religions and their tolerance. With my family I live in an Indian area, it's lovely, great. Racism is still a big problem but I would like my children to grow up here." [Zhiehong (student in Shanghai)]: "I don't consider Shanghai pretty, but I like its architecture. My house? It's like a cube. I dream of a bigger and brighter house, somewhere in the country, full of trees."

RECOVERY The elevated Minhocao highway, which runs across the city centre of [São Paulo], is closed to traffic at weekends. During these days the Paulistas reclaim the tarmac: the highway is transformed into a public place to be used for sport, barbecue and even strolls on a sunny Sunday afternoon. In [Tokyo] scarce space is used inventively by locating businesses underneath infrastructure. Driving schools are located on roofs of supermarkets, golf courses located above parking places. In [Bangkok] illegal restaurants and businesses can be found everywhere under elevated infrastructure. An estimated one million inhabitants of [Cairo] lives in the tombs and mausoleums of the City of the Dead. Services are provided: shops, mosques and street vendors, and the City provides electricity and water. Some tombs contain television sets and stereos. About 5,000 live in [New York]'s abandoned subway tunnels; they are called the 'mole people'.[33]

SUBURBIA [growth] Although cities are getting bigger all over the world, they do not all grow in the same way. North American cities like Los Angeles and Chicago do not simply increase the number of their inhabitants but rather expand the territory they occupy. Suburbanisation has led to massive development, widespread road building and increased use of cars. In suburbia the

Bangkok

V

Moscow

Mumbai

Shanghai

Shanghai

Bangkok

Rio de Janeiro

Singapore

Kuala Lumpur

Cairo

New York

São Paulo

U

Kuala Lumpur

Shanghai

Tokyo

Tokyo

Beijing 11,7 million

Los Angeles

Singapore

Y

Z

Buenos Aires 6,6 million

Mumbai

Tokyo

Hong Kong

Bangkok

Shanghai

X

New York

Mexico City

Mumbai 17,4 million

Tokyo

Bangkok

Teen

Santiago

W

Los Angeles 13 million

Johannesburg

Los Angeles

Shanghai

São Paulo 17,5 million

Bangkok

Mexico City

Santiago

Tokyo

landscape is monotonous; there is an endless repetition of the individual dream, a house, garden and a car. [United States] If the entire American population were to live in suburbia, with an acre of land per household, it would still occupy less than 5% of the contiguous 48 states. [New York]'s suburbs extend across the whole state of New Jersey into eastern Pennsylvania, a distance of almost 100 miles from Times Square.

TRANSFORMATION [Shanghai] has transformed its skyline from the two to four storeys of ten years ago, to become a metropolis of more than 2,400 ten-storey buildings. It is said that until the Asian crisis reached Shanghai in 1997, one fifth of the world's construction cranes could have been found there.[34] In [Tokyo] each day 12,000 sq meters of building are demolished and 63,000 sq meters are built.[35] The Boat Quay, one of the last remnants of the old city, is now completely restored and has become a tourist attraction in the centre of [Singapore].

URBANISATION [urban world] In 1900 only one tenth of the world's population lived in cities. At the turn of the millennium half the population lived in cities and, according to the latest projections made by the United Nations, by 2015 65% of the world's population, 3.5 billion people, will live in cities. In 1950, six of the ten largest cities were in the [US & Europe]. By 2015, all of the top ten will be located in other parts of the world. The number of [mega cities] – cities with at least 8 million inhabitants – has risen from just 2 in 1950 (New York and London) to 23 in 1995, 17 of which are in the developing world. This number is projected to grow to 36 by 2015, 23 of which will be located in [Asia]. [Africa] has the highest urban growth rate of all the regions of the world, at 5% per year.[36]

VEHICLE [automobiles] a rough estimate of the number of cars on earth comes to 500 million. Fifty years ago the number was half of this. It is estimated that the number will double in the next 25 years. The average speed in [London] in 1899 was 11 mph; in 1999 the average speed was still 11 mph.[37]

WEDDING In [Japan] over the last 50 years the number of arranged marriages ('omiai') has decreased by 71%, largely because of the influence of Western culture, where romantic marriages are the norm. Divorce rates are as high as 50%. In the [United States] over 2,000 American men per year find their soul mates by leafing through a glossy catalogue of women who usually come from Latin America, Asia or Eastern Europe. In [Singapore] Filipinos are deported if they attempt to marry a Singaporean national.[38]

X-CLUDED In 1973, 1.3% of the population of [São Paulo] lived in favelas, today the figure is 20%.[39] [Johannesburg] After the inner-city electricity plant was left abandoned in Johannesburg, it took over 2,000 homeless people only two days to construct a two-level village in it. Among them a 'mayor' and security people were chosen. Construction of a tunnel, heading for the safe of the National Bank, 400m away started immediately. After a week the police discovered the construction of the tunnel and the plant was cleared.[40] About 6000 10- to 16-year-olds serve as armed soldiers for rival drug gangs in [Rio de Janeiro]'s shantytowns. Between 1978 and 2000, at least 49,913 people in Rio died from small-arms fire, although many more child casualties of gang violence are believed to be buried in unmarked graves around the city. [Rocinha] favela, one of the 400 in Rio de Janeiro, is the "first world of favelas" – South America's largest and most developed slum. Varying counts put the population anywhere between 150,000 and 250,000 people. In 1998 Rocinha, was awarded the title of Brazil's 'best managed community'.

YOUNG In the [United States] 22% of all children between 12 and 18 years use an anti-depression medicine. In [Argentina] 33% of all teens have an eating disorder. One of ten girls suffers from anorexia or bulimia. This is five times as high as the European figure.[41] [Teen magazines] serve as guides to teenage life styles. They identify trends and define what is cool and what not. They present the latest fashions and gadgets from all over and discuss school, sport and the latest video games. They include pin-up photos and posters of music and film idols and give instruction on how to put on make up and how to ensure that 'the first time' is successful and enjoyable.[42]

ZZZZ

Notes

[1] Online. Available, www.tourismconcern.org.uk/resources/infocus_the_future_tourismin2002.htm
[2] Online. Available, www.travelweekly.com
[3] World Tourism Organisation. Online. Available, www.world-tourism.org
[4] Online. Available, www.oneworld.net/guides/TNCs/front.shtml
[5] P. Hall, *Doing business around the World*, USA, Online. Available, www.phdirect.com
[6] M. van Bracht, "Even India hellen..." broadcasting by VPRO's DNW
[7] according to the Coca Cola Company, see http://www.Cocacola.com
[8] according to the Coca Cola Company, see http://www.Coocacola.com
[9] Online. Available, www.orientaltravel.com.hk/tours/HongKong/Spendid_China.htm
[10] Online. Available, www.apc.org/english/rights/monitors.shtml
Online. Available, www.trendsreport.net/wireless/2.html
Online. Available, www.doc.ic.ac.uk/~nd/surprise_97/journal/vol4/kaa2/#Γ
Online. Available, www.gsmworld.com/news/press_2001/press_releases_22.shtml, http://unstats.un.org/unsd/
[11] Online. Available, www.sunday.com
[12] M. Effting, J.P. Geelen, 'Contact en nu meteen!', *De Volkskrant*, 14 September, 2002
[13] Online. Available, www.demographia.com
[14] P. Meurs, 'Bouwen aan een ongelijke wereld', in: *De Architect*, Den Haag: tenHagen&Stam bv, September 2003
[15] Online. Available, www.demographia.com/db-intluadens-rank.htm
[16] P. Riethmuller, Department of Economics, University of Brisbane
[17] Online. Available, www.china.org.cn/english/2001/Aug/17347.htm
[18] Online. Available, www.airlinemeals.net/
[19] *Colors Magazine*, issue 36, February–March 2000
[20] E. Etxebarria, director of the Bilbao Office of Tourism and Conventions
[21] Online. Available, www.time.com/time/europe/magazine/2000/1030/travel/design.html
[22] *National Geographic*, Vol 196 (2), August 1999
[23] Ibid.
[24] W. Davis, *Light at the Edge of the World: A journey through the Realm of vanishing Cultures*, Washington: National Geographic Society, 2002
[25] *Colors Magazine*, February–March 2000
[26] 'Peking plant de bouw van vier megasteden' *De Volkskrant*, 29.03.2001
[27] Online. Available, http://theory.tifr.res.in/bombay/physical/geo/new-bombay.html
[28] Online. Available, www.changemakers.net/library/temp/washpost061101.cfm
[29] Online. Available, www.colby.edu/sts/st215/8.1view/sld016.htm
[30] Online. Available, http://lonelyplanet.lycos.com/indian_subcontinent/mumbai/history.html
[31] Online. Available, www.dnw.nl
[32] Online. Available, www.unesco.org/courier/2000_11/uk/dici.htm
[33] Online. Available, www.disinfo.com/pages/dossier/id350/pg1/
[34] 2G *instant China*, city: publisher, no 10, 1999
[35] Online. Available, www.dnw.nl
[36] Online. Available, United Nations website
[37] Advertisement in London metro, 2001
[38] Most facts from *Colors Magazine* issue 20; 'Wedding', 1997.
[39] J. Bosch, et al, *Eating Brazil*, Rotterdam: 010 publishers, 2001, p. 105
[40] Anecdote, Urban Futures conference, South Africa, 2001
[41] Online. Available, www.dnw.nl
[42] Summary of all collected magazines

The Image of Metropolis
NEXT Architects
Bart Reuser | Marijn Schenk | Michel Schreinemachers | John van de Water

Introduction

'The Image of Metropolis' is the result of a four-month tour of twenty-six metropolises undertaken by NEXT architects.[1] Our purpose was to research the ways in which metropolises are beginning to adopt a similar form under the influence of globalization and extreme urbanization. Each metropolis was systematically documented visually according to more than seventy themes, and by carrying out interviews and collecting information in a wide range of media. The ABC represents twenty-six contemporary phenomena, utilizing diverse collected information, to form an inventory of the appearance of the metropolis. We attempt to map here the relations between the phenomena, speculate on the transformation of metropolitan society, and examine some spatial and social implications of the ways in which a metropolis influenced by globalization is experienced, used and interpreted. Finally, there is a summary of design considerations.

Globalization

It is possible to argue that globalization is less a neutral idea relating to processes found in the contemporary world, more a doctrine and an instrumental idea, feeding into and fed by a neo-liberal ideology. The driving forces behind globalization, besides a neo-liberal political agenda, are technological development and consumption. As a consequence of the strategic coordination and linking of economies, globalization has produced a world economy which is in a position to function in a highly integrated manner in real time and on a global scale. With the emergence of this so-called 'network economy', old social and spatial relations lose their strategic significance and their meanings. Conceptual constructs such as 'network society' and 'network city' attempt to describe a new regime of relations and connections.

If we look at the effects of globalization on the world, the world appears marked by over and under development. In relation to the uneven spread of prosperity, Nobel Prize Winner for Economics, Joseph Stiglitz, speaks of the existence of a 'global administration', but the absence of a 'global parliament'.[2] 'We have created a machine that is operated by no one', says Manuel Castells.[3]

Metropolises play lead roles in this process of globalization. In these centers of urbanization there exists a field of tension where an exchange occurs between local and global influences and where the consequences for the city can be best identified. The metropolis as a connective and physical artifact provides the grounding for a networked dynamic which informs and transforms urban society. Under the influence of globalization this society transforms and modernizes to an ever-greater degree and with ever-increasing speed. This is characterized by two forms of fragmentation: social and spatial.

Deltametropolis/Randstad, Moscow, Cairo, Johannesburg, Mumbai, Bangkok, Kuala Lumpur, Singapore, Hong Kong, Shenzhen, Guangzhou, Shanghai, Beijing, Tokyo, Osaka, Kyoto, Los Angeles, Chicago, Mexico City, New York, Santiago, Buenos Aires, São Paulo, Rio de Janeiro, Brasilia. The trip was made possible thanks to the financial support of the Dutch Foundation for Visual Arts, Design and Architecture in Amsterdam and the Van Esteren-Fluck & Van Lohuizen Foundation in The Hague

J.E. Stiglitz, *Globalisation Its Discontents*, Penguin, 2003

W. Oosterbaan 'We hebben een machine gemaakt die door niemand beheerst wordt', interview *NRC*, 17th Oct 2001

Fragmentation

Social fragmentation is fed by a global 'ecology of fear'. When a large part of the world's population was able to watch live as the twin towers of the World Trade Center in New York collapsed to the ground, for many of them the idea of a secure, centered world was shattered in an instant. At that moment Mike Davis' Ecology of Fear[4] transcended the scale of its intellectual origins, Los Angeles, and became acutely global. War had been declared on 'freedom and democracy' and around the world anxiety attended living and working in urban areas.

The ecology of fear is fertile ground for the 'capsular society'.[5] Cocooning and the degree of uniformity it produces in our lives creates the visible affirmation of us all being the same, or at least of being together with others who are the same.[6] Because the 'not same' are always somewhere else, they mutate into an abstraction and dark phantoms of the unknown. René Boomkens demonstrates that, as the 'not same' becomes abstracted, tolerance and humanity give way to an anxiety psychosis. The more individuals protect and shield themselves, the greater will be the psychic impact of any breach of their defenses; capsular society finds itself caught in a vicious circle.

Spatial fragmentation arises through explosive urban growth and changing relations between urban areas.[7] The enlargement of scale is not only physical, but mental too; new forms of infrastructure allow a city to be used with a speed that causes the relationship to the context to disappear.[8] Accessibility conquers proximity, resulting in an implosion of space and a shattered morphology. For the city dweller, all this transforms the experience of the metropolis into a mosaic of urban spaces which are apparently no longer connected. New urban junctions and enclaves have emerged, interspersed with discontinued, apparently meaningless bits of city.

Spatial connections in this capsular society access bordered enclaves, which are linked into 'the network' and surrounded by voids.[9] The forms behind this development are what some see as the segregation machines of our times: gated communities and shopping malls.[10] Drive-in typologies and the car as cocoon complete the secure link between destinations. Alongside this conditioned, contained world there exists the metropolitan slum; similarly exclusive, sealed, and often self-sustaining.[11]

The above developments are part of metropolises worldwide. They underline the view that the city as a social and spatial unit is losing meaning. But this suggestion needs to be looked at critically. Paradoxically, in this time of social and spatial fragmentation, new forms of cohesion have emerged. If we look at metropolitan communities from the viewpoint of the dynamics through which new forms of collectivity and new meanings may arise and disappear, the picture is somewhat different.

New collectivity

Understanding a new collectivity requires a shift in thinking. Collectivity may presume a social unity which serves exclusion and fragmentation rather than diversity and the drawing together of differences. We can therefore no longer reason from the position

[4] M. Davies, *Ecology of Fear: Los Angeles and the Imagination of Disaster*, New York: Vintage Books, 1999

[5] R. Boomkens, 'De angstmachine', *Het Parool*, 28th June 2003

[6] See chapter 'ABC'

[7] See 'Urbanization' in chapter 'ABC'

[8] See 'Vehicle and Invention' in chapter 'ABC'

[9] W. Oosterbaan, op. cit.

[10] See 'Gated', and 'Public Space' in chapter 'ABC'

[11] See 'X-cluded' in chapter 'ABC'

that the protection of social cohesion is desirable, but from the inevitability of difference. Paradoxically, it is in the acceptance of difference that an open permeable social cohesion exists. Three random supports for this tendency may be: ideology, virtuality, and lifestyle, as the following examples show. There is a change in strategy in anti-globalization politics; from an in general ineffective cry of, 'No to globalization!', during demonstrations at world economics summits, to increasingly successful protests at the national and local levels.[12] At the local scale, reclaim-the-streets groups are employing light-hearted tactics to temporarily take back streets from traffic and commerce in protest against the loss of public space resulting from commercialization and privatization.[13]

It is now possible to be connected to others without being restricted by the constraints of time and physical space. However particular someone's tastes and preferences may be, they will always be able to find kindred spirits and allies through the Internet. Identities become simpler, more manipulable and more specific. What is interesting in this context is the existence and rise of the so-called MUDs, Multi-User Dungeons, or 'Internet Cities'[14]

But the physical world too is united, for instance, through lifestyle. Ethan Watters describes one of the fastest growing social classes in the United States, known to demographers as the 'never-marrieds'.[15] Watters participates in a debate about the nature of social cohesion in contemporary American society and gives us an insight into the rise of a variegated collective of highly educated, single people who live and work in all kinds of groupings and collectivities, right into middle age.

In the examples above, the traditional idea of community is becoming increasingly superceded by others. 'Community' presumes a large number of shared relations and is less dynamic and flexible than 'collectivity', which implies a wider range of relationships that bind people together. Many different forms of collectivity are possible, from 'light' varieties to 'heavy' ones, which emerge out of the dynamics of pluriform urban dwellers' real life patterns and preferences.

G. Wehrfritz, 'All protest local', Newsweek special tion, 'Issues 2004'

Online. Available, http://vw.reclaimthestreets.net/

H. Rheingold, The Virtual mmunity: Homesteading on e Electronic Frontier, mbridge, MA: MIT Press, 00

E. Watters, ban Tribes: A Generation defines Friendship, Family, d Commitment, New York: omsbury, 2003

M. Effting and J.P. Geelen, kskrant, op. cit.

M. Hajer, A. Reijndorp, Search of New Public main, Rotterdam: NAi lishers, 2000

Collectivity arises through a new use of the city in which a greater formality and structuring of meeting gives way to more fleeting exchanges, and use gives way to appropriation. The individual has left behind the nineteenth century flâneur and has mutated into a twenty-first-century 'dolphin'. The dolphin metaphor is intended to illuminate the way young people use, live and experience the city.[16] The integration of the mobile phone into daily life, and the accompanying easing of the need to fix appointments and locations in advance, has been the spur for this development. Whereas the flâneur strolled through defined urban spaces, like the passages, the dolphin floats willfully and opportunistically through the urban expanse of the metropolis, tied to no particular space. Dolphins gather in schools in the new public domain.[17] This public domain is opportunistically assembled out of individual movements and experience and is tied to immediate individual need rather than collective meaning. The nature of the public domain is therefore not static, but is constantly changing, and new meanings are continuously being generated. The places where the new public domain emerges may be between the enclaves, or on their borders; in the leftover spaces and non-places of the urban field. The anonymous and indefinite character of these spaces seem to make them an ideal ground from which to develop new socio-spatial practices. Here new meanings are continually produced as new users repeatedly reinterpret and reorganize the spaces.[18] Besides the social potential of the unnamed places, highly accessible posi tions within the network also offer potential: nodes where different population groups stay for a short time, such as airports, stations, and other transport interchanges. In these intensively visited and condensed spaces there emerges an intense friction between workers and local visitors, the homeless, tourists and business people, which potentially makes them the new 'city squares' of tomorrow.

Design considerations

If the social cohesion of the metropolis is reliant on a public domain of unnamed places and nodes in the metropolitan network, will the city itself add nothing beyond the resistance of travel time and distance? A major design task is implied in this question, or at least a detailed design analysis. Traditional urban design elements, such as boule-vards and squares, may not answer all the questions and an extended design vocabu-lary may be required. The question of whether collectivity – however 'light' – can be created in an urban plan also becomes relevant at this point, as does the question of the designer's role in establishing the conditions of the public domain.

Human beings are themselves part of a constant process of transformation: the global population is almost entirely renewed every seventy years and every twenty-five years a new generation nestles into the structures of society. Changes in the population accompany changes in the living environment. Every living environment is built and changes around different sectors, each with its own rhythms. Up till now it has been the users who changed quickest, while the structure of the city developed more grad-ually. It was the gradual changing of the urban structure that provided a sense of con-tinuity and the background space for the quicker transformations of an urban society. A sustainable support for urban design is a framework containing an optimum space for social and programmatic uit. It is the task of urban design to define this framework and to reinforce it. This will facilitate reaction to and anticipation of social developments, allowing transformations to take place without complete revisions of the main struc-ture.

Today more than ever, the designer needs to learn to work within a context of dynamic transformations. Technological development has brought with it a shrinking of the world, which has increased the importance of the dwelling as the operations base with-in the network society. The detaching of functional and social relations from local con-texts means social life and interaction occurs at a higher level and on its own terms. Conversely, the increase in activities that take place in and around the home offers opportunities for a re-evaluation of the local context.[19] It is up to designers to work with new opportunities and developments, to deal with the world as it is, while creat-ing open environments capable of accommodating future social transformation. The

[18] See 'Recovery' in chapter 'ABC'

[19] I. Nio, 'Het verlangen naar collectiviteit' , Stedebouw & Ruimtelijke Ordening 3, 2003, Weemoed, p. 40

dolphin attitude and the ability of mobile and connected individuals to 'float' through the city means that places in metropolises can be turned to different uses at a much faster rate than before. Collectivity between people is less linked to fixed locations, and media and communications are using new technologies to reach across space. Places can be 'loaded' with a particular image, and only the accessibility of the place need be of major significance: deserted dock areas become temporary beaches, defunct industrial areas become artists' colonies, decommissioned nuclear power stations become amusement parks and gas-stations locations for instant pop-concerts.

The Editors

Job van Eldijk holds a MSc in Urbanism and Architecture from the Delft University of Technology. He organized the Millennium Cities lecture series from which this book originates. He has also been involved in the organization of the 1st Architecture Biennale Rotterdam in 2003.

Stephen Read worked as an architect in South Africa before moving to the Netherlands where he obtained his PhD at Delft University of Technology in 1996. He spent the next year at The Bartlett, University College London on a European Union IICR Fellowship, and has worked since then as a teacher and researcher in the Urbanism department at Delft. He is researching the idea of productive urban space and is involved with a book about the design of cities as dynamic organizations.

Jürgen Rosemann holds the chair of Urban Renewal & Management at the Faculty of Architecture, Delft University of Technology. He received his education as an architect and urban planner in Germany. He has acted as architect, researcher and consultant in various urban renewal projects in Berlin, Cologne and Frankfurt and lectured at the TU Hanover and at the Hochschule der Künste in Berlin. He has been visiting professor at universities in Vienna, Venice, São Paulo and Buenos Aires and is a member of the founding board of the University of Oldenburg. Presently he is research coordinator of the department of Urbanism in Delft and chairman of the board of governors of the Berlage Institute in Rotterdam. He has published in the fields of globalization, urban transformation and management, urban renewal, housing and international comparative research.

The Authors

Ramesh Kumar Biswas (PhD) studied architecture, art and urban design in Delhi, Edinburgh and Graz. His architecture practice has offices in Vienna, Berlin and Kuala Lumpur. He has been visiting professor at the École Nationale des Ponts et Chaussées, Paris, in Tokyo, Sydney, at the Bauhaus, and has lectured in leading universities all over the world. He advises on development projects in Africa and was named in 1998 by heads of government of the European Union and Asia as one of the '100 Asia-Europe Young Leaders'. His books include: *Magical Hands; Food of The Gods; M1:333; Malaysia* (2003); *Metropolis Now!* (2001). Forthcoming books include: *Food and the City* and *Cities in Crisis*. He has published essays in numerous books and journals, and has been guest editor of StadtBauwelt.

Stefano Boeri (PhD IUAV Venice 1989) is an architect and urban planner. He teaches Urban Design at Universities in Venice and Lausanne, and is visiting professor at the Berlage Institute Rotterdam. He has arranged numerous interdisciplinary exhibitions and has been the initiator of various research projects, among them Uncertain States of Europe (USE) and Border Device(s). He has set up the network Multiplicity, from which the installation Solid Sea has been exhibited at the documenta XI in Kassel. He has lectured widely in Europe, Japan and the USA and has published articles and essays in specialized and general-interest magazines, as well as several books, including

Mutations. His office is involved in transformation projects in the port areas of Genoa, Naples, Mytilene, Salerno and Trieste.

M. Christine Boyer is a city planner and computer scientist whose interests include the history of urbanism, cybernetics, memory and perception. She joined the School of Architecture at Princeton University in 1991. She has been professor and chair of the City and Regional Planning Program at Pratt Institute and has taught at Cooper Union, Columbia University and GSD, Harvard University. She has written extensively about urbanism and her publications include *Dreaming the Rational City: The Myth of American City Planning* (1983); *Manhattan Manners: Architecture and Style 1850-1900* (1985); *The City of Collective Memory* (1993) and *CyberCities: Visual Perception in the Age of Electronic Communication* (1995). She is currently researching a book on the rhetorics of Le Corbusier, tentatively titled The City Plans of Modernism; and a series of collected essays entitled Twice-Told Stories: Cities and Cinema.

Lindsay Bremner holds the chair in Architecture at the University of Witwatersrand, Johannesburg. She has a Masters of Architecture from the University of Witwatersrand and is currently registered for a Senior Doctorate at the same university. She has been invited to lecture in Argentina, Cuba, Germany, Nigeria, Spain, South Africa, and Turkey, and is the co-editor of the book *Emerging Johannesburg* (2003). Her own book, *Johannesburg – One City Colliding Worlds* (2004) was published recently. From 1993 to 1997, she served on the Executive Committee of the Greater Johannesburg Metropolitan Council, during which time she chaired the Planning, Housing, Urbanization, and Environmental Management Committees.

Gary Chang founded the practice EDGE in 1994 and works as Associate Professor at the University of Hong Kong. His work has been exhibited at numerous international symposiums and expositions including the Venice Biennial in 2000 and 2002, and Archilab 2001 in Orléans. He has received various awards including the ar+d High Commendation (2002) for the Light Hotel, Dedalo-Minosse International Prize in Vicenza (2002) for the Suitcase House by the Great Wall in Beijing and the Hong Kong Institute of Architects President's Prize (1996) for the Broadway Cinemàthéque. His most recent projects include M-Club and M-Gym in Doha (2003), Kung-Fu Tea Set for Alessi, Tea and Coffee Towers (2000-2003) and the Gifu Kitagata Housing, North Block (2002).

Penelope Dean is a registered architect and PhD candidate in Critical Studies in Architectural Culture at the University of California, Los Angeles (UCLA). She holds a Master of Architecture degree from the Berlage Institute, Rotterdam (1997) and worked for the Dutch architecture office MVRDV from 1998 to 2002. She has published on architecture and urbanism in the international journals Archis, Daidalos, OASE, Architecture Australia and Trans and currently guest edits issues of the Berlage Institute's magazine Hunch.

Dirk Frieling was Professor of Urban and Regional Planning at Delft University of Technology. He has been director of the research office *ABF Strategie*. Presently he is linked with the Vereniging Deltametropool. In the 1980s Frieling was one of the founders of *Stichting Nederland Nu Als Untwerp*. Together with five other professors he has been an initiator of the foundation *Het Metropolitane Debat*. Until a few years ago he worked as a consultant for the Urban Planning Department of the Municipality of Amsterdam.

Andreas Huyssen is the Villard Professor of German and Comparative Literature at Columbia University where he also served as director of the Center for Comparative Literature and Society. He is one of the founding editors of New German Critique. His books in English include *After the Great Divide: Modernism, Mass Culture, Postmodernism* (1986), *Twilight Memories: Marking Time in a Culture of Amnesia* (1995), and *Present Pasts: Urban Palimpsests and the Politics of Memory* (2003).

Jim Masselos is an Honorary Reader in History at the University of Sydney where he previously lectured. He did his PhD on a Commonwealth Fellowship at the University of Bombay. He is the author of *Indian Nationalism: a History* (2002), *Towards Nationalism: Group Affiliations and the Politics of Public Associations in Nineteenth Century Western India* (1974) and (with Jackie Menzies and Pratapaditya Pal) *Dancing to the Flute: Music and Dance in Indian Art* (1997), (with Narayani Gupta) *Beato's Delhi 1857, 1997* (2000). He has edited *Popular Art in Asia: The People as Patrons* (1983), *Struggling and Ruling: The Indian National Congress, 1885-1985* (1987) and India: *Creating a Modern Nation* (1990).

NEXT Architects (Bart Reuser, Marijn Schenk, Michel Schreinemachers and John van de Water) is a young Dutch architectural firm which works on projects over a wide range of scale. Their work is characterized by an exploration of new concepts which anticipate contemporary developments. The architects have integrated design with a research practice in order to do this. Recent projects include two bridges in Enschede, the Netherlands, an atlas: Sense of Place: Rotterdam, and a 'Fatlamp' for Droog Design. Awards include a first prize in the Archiprix 2000, a first prize for a Belvedere-tower in Leeuwarden. Projects have been exhibited in Berlin, New York, Shanghai, Kuala Lumpur and Johannesburg among other places.

Saskia Sassen is the Ralph Lewis Professor of Sociology at the University of Chicago, and Centennial Visiting Professor at the London School of Economics. Her most recent books are *Guests and Aliens* (2000), *Globalization and its Discontents* (1998) and her edited book *Global Networks/Linked Cities* (2002). Her best-known work *The Global City* has been brought out in an updated edition in 2001. She is co-director of the Economy Section of the Global Chicago Project, a Member of the National Academy of Sciences Panel on Urban Data Sets, a Member of the Council of Foreign Relations, and Chair of the newly formed Information Technology, International Cooperation and Global Security Committee of the SSRC.

Richard Sennett received his PhD from Harvard University in 1969. He is Professor of Social and Cultural Theory, Professor of Sociology and Social Policy, and Chair of the Cities Programme at The London School of Economics. At the New York University he is Professor of Sociology and University Professor of the Humanities. His numerous publications, both non-fiction and fiction, include: *Respect in a World of Inequality* (2004), *The Corrosion of Character: The Transformation of Work in Modern Capitalism* (1998), *Flesh and Stone: The Body and the City* (1994), *The Conscience of the Eye: Urban Design and the Social Life of Cities* (1990), *Palais-Royal* (1987), *Authority* (1980), *The Fall of Public Man* (1977), *The Hidden Injuries of Class and The Uses of Disorder* (1970).

AbdouMaliq Simone presently holds academic appointments at the Graduate Program in International Affairs, New School University, New York and the Institute of Social and Economic Research, University of Witwatersrand. He has taught at the University of Khartoum, University of Ghana, University of the Western Cape, and the City University of New York, and has worked for several African NGOs and regional institutions. He has been the recipient of Rockefeller and Ford Foundation visiting fellowships at New York, Columbia and Yale universities. His publications include *In Whose Image?: Political Islam and Urban Practices in Sudan* (1994) and *For the City Yet to Come: Changing Urban Life in Africa* (2004).

STEALTH Group comprises Ana Dzokic, Milica Topalovic, Marc Neelen and Ivan Kucina. They have initiated several joint projects that deal with the dynamics of contemporary urban transformations. It was out of simultaneous research projects at the Berlage Institute, Rotterdam and the Faculty of Architecture at the University of Belgrade that their practice evolved. Their projects bring together concepts and expertise from diverse fields such as architecture, urbanism, city management, software development and media.

Erik Swyngedouw obtained his PhD from Johns Hopkins University. He is University Reader in Economic Geography at Oxford University, and Fellow and Tutor in Human Geography at St Peter's College. His research interests cover a variety of topics with political economic and political–ecological themes. The central concern of his work is the integration of space and nature into critical social theory. Recent work in economic geography, has included the analysis of economic globalization, urban restructuring, and urban governance. He has worked in Latin-America, the US and, more recently, in Spain. Recent books include the co-authored *Towards Global Localization, The Urbanization of Injustice, The Globalized City* (2003), and *Social Power and the Urbanization of Water* (2004).

Kazys Varnelis teaches at SCI-Arc, Los Angeles. He is an historian of architecture and urbanism whose recent interest has been an investigation into architecture's relationship to global capitalism and the influence of telecommunications on the shape of the city. His particular object of research is Los Angeles. These interests are explored in two forthcoming books, *Simultaneous Environments: Architecture and Urbanism in Los Angeles, 1990–2005* and *Late Modernism: Postwar Architecture and Capital.* Varnelis is a founding member of Architecture Urbanism Design Collaborative (AUDC), a non-profit research collective. AUDC's projects have been featured in *306090: A Journal of Emergent Architecture and Design*, in *Form + Function*, a group show at Chapman College in 2003 and in *Textfield* magazine.

Illustration credits

The authors and publishers gratefully acknowledge the following for permission to reproduce material in the book. Every effort has been made to contact copyright holders for their permission to reprint material in this book. The publishers would be grateful to hear from any copyright holder who is not acknowledged here and will undertake to rectify any errors or omissions in future editions of the book.

From Randstad to Deltametropolis
Sdu Uitgevers, figures 1, 2, 3, 4, 5, 6
Serge Schoemaker and Jarrik Oudorp, figures 9, 10
NEXT Architects, figures 11, 12, 13, 14, 15, 16

Remaking Johannesburg
The Geological Society of South Africa, figure 3
MuseuMAfricA, figures 4, 5, 10
Library of the University of the Witwatersrand, figures 9, 11, 12
Gideon Mendel, figure 13

The Construction of Sydney's Global Image
Bart Lootsma, figure 4

The Voids of Berlin
Architecture Library Columbia University, figures 4, 6
Studio Daniel Libeskind, figures 8, 9
Elizabeth Felicella, figure 7

Los Angeles, Cluster City
NASA, figure 5
Guthrie + Buresh, figure 8

Local Navigation in Douala
Sébastien Venel, figure title page, 3
Eloi Chafaï, figures 1, 4
Sandrine Dolle, figures 2, 5

Milan, Urban Footnotes
Peter Fischli and David Weiss, figure 1
Guido Guidi, figure 2
Thomas Struth, figure 3
Mimmo Jodice, figures 4, 5

Gabriele Basilico, figure 6
John Davies, figures 7, 8
Paul Graham, figures 9, 10, 11, 12
Vincenzo Castella, figure 13

Belgrade: Evolution in an Urban Jungle
Courtesy: Bas Princen, Sonja Milojevic, Natasa Rajkovic, Marko Pajagic, Aca Petrovic, Milan Bozic, Vedran Latincic, Marija Saric, Velimir Manjulov.

References data blocks
The statistics are intended only as a general indication of differences between the cities discussed in this publication. Comparison of a more detailed nature is impossible since the definitions, methods of measurement and reliability of the different sources from which the statistics originate vary greatly.

Deltametropolis

Number of inhabitants	Key figures Regio Randstad 2002
Area	ibid.
Density	Calculation editors
Population urbanized (national)	Population Division of the United Nations Secretariat, *World Urbanization Prospects: The 2003 Revision.* Online. Available at http://unstats.un.org

Johannesburg/Johannesburg Municipality

Number of inhabitants	*Integrated Development Plan 2003/4,* Online. Available at http://www.joburg.org.za
Area	---
Density	Calculation editors
Population urbanized (national)	Population Division of the United Nations Secretariat, *World Urbanization Prospects: The 2003 Revision.* Online. Available at http://unstats.un.org

Sydney

Number of inhabitants	Australian Bureau of Statistics, 2001, Online. Available at http://www.abs.gov.au
Area	---
Density	Calculation editors
Population urbanized (national)	Population Division of the United Nations Secretariat, *World Urbanization Prospects: The 2003 Revision.* Online. Available at http://unstats.un.org

Kuala Lumpur

Number of inhabitants	*Statistical handbook Malaysia, 2003*, Kuala Lumpur, Malaysia: Jabatan Perangkaan, 2003
Area	---
Density	Calculation editors
Population urbanized (national)	Population Division of the United Nations Secretariat, *World Urbanization Prospects: The 2003 Revision.* Online. Available at http://unstats.un.org

Berlin

Number of inhabitants	2003, The Berlin State Statistical Office, Online. Available at http://www.statistik-berlin.de
Area	---
Density	Calculation editors
Population urbanized (national)	Population Division of the United Nations Secretariat, *World Urbanization Prospects: The 2003 Revision.* Online. Available at http://unstats.un.org

Mumbai

Number of inhabitants	Mumbai Metropolitan Region Development Authority, 2001. Online. Available at http://www.mmrdamumbai.org
Area	---
Density	Calculation editors
Population urbanized (national)	Population Division of the United Nations Secretariat, *World Urbanization Prospects: The 2003 Revision.* Online. Available at http://unstats.un.org

Los Angeles

Number of inhabitants	2000, US Census. Online. Available at http://www.census.gov
Area	---
Density	Calculation editors
Population urbanized (national)	Population Division of the United Nations Secretariat, *World Urbanization Prospects: The 2003 Revision.* Online. Available at http://unstats.un.org

Amsterdam

Number of inhabitants	O + S, 2003. Online. Available at http://www.onstat.amsterdam.nl
Area	---
Density	Calculation editors
Population urbanized (national)	Population Division of the United Nations Secretariat, *World Urbanization Prospects: The 2003 Revision.* Online. Available at http://unstats.un.org

Douala

Number of inhabitants	UN Habitat *Global Report on Human Settlements 2000*, Oxford: OUP, 1999
Area	World Dev. Report 1999, World Bank
Density	Calculation editors
Population urbanized (national)	Population Division of the United Nations Secretariat, *World Urbanization Prospects: The 2003 Revision.* Online. Available at http://unstats.un.org

Belgrade

Number of inhabitants	*The Statistic yearbook of Belgrade*, 2000
Area	*ibid.*
Density	Calculation editors

Population urbanized (national)	Population Division of the United Nations Secretariat, *World Urbanization Prospects: The 2003 Revision.* Online. Available at http://unstats.un.org

Hong Kong

Number of inhabitants	Government of the special Hong Kong Administrative Region, *Hong Kong in figures*, 2004 edition. Online. Available at http://www.info.gov.hk/
Area	---
Density	Calculation editors
Population urbanized (national)	Population Division of the United Nations Secretariat, *World Urbanization Prospects: The 2003 Revision.* Online. Available at http://unstats.un.org

Milan

Number of inhabitants	Settore statistica, servizio studie recherché, Milano, 2001. Online. Available at http://www.comune.milano.it/statistica/
Area	---
Density	Calculation editors
Population urbanized (national)	Population Division of the United Nations Secretariat, *World Urbanization Prospects: The 2003 Revision.* Online. Available at http://unstats.un.org

Index